THE FALL OF THE NAPOLEONIC KINGDOM OF ITALY (1814)

BY

R. JOHN RATH, Ph. D.

Mississippi State College for Women

NEW YORK

COLUMBIA UNIVERSITY PRESS

LONDON: P. S. KING & SON, LTD.

1941

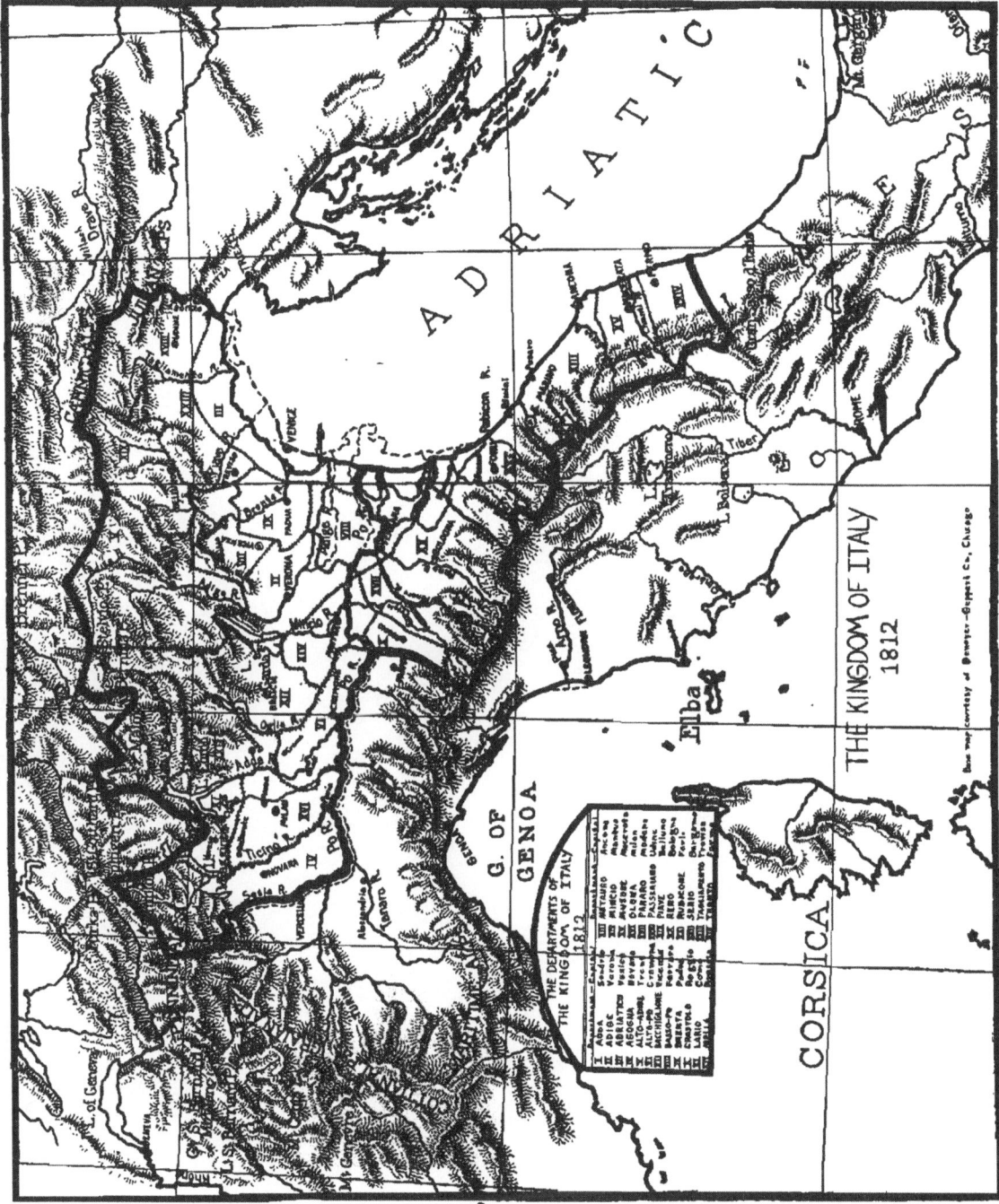

ADRIATIC

THE KINGDOM OF ITALY
1812

CORSICA

G. OF
GENOA

Elba

Tiber

THE DEPARTMENTS OF
THE KINGDOM OF ITALY
1812

I   Adda
II   ADIGE
III   ADRIATICO
IV   AGOGNA
V   ALTO-ADIGE
VI   BACCHIGLIONE
VII   BASSANO
VIII   BRENTA
IX   CROSTOLO
X   LARIO

XI   METAURO
XII   MINCIO
XIII   MUSONE
XIV   OLONA
XV   PANARO
XVI   PASSARIANO
XVII   PIAVE
XVIII   PO
XIX   REGGIO
XX   RENO
XXI   RUBICONE
XXII   SERIO
XXIII   TAGLIAMENTO
XXIV   TARO

Ancona
Basso
Passerio
Milan
Lario
Bellune
Bologna
Ferri
Parma

To

ISABEL

PREFACE

In the spring of 1814, the Kingdom of Italy, created by Napoleon in 1805, was conquered by the armies of the Allied Powers. The Venetian departments of the kingdom had been occupied by Austrian troops since October, 1813. The territory west of the Mincio and north of the Po, however, remained under French control until April, 1814. When, after Napoleon's defeat by the Allies, Prince Eugene Beauharnais, the French Emperor's viceroy in the kingdom, attempted to secure the creation of a new Kingdom of Italy with him as sovereign, the anti-French parties cooperated in staging a revolution in Milan which brought about a violent overthrow of Eugene's government. To take the place of the deposed French regime, the Milanese communal council established a provisional government for the parts of the kingdom still unoccupied by the Austrian army and invited Austrian and English officials to come to the capital of the Kingdom of Italy to help maintain order. In the meantime, the news of the great amount of liberal agitation in Milan caused the governments of the Allied Powers, who had agreed in July, 1813, upon giving Venetia to the Habsburgs, definitely to decide to give Lombardy as well. In late May and early June, 1814, the Habsburgs finally took control of the whole kingdom.

It is the purpose of this monograph to trace the various steps which led to the overthrow of the French-Italian government and to the establishment of Austrian control in the Kingdom of Italy. Such a study necessarily involves the raising of various seemingly unrelated questions. What were the conditions which existed in the kingdom just before its final demise? What were the causes of the Milanese revolution? How did the events which took place before, during, and immediately after the revolution demonstrate the existence of liberal and national sentiment in northern and northeastern Italy? How did they influence the Allied Powers in deciding the fate of the kingdom? What were the actions of the Austrian and

British officials in Milan during the period between the time of the Milanese revolution and the time that the decision of the Allies to give Lombardy, as well as Venetia, to Austria was announced? Why did a rift develop after the revolution between the members of the Milanese provisional government and the Austrian officials? Why did the Venetians, who had been under provisional Austrian military control since the fall of 1813, become dissatisfied with the Habsburg government? It is the writer's intention in this work to answer these and similar questions pertinent to the story of the overthrow of Napoleon's Kingdom of Italy.

Parts of the story, such as the Milanese revolution of April 20, 1814, have been fairly well covered by such accounts as Francesco Lemmi's *La restaurazione austriaca a Milano nel 1814* (Bologna, 1902), Baron von Helfert's *La caduta della dominazione francese nell'alta Italia e la congiura militare bresciano-milanese nel 1814* (Bologna, 1894), and Domenico Spadoni's *Milano e la congiura militare nel 1814 per l'indipendenza italiana: Il moto del 20 aprile e l'occupazione austriaca* (Modena, 1936). In such places, the writer has, however, been able to use some source material which was not available to these authors. Other phases, particularly the early Austrian activities in the Venetian departments, have been wholly neglected.

The writer is deeply indebted to several sources for this study. In the first place, he wishes to express his obligations to Francesco Lemmi, Baron von Helfert, Domenico Spadoni, Giuseppe Gallavresi, Alessandro Luzio, and the many other Italian and Austrian scholars whose writings have been so helpful. In particular does he wish to express his appreciation to the Social Science Research Council, from which he received a Pre-Doctoral Field Fellowship in 1937-38, which permitted him to explore various archives and libraries in Vienna, Venice, Milan, and Rome. Part of the material which he collected while holder of this fellowship is incorporated in this study. He also wishes to thank the librarians and officials of the *Oester-*

reichische, Staats Bibliothek, the *Haus Hof und Staats Archiv,*
the *Kriegs Archiv,* the *Hofkammer Archiv,* and the *Archiv des
Ministeriums des Innern,* of Vienna; the *Archivio di Stato,*
and the *Biblioteca di San Marco,* of Venice; the *Biblioteca
Nazionale,* and the *Biblioteca del Risorgimento Italiano,* of
Rome; the *Archivio di Stato,* the *Biblioteca del Risorgimento
Italiano,* the *Biblioteca Braidense,* and the *Biblioteca Ambrosiana,* of Milan; the Princeton University Library; the
Columbia University Library; the University of California
Library; and the Widener Library of Harvard University for
the kind and helpful manner in which they put their material
at his disposal. The librarians at the University of Kansas
and the College of Puget Sound were helpful in assisting the
writer in obtaining books through the Inter-Library Exchange
Association. Permission to use the base map in the frontis-
piece has been given by the Denoyer-Geppert Company,
Chicago.

In his research and writing, the writer has received the
valuable assistance of various persons. Much credit is due Dr.
Frank E. Melvin, of the University of Kansas, under whose
able tutelage this study was begun. Dr. Franklin C. Palm, of
the University of California, gave many worthwhile suggestions and criticisms during the early stages of the work. Dr.
Carlton J. H. Hayes, of Columbia University, in his courses
gave both inspiration and information which were indispensable. In addition, Professor Hayes has made many excellent
and helpful suggestions in the writing of this work and in the
correction of the proof. Drs. Shephard B. Clough, Leo J.
Wollemborg, Giuseppe Prezzolini, Charles C. Cole, and
Michael Florinsky, of Columbia University; Dr. Walter C.
Langsam, of Union College; and Dr. Virgil L. Jones, of the
University of Arkansas, have read the manuscript and offered
valuable suggestions. Miss Jeanette Lee, a student at Linden-
wood College, has assisted in making the map of the Kingdom
of Italy. Finally, to my wife must go my thanks for tedious
hours of labor in typing and proof reading, and for the encouragement which was so valuable for the completion of
the work.

TABLE OF CONTENTS

CHAPTER I

THE KINGDOM OF ITALY

In the spring of 1796, when Napoleon Bonaparte marched into the plains of northern Italy at the head of his army of 38,000 men,[1] a new era began in the Apennine peninsula. Before Napoleon's astoundingly rapid conquest, Italy, divided as it was into nine different sovereignties, each with its own political system and each with its own culture, had been little more than a geographic expression; now it was to have the first taste of political unity since the days of the Roman Empire. During the period of the Napoleonic Empire, the nine parts were to be reduced to three—the part annexed to France proper, the Kingdom of Naples, and the Kingdom of Italy—each of them dependent upon the central authorities in Paris.

The northeastern and north central parts of Italy, which are the subject of our discussion, experienced several changes in their form of government and territorial configuration before they were finally made into the Kingdom of Italy. Immediately after Bonaparte's entry into Italy in 1796, revolutionists in Modena, Ferrara, Reggio, and Bologna created the Cispadane Republic; and the inhabitants of Milan, Mantua, Bergamo, Brescia, and Crema were grouped together in the Transpadane Republic. In 1797, Napoleon combined these two infant republics into one large trans-Alpine state, the Cisalpine Republic, and, at the same time, gave the old Venetian territory situated between the Adige and Po rivers to Austria as an indemnity for her loss of Belgium and the Duchy of Lombardy.[2]

1 Driault, J. Édouard, *Napoléon en Italie (1800-1812)* (Paris, 1906), 1.

2 Treaty of Campo-Formio, October 17, 1797, D'Angeberg, Comte, *Recueil des traités, conventions et actes diplomatiques concernant l'Autriche et l'Italie* (Paris, 1859), 77 The Duchy of Lombardy had been created by the Austrians in 1786 through the union of the duchies of Milan and Mantua, which had been acquired by the Habsburgs in the Treaty of Utrecht of April 11, 1713 *Ibid.*, 6, 56-8.

13

The newly created Cisalpine Republic did not long remain undisturbed. In 1799, after the formation of the second coalition against France, an Allied army overran northern Italy, overthrew the Republic, restored the Austrian laws, and inflicted severe punishments upon the supporters of the French. The next year the Habsburgs were again evicted from this territory when Napoleon, who had returned from Egypt and had been made First Consul, defeated the Allied armies at Marengo and decreed the re-establishment of the Cisalpine Republic.

In 1802, the Cisalpine Republic was transformed into the Italian Republic, with Bonaparte as president and the Milanese Francesco Melzi d'Eril as vice-president.[3] After Napoleon became Emperor of France in May, 1804, he decided to transform the Italian Republic into a kingdom. First, Napoleon offered the crown to his oldest brother, Joseph, and then to Louis, another brother, but both refused it. Thereupon, he decided to take the crown himself. To an Italian deputation summoned to Paris, he revealed his determination early in 1805. On March 17, a constitutional statute was issued calling the French Emperor to the throne of Italy on condition that the kingdom would be kept forever distinct from the Empire and that on the conclusion of peace Napoleon would resign in favor of either his natural or adopted son.[4] On May 26, amidst

3 For important works on the creation of the Italian Republic, see Pingaud, Albert, *Bonaparte, président de la République italienne* (Paris, 1914); Koch, Gottfried, *Die Entstehung der italienischen Republik, 1801/2* (no place or date given); and Pedrotti, Pietro, *Francesco Melzi d'Eril e la Repubblica Italiana* (Roma, 1937).

4 Constitutional statute of March 17, 1805, Driault, *op. cit.*, 315; Coraccini, Frédéric, *Histoire de l'administration du royaume d'Italie pendant la domination française* (Paris, 1823), 34-5. This latter book is a French translation of Coraccini, Federico, *Storia dell'amministrazione del regno d'Italia durante il dominio francese* (Lugano, 1823). It was also published under the following title: *Mémoires sur la cour du Prince Eugène et sur le royaume d'Italie pendant la domination de Napoléon Bonaparte.* Par un Français attaché à la cour du vice-roi d'Italie (Paris, 1826). The authorship of this work is usually attributed to Jean La Folie, an administrative official of the Kingdom of Italy. Arrigo Solmi, however, asserts that the real author of this book was Giuseppe Valeriani. See Solmi's article entitled " Sul vero autore

the joyful acclamations of the people, Napoleon was formally crowned king in the Milanese cathedral.

When first created, the Kingdom of Italy included the territory that had comprised the former Italian Republic, namely: all of the former Duchy of Lombardy; Novara and Lomellina, situated between the Ticino and the Sesia; the former Venetian territory west of the Adige; the valleys of Bormio, Chiavenna, and the Valtelline; the former Duchy of Modena; and the papal Legations of Bologna, Ferrara, and Romagna. Additions, however, were soon made. The first of these was the city of Venice and the remaining Venetian territory on the mainland which had been taken from Austria in the Treaty of Pressburg (December 26, 1805).[5] In 1806 Dalmatia was incorporated into the kingdom, but later in the same year it was turned over to General Marmont, and in 1809 added to the command of the governor of Dalmatia. In 1808 the papal March of Ancona and the papal Duchies of Macerata, Fermo, and Urbino, and in 1810 the South Tyrol were united with the kingdom. Thereafter no more territorial additions were made.

Very few of the different parts of the newly created Kingdom of Italy had previously been combined in a single political entity. Prior to the French Revolution they had been governed by diverse authorities. The valleys of Bormio, Chiavenna, and the Valtelline had been a part of the Swiss canton of the Grisons. The Sardinian territories of Novara and Lomellina had experienced the cautious reforms of Charles Emmanuel III and Victor Amadeus III. Modena had been under the conservative and peaceful guidance of Duke Ercole Rinaldo III. The Legations of Bologna, Ferrara, and Romagna, the March of Ancona, and the Duchies of Macerata, Fermo, and Urbino had been ruled by the intolerant, conservative, and priest-ridden government of the papacy; whereas the Tyrol,

della 'Storia dell'amministrazione del Regno d'Italia durante il dominio francese,'" in his *L'idea dell'unità italiana nell'età napoleonica* (Modena, 1934), 145-58.

5 D'Angeberg, *op. cit.*, 93-5

like the other Habsburg lands, had been subjected first to the reforming temperament of Emperor Joseph II and then to the cautious conservatism of Leopold II and Francis II.

Venice had sunk into almost complete stagnation. The government of the republic had been in the hands of the aristocracy, which, through its influence on the grand council, the senate, the *signoria,* the council of ten, and the doge, had striven to maintain the existing edifice of special privileges. Under the tutelage of this privileged class Venice had become moribund. Her army had dwindled to a few undisciplined and inefficient regiments; commerce had declined tremendously; industry and manufacture were almost nonexistent. Gayety, luxury, and vice reigned triumphant; many of the young blades of Europe went thither to carouse.

Contrasting sharply with conditions in the Venetian Republic were those in Lombardy, a Habsburg possession before its acquisition by the French. The reforms of Maria Theresa (1740-80) and Joseph II (1780-90) had done much to repair the damage inflicted upon the country by previous Spanish misrule. The administration of justice had been improved by establishing separate courts to try civil and criminal cases and by abolishing torture and secret trials. Learning had been encouraged by the founding of new schools and the improvement of existing ones. Agriculture had been encouraged by the draining of swamps, the giving of prizes for agricultural improvements, and the reassessing of land taxes in such a way that the taxes paid were proportionate to the actual value of the land. Commerce had been encouraged by the construction of canals and the abolition of most of the inland tolls between various cities and communities. Industry had been improved by reducing to a small sum many of the duties on raw materials and by abolishing export duties on many Italian manufactures.[6] Well governed as it had been, and endowed by nature with the

6 See especially Simonyi, Ludwig von, *Das Lombardisch-Venezianische Koenigreich: Charakteristisch- Artistisch- Topographisch- Statistisch- und Historisch* (Mailand, 1844-46), II, 400-8.

extremely fertile Po valley,[7] Lombardy was by far the wealthiest portion of the Kingdom of Italy.

Although the various parts of the kingdom differed from each other to a remarkable extent, as we have seen, Napoleon, nevertheless, welded them together, like the other territories under his control, into a highly centralized political unity directly under his own personal supervision. Nominally, the most important authority in the kingdom was the senate, the members of which were chosen by the King of Italy. To it were presented proposed statutes and laws, treaties of peace, alliance, and commerce, declarations of war, conventions providing for the cession of territories, and the accounts of the various ministers. It decided the punishments which were to be meted out for excesses or abuses in ecclesiastical jurisdiction and for conspiracies against civil liberty. Above the senate were the electoral colleges, divided into the three separate bodies of landed proprietors, tradespeople, and " intellectuals," to which was assigned the duty of deciding whether or not the decisions of the senate were constitutional, whether or not any officials had misused public funds, and whether or not malfeasant public servants should be suspended from office.

The senate and electoral colleges were to represent the will of the people. There were still other bodies directly subject to the king. One of these was the council of state, which was presided over by Napoleon himself and which had the duty of advising the government on judicial, religious, financial, administrative, military, and naval matters. There were also seven ministers of state, each of whom owed his appointment to the king: a minister of justice, a minister of foreign affairs, a minister of interior, a minister of finance, a minister of war

7 For excellent discussions of the highly developed agricultural industry in Lombardy in the early part of the nineteenth century, see Greenfield, Kent Roberts, *Economics and Liberalism in the Risorgimento. A Study of Nationalism in Lombardy, 1814-1848* (Baltimore, Md., 1934), 1-35; and the article entitled "Agriculture and Statistics of Italy (A Review of Chateauvieux, Frédéric Sullin de, *Lettres écrites d'Italia en 1812 et 1813, à M. Charles Pictet,...,*" *The Edinburg Review,* XXVIII (1817), 32-9.

and marine, a minister of the treasury, and a minister of religion.

To facilitate local administration, the kingdom was divided into twenty-four departments, each presided over by a prefect, who represented the central government in his department. Every department was divided into several districts, in each of which, except the one in which the prefect resided, was a vice-prefect to represent his superior in that district and to carry out and enforce all laws and ordinances. Every district was divided into cantons, in each of which was a justice of peace and in most of which there was, in addition, a tax registrar to apportion and levy all taxes. In turn, the cantons were divided into communes, the smallest of the governmental subdivisions, in each of which there was, to represent the central authority, a municipal representative.[8]

Highly centralized as the government of the Kingdom of Italy was, it is evident that all ultimate power lay in the hands of the King of Italy, Napoleon himself. The type of officials whom Napoleon chose to represent him in Italy shows that the French Emperor intended to be supreme. Foremost among these officials was the handsome and debonaire Prince Eugene Beauharnais, Napoleon's young stepson, whom he made his viceroy in the kingdom. Although Beauharnais, in the opinion of Ugo Foscolo, was " endowed with good common sense and with a courage that was perplexing to those who did not understand him," he was easily " dominated by minds and

8 Reuss to Ugarte, Udine, February 11, 1814, *Haus- Hof- und Staats-Archiv* (In future references this archive will be cited as *Staats-Archiv.*), Vienna, *Kaiser Franz Akten*, Fasc. 27, Sect. 1, Fo. 20-1; Cantù, Cesare, *Della indipendenza italiana cronistoria* (Torino, 1872-77), I, 410-23; " Statistische Auskuenfte ueber die Oesterreichischen-Italienischen Provinzen nach dem Leitfaden der Hohen C. O. H. C. vom 18. August 1814," Helfert, Fhr. v., *Kaiser Franz I von Oesterreich und die Stiftung des Lombardo-Venetianischen Koenigreichs* (Innsbruck, 1901), Appendix I, 525-35. The latter report, printed verbatim in Helfert, was referred to by the Austrian government when it created a new government for its reacquired Lombardo-Venetian provinces.

spirits superior to his own," [9] and was totally without political experience. He by no means had all the necessary characteristics of a great statesman, but he possessed that attribute which Bonaparte demanded of his chief emissary in Italy: dogged loyalty to his chieftain.[10] With Eugene as viceroy, Napoleon's own position in the kingdom was clear. Napoleon was to be the executive and administrator; Eugene, his chief spokesman and lieutenant.

In order to give his viceroy a dependable guide, the French Emperor appointed Étienne Méjean, the secretary of the prefecture of the department of the Seine, as Eugene's private secretary. Not only was Méjean a capable administrator, but he could always be depended upon to follow Napoleon's instructions to the best of his ability. A genial person, with conciliatory and moderate opinions, he was a good choice for the position of the viceroy's chief adviser in directing the affairs of the kingdom.

Next to Prince Eugene and perhaps Méjean, the Milanese nobleman Francesco Melzi d'Eril was undoubtedly the most influential man in the kingdom. Growing up during the time of the benevolent rule of Maria Theresa and Joseph II, Melzi, after the outbreak of the French Revolution, became one of the most important statesmen in northern Italy, and, in 1802, when the Italian Republic was created, he became its vicepresident. With the creation of the Kingdom of Italy, he was made Grand Chamberlain of the kingdom and Duke of Lodi. He became the viceroy's most sagacious monitor and exerted a salutary influence upon the affairs of state. Often too pessimistic and many times greatly handicapped because of gout, he was, nevertheless, Eugene's best informed and most astute counsellor.[11]

9 Quoted in Lemmi, Francesco, *La restaurazione austriaca a Milano nel 1814* (Bologna, 1902), 28.

10 Castro, Giovanni de, *Principio di secolo: Storia della caduta del regno italico* (2nd ed., Milano, 1897), 6-7.

11 Bonfadini, R[omualdo], *Mezzo secolo di patriotismo. Saggi storici* (Milano, 1886), 67-70.

In addition to these men, there were several other officials who played an important rôle in the government. Foremost among them were the ministers of state. Of these, Luosi was minister of justice; Felici, of the interior; Bovara, of religion; Prina, of finance; Veneri, of the treasury; Pino, of war and marine; and Marescalchi, of foreign affairs. Then, there was Aldini, the secretary of state, who had his headquarters in Paris, and whose duty it was to prepare decrees and to transmit the Emperor's orders to the government at Milan. Also with considerable influence were Guicciardi, the director of the police; Darnay, the director of the posts; Moscati, the director of public instruction; Paradisi, the director of bridges and highways; Barbò, the director of direct taxes and of the administration of the tax estimate; and Lambertenghi, the director of the customs.[12]

Some of these officials, such as Prince Eugene and Melzi, were liked and respected by the Italians; others were intensely disliked. Among the latter was the director of the posts, Darnay, who was accused of opening private letters and of violating the secrecy of the mail.[13] Equally opprobrious were Vaccari, who during the last days of the kingdom took Felici's place as minister of interior, and Paradisi, who was elevated to the position of president of the senate. They were accused of being megalomaniacs, and since they were Modenese, the Milanese populace also stigmatized them as foreigners. Méjean, too, was abominated. He was a Frenchman and a pliant cat's-paw of Napoleon.[14]

The most despised of all, however, was the minister of finance, Giuseppe Prina. Although he was a dexterous administrator, capable in financial matters, intelligent, honorable, and hard-working, Prina was hated for his obsequiousness to

12 Coraccini, *op. cit.*, 51-3, 221.

13 *Ibid.*, 221-22.

14 Helfert, Barone von, *La caduta della dominazione francese nell'alta Italia e la congiura militare bresciano-milanese nel 1814* (Bologna, 1894), 22-3.

Napoleon, and was held responsible for the increase of the taxes during the last days of the Empire.

The situation that confronted the officials of Napoleon, in Italy as well as in the other countries under the domination of the French Emperor, was the creation of a new order, the making of which always causes dislocations and brings both goodwill and hatred for those who do it. Before the Russian debacle in the fall of 1812, the old political laws of Italy, the same as elsewhere, were destroyed, and the country was moulded and broken and moulded anew. The last vestiges of feudalism were wiped out. Justice according to the ideas of the rising bourgeoisie was instituted; civil equality was established. The administration was well ordered and energetic; the laws were clear and just. The introduction of the French civil and commercial codes, the systematic and efficacious repression of brigandage, and the construction and repairing of roads and bridges helped to stimulate commerce and industry; whereas the direct intervention of French authorities in constructing canals and dams, in giving prizes for agricultural improvements, and in improving the existing irrigation system, encouraged agriculture. New primary and secondary schools were established, and the universities of Pavia, Bologna, and Padua acquired an importance which they had not had for centuries. The city of Milan especially profited from the changes. Prior to Bonaparte's Italian campaign, it was a provincial capital; now it was the center of a large, thriving, and pretentious kingdom and of a brilliant and pompous court life such as the city had never seen.

Reforms such as these were beneficial to the inhabitants of the Kingdom of Italy, and many Italians were well pleased with them. Other creations and policies of the new French masters, however, were burdensome and annoying and tended to produce a considerable amount of dissatisfaction. One grievance for many persons was the lack of political liberty in the kingdom. The council of state prepared the laws, the viceroy promulgated them, the senate registered them, the ministers made them applicable, and the prefects and vice-prefects enforced them throughout the kingdom. The presence everywhere of an arbitrary police curbed all opposition to the regime, and the omnipresent censorship effectively prevented any expression of discontent.

More exasperating were the heavy military and economic burdens laid upon the shoulders of the inhabitants of the kingdom. Napoleon never took pains to conceal from his viceroy that his interest in Italy was wholly confined to what the Italian people "could furnish him in money and men for his European wars."[15] He admonished Prince Eugene to bear in mind that he was always to consider "*France above all*," and that he was to make Italy's interests inseparable from those of France.[16]

Since Napoleon took such an attitude, it was to be expected that he made ever increasing demands for more Italian soldiers for his army. Beginning in 1801, each year brought about a new request for more men. By 1812 the Kingdom of Italy had furnished a total of 91,788 men to Napoleon's military forces.[17] Of these, 22,000 were killed in the Peninsular War. Twenty-seven thousand went with the viceroy and General Pino to Russia, scarcely 1,000 of whom returned to their native land.[18] The Italians, the same as the Germans, the Dutch, the Poles, and other peoples under Napoleonic domination, had to shed their blood for causes other than their own.

The Italians also had to endure the same onerous economic burdens as other subjects of the French Emperor. Government expenses in the Kingdom of Italy slowly but steadily increased. In 1805, the total annual expenditures had amounted to 103,-

15 Tarlé, Eugène, *Le Blocus continental et le Royaume d'Italie. La Situation économique de l'Italie sous Napoléon Ier, d'après des documents inédits* (Paris, 1928), 14.

16 Letter of August 23, 1810, Du Casse, A., *Mémoires et correspondance politique et militaire du Prince Eugène* (Paris, 1858-60), VI, 367-68. Also see Tarlé, *op. cit.*, 20.

17 Tarlé, *op. cit.*, 33.

18 Helfert, *La caduta, op. cit.*, 6-7.

282,143 lire. By 1809, they had risen to 136,000,000, and by 1812, to 144,000,000 lire.[19] In 1812, less than one-half of the sums disbursed was used to defray the normal ordinary expenses of the kingdom. Of the 144,000,000 lire spent in that year, 46,000,000 lire went to the army and navy, 30,000,000 lire were turned over directly to the imperial treasury in Paris, and 22,000,000 were allocated towards servicing the public debt, of which a large amount had been charged to the Italian treasury.[20]

This augmentation in expenditures, which could be met only by increased taxation, would perhaps in itself not have been too burdensome,[21] had not Napoleon's policy of exploiting the Kingdom of Italy for the general interests of the Empire noticeably harmed its commerce and industry.[22] Although such improvements as the introduction of French civil and commercial codes helped to stimulate business, other policies of the French government served to hinder and injure it. The incessant conscription took many workers away from farm and factory. The arbitrary confiscation of merchandise, and the frequent checks and hindrances placed upon commerce tended to create a sense of insecurity which was prejudicial to business expansion. The vexatious regulations in the customs administration discouraged trade to countries on the con-

19 Tarlé, *op. cit.*, 29.

20 *Ibid.*, 30-1.

21 Giuseppe Pecchio, in his *Saggio storico sull'amministrazione finanziaria dell'ex-regno d'Italia dal 1802 al 1814* (2nd ed., London, 1826), maintains that his contemporaries had greatly exaggerated the deleterious effects of the financial policies of the Kingdom of Italy, and that the financial measures of the Napoleonic government in Italy were, on the whole, reasonably moderate and just. Augusto Sandonà, in his book entitled *Il Regno Lombardo Veneto 1814-1859, la costituzione e l'amministrazione* (Milano, 1912), 60, on the other hand, says that the exactions of the government were so heavy that in 1812 the land taxes alone absorbed twenty-five per cent of the income, and that in 1813 this proportion rose to twenty-nine per cent, and in 1814, to thirty-two per cent. The position taken by Tarlé is in between these two widely differing points of view.

22 Tarlé, *op. cit.*, 25.

tinent of Europe,[23] and the continental blockade ruined not only the shipping industry but also industries such as the manufacture of articles made of silk, the prosperity of which was dependent upon the British market.[24] Other industries were damaged by Napoleon's policy of favoring native French industries by all possible means and of making Italy merely an economic dependency of France.[25]

Agriculture, on the other hand, because of the fact that the Emperor tried to make Italy a vast granary of food for the French industrial population, was relatively little hurt by Napoleon's commercial policies,[26] but by 1813 persons making their living from the soil were also beginning to feel the pinch of hard times. The inclement weather during the spring and summer of that year ruined the crops, and frequent hail storms, an early frost, and early autumn snows severely injured " the

23 *Ibid.*, 370.

24 *Ibid.*, 368-69. The total sums realized from the sale of silk articles in both foreign and domestic trade in 1806, just before the institution of the continental blockade, was 14,586,100 lire. By 1811 this sum had shrunk to 6,288,096 lire. *Ibid.*, 242-43.

25 *Ibid.*, 367. The effects of Napoleon's policy are reflected in the following figures, obtained from *ibid.*, 249-50, 299-300, 277, 330, and 346, of the imports and exports of some of the chief products of the Kingdom of Italy in the year 1812:

	Raw silk	Cotton goods	Wool and woollen goods	Leather goods, hides, and furs	Metals and metal goods
Value of exports (in lire)	59,382,502	17,189,565	4,043,289	910,981	2,778,091
Value of imports (in lire)	3,765,480	23,729,484	21,084,715	6,851,802	5,206,422
Amount of imports obtained from France (in lire)	2,490,000	14,490,000	15,390,000	2,420,000	2,270,000

Tarlé, *op. cit.*, 234, also says that in 1812, 80,294,000.00 lire of the 138,067,143.78 lire worth of the total imports of the Kingdom of Italy came from the French Empire. Of the total exports of the kingdom, which amounted to 140,724,461.09 lire, 66,340,000.00 lire went to the French Empire.

26 *Ibid.*, 95-6, 367.

few sprouts of late maturation."[27] Thus agriculture, too, like industry and commerce, was not in a prosperous condition on the eve of the overthrow of the Napoleonic regime.

Under such conditions a lowered standard of living and business failures were inevitable. As early as the beginning of 1813, the Milanese priest Mantovani noted in his diary that the cost of primary necessities, such as food, was very dear.[28] With high prices came an avalanche of business failures. In May, 1813, the Bignami house, one of the largest financial institutions in the city of Milan, crashed.[29] By the beginning of June, 1813, nineteen large business houses had failed in the cities of Milan and Venice alone.[30] A succession of bankruptcies and the disastrous war of the fall of 1813, which was conducted in the Kingdom of Italy itself, brought misery to the country. By October, 1813, the royal treasury was bankrupt,[31] commerce and industry were in a wretched condition, and large numbers of people, especially in the mountain valleys of the Venetian departments, were on the verge of starvation.[32] Thus,

27 Prefect of Bacchiglione to Thurn, Vicenza, December 10, 1813, *Archivio di Stato*, Venice, *Pubblico Politico*, 1813, Fasc. VIII-IX, Rub. 14, No. 27,798; Prefect of Piave to Central Government, Udine, January 26, 1814, *Archivio di Stato*, Venice, *Polizia*, 1814, Busta XXXIX, Fasc. 68, No. 3067.

28 Cited in Lemmi, *op. cit.*, 44-5.

29 *Ibid.*, 45.

30 Tarlé, *op. cit.*, 238.

31 *Ibid.*, 31. Also see Cusani, Francesco, *Storia di Milano dall'origine ai nostri giorni e cenni storico-statistici sulle città e province lombarde* (Milano, 1861-84), VII, 22-5.

32 There are literally dozens of documents in the *Archivio di Stato* of Venice which indicate the appalling lack of food in many districts. Among them, note especially the following: Prefect of Piave to Central Government, Udine, January 26, 1814, *Polizia*, 1814, Busta XXXIX, Fasc. 68, No. 3067; Prefect of Bacchiglione to Thurn, Vicenza, December 10, 1813, *Pubblico Politico*, 1813, Fasc. VIII-IX, Rub. 14, No. 27,798; Mayor of Nogarle to Reuss, n. d., enclosed in Prefect of Bacchiglione to Reuss, Vicenza, February 18, 1814, *Imposte*, 1814, Busta XXXII, Fasc. 8, No. 1834; Prefect of Tagliamento to Reuss, Treviso, December 30, 1813, *ibid.*, Fasc. 23, No. 22,634; and Inhabitants of Megliadino S. Videnzio (the letter bears thirty-seven signatures) to Reuss, n. d., *ibid.*, Fasc. 76, No. 3139.

several months before the final defeat of Napoleon's armies and, with it, the overthrow of the French government in Italy, the Kingdom of Italy, like other countries under Napoleon's control, was in a state of almost complete prostration, and a considerable number of its inhabitants were crying for relief from the heavy exactions from which they were suffering.

CHAPTER II

THE STIRRING UP OF A LIBERAL AND NATIONAL SENTIMENT

EXHAUSTED and disgruntled as many Italians were with the constant warfare, the disquieting censorship of press and speech, the burdensome conscription, and Napoleon's policy of exploiting Italy for the benefit of France, the Kingdom of Italy, like other countries under French control, during the last few years of its existence, became a fertile field for anti-French propaganda and intrigue. In line with the new spirit of liberalism which had spread among various intellectual circles of Europe after the outbreak of the French Revolution, the opposition to the Napoleonic regime was mainly liberal and national in form. Much of this anti-French sentiment in Italy was stirred up by three different groups which frequently worked in conjunction with one another: the national writers, British agents, and the secret societies. By the fall of 1813 and the spring of 1814, the work of the opposition was so effective that a spirit of revolt had permeated a not inconsiderable number of influential people.

During the Revolutionary and Napoleonic period, many litterateurs, in Italy as well as elsewhere, busied themselves with preaching the new liberal and national doctrines. It is true that several vague and inchoate plans for the unification of Italy had been formulated long before the outbreak of the French Revolution,[1] but it was only after Bonaparte had

1 This was particularly true in the period immediately following the War of Spanish Succession. Even in the period preceding the outbreak of the French Revolution, a rather considerable amount of patriotism was expressed by Italian writers. Megaro, Gaudence, *Vittorio Alfieri, Forerunner of Italian Nationalism* (New York, 1930), 16-20; Solmi, Arrigo, "L'idea dell'unità italiana nell'età napoleonica," in his collection of essays published under the same title (Modena, 1934), 33-4. Solmi's article was first published in the *Rassegna storica del Risorgimento*, Anno XX (gennaio-marzo 1933), 1-19. All my citations to Solmi's article are to the first of the two sources. Also see Ghisalberti, Alberto, *Gli albori del Risorgimento italiano (1700-1815)* (Roma, 1931), 78-89.

marched his troops into the Apennine peninsula in 1796 that the dreams of a liberal and united Italy aroused spirited and determined action. Immediately following Bonaparte's Italian campaign, patriotic societies sprang up as if by magic in all parts of the peninsula. Knights-errant of " liberty, equality, and fraternity " planted liberty trees in parks, public squares, and the open countryside, and began heralding the advent of the new freedom with much gusto, while misty-eyed dreamers began telling receptive audiences of the better world that was to come.

After the excesses of the Italian revolutionary governments had disgusted many Italian liberals, and after the Austro-Russian reaction of 1799-1800 had forced many of the Italian patriots to flee from their native haunts to a more secure exile, some of the Italian supporters of the French, however, began to realize that national liberty was not to be gained by reverently paying homage to their new taskmasters and slavishly worshipping them. They came to interpret the terms " liberty, equality, and fraternity " as meaning " the liberation of the country from its foreign domination, and not the liberation of the individual from all the bonds and limits with which law, manners, and customs have surrounded him." [2] Liberty came to be " interpreted in the sense of nationality." [3] Nationalism and not internationalism was to be the product of the French Revolution, not only in Italy but in all Europe.

Just as Spanish and German litterateurs tried to arouse a feeling of intense patriotism among the Spaniards and Germans, a coterie of Italian writers strove to make their countrymen conscious of their Italianism. Some admonished their fellow citizens to delete all non-Italian words from their vocabularies.[4] Others penned quips attacking the French Em-

2 Ferrero, Guglielmo, " L'effet de la révolution française sur l'Italie," *Revue Bleu,* February 5, 1928, 66.

3 Hazard, Paul, *La révolution française et les lettres italiennes, 1789-1815* (Paris, 1910), xvii.

4 See *ibid.,* 113, 230-43, for examples of the writings of these Italian patriots.

peror and holding his cohorts in Italy up for ridicule.[5] Still others pleaded for the Italians to unite themselves together in a single liberal state.

Standing very high in the ranks of the new liberal and national writers were Melchiorre Gioia, Vincenzo Monti, Vittorio Alfieri, Vincenzo Cuoco, and Ugo Foscolo. The first of these, Melchiorre Gioia, in his *Dissertazione su quale dei governi liberi meglio convenga all'Italia,* which was published in Milan in 1797, presented to his countrymen what has been referred to as " the first real program of the Risorgimento." [6] He advocated complete independence from foreign rule, and the unification of the whole of Italy, not into a federation of states, but into a single centralized state under a republican form of government.[7]

Vincenzo Monti, at first an admiring eulogist and later a caustic opponent of the French, penned pages in praise of the virtues of the Italian nation.[8] In particular did he extol the greatness of Italian scientific and philosophical productions, although he reviled the Italian people for having been disunited for so long and for not having prevented foreigners from shedding Italian blood for interests which were totally foreign to Italy.[9]

Vittorio Alfieri, at first sympathetic to the French revolutionary movement, later came to " hate the French," as he expressed himself, " as much as I love liberty," [10] and began

5 See *ibid.,* 260-88, for good examples of this.

6 Villari, Luigi, *The Development of Political Ideas in Italy in the Nineteenth Century* (London, 1926), 6. Also see Ferrari, Aldo, *L'esplosione rivoluzionaria del Risorgimento italiano (1789-1815)* (Milano, 1925), 427-28.

7 Good extracts from Gioia's work, containing summaries of his main arguments, can be found in Carducci, Giosue, *Letture del risorgimento italiano* (Bologna, 1896-97), I, 130-45; and in Rota, Ettore, *Il problema italiano dal 1700 al 1815 (L'idea unitaria)* (Milano, 1938), 103-7.

8 Hazard, *op. cit.,* 288-90.

9 In his *Dell'obbligo di onorare i primi scopritori del vero in fatto di scienze,* an extract from which is published in Carducci, *op. cit.,* I, 256-70.

10 Megaro, *op. cit.,* 116.

to write treatises abounding in virulent denunciations of the French Revolution and of the French people.[11] He insisted that the Italians could have no *patria* until they had first expelled the French from their sacred soil.[12] In Alfieri's opinion, hatred of the foreigners and their expulsion from the country were the *sine qua non* of national independence.[13] But before their national redemption could be accomplished, the Italians would, furthermore, have to formulate and adopt national ideals. They would have to stop imitating the French language and customs,[14] and would have to free themselves from the intellectual domination of France.[15] Only then, Alfieri contended, could the Italians create a new life, wholly Italian in form, and bring about the regeneration of their country.

Perhaps even more effective than Alfieri in stirring up a liberal and national sentiment in Italy was Vincenzo Cuoco. Cuoco's *Saggio storico sulla rivoluzione napoletana*, written in Milan in 1800-1801, is said to have inspired the national consciousness of some of the greatest figures of the Italian Risorgimento from Manzoni to Mazzini.[16] In this forceful book, Cuoco emphatically asserted that the Kingdom of Naples fell prey to the French, not because of the great daring and consummate skill of the French army, but because the French had had no great people to oppose them. That sentiment of pride which renders individuals capable of performing the greatest deeds and inspires nations with resoluteness had been entirely extirpated in the Neapolitan kingdom. Before the Gallican tarantula could be annihilated in Italy, the Italians had to give up slavishly imitating foreign cultures and habits. They had to feel Italian, think Italian, write Italian, act Italian. Unification could come only from the " inner forces " of the

11 *Ibid.*, 34-6.
12 *Ibid.*, 96, 100.
13 *Ibid.*, 102.
14 *Ibid.*, 106-7.
15 *Ibid.*, 122.
16 Solmi, " L'idea dell'unità," *loc cit.*, 70.

people themselves. Only after Italy was united into a single state could the Italians be free to enjoy the blessings of happiness.[17]

By no means the least important among the great national writers in Revolutionary and Napoleonic Italy was Ugo Foscolo, who, deeply shocked by Napoleon's betrayal of his native country, Venice,[18] had gone to Milan to embark upon his literary career. Firmly convinced that only through independence and unification could Italy ever become strong, Foscolo applied himself assiduously to the task of national regeneration. In his " Oration to Bonaparte," written in 1802, he courageously accused the French Emperor of being responsible for the miseries of the Cisalpine Republic and appealed to him to devote himself seriously to the cause of independence.[19] In other books and articles he tried, first of all, to convince the French that their own interests would best be served through an independent Italy, and then, failing in this attempt, he exhorted his fellow countrymen to make their land a united and independent nation through their own efforts. Finally he became convinced that Italy could never be united or independent so long as the French rule existed, and actively entered the ranks of the conspirators who were plotting the overthrow of the French regime.[20]

To expel the foreigners from Italian soil, to create an " Italian " culture and " feeling," and to unite all Italians in a single state was the program of the patriotic Italian writers. The British agents, the second of the three groups spreading liberal and national ideas in Italy, on the other hand, tried to capitalize upon the sentiment of independence which national propagandists had already inculcated in the Italians to stir up

17 Hazard, *op. cit.*, 220-26.

18 Foscolo's thoughts at the time of his exile are expressed in his " Sfoghi d'un fuoruscito veneto," in his *Ultime lettere di Jacopo Ortis*. Reprinted in Carducci, *op. cit.*, I, 168-90.

19 See Carducci, *op. cit.*, I, 193-204.

20 Solmi, Arrigo, " Ugo Foscolo e l'unità dell'Italia," in his *L'idea dell' unità italiana nell'età napoleonica, op. cit.*, 97-141.

a revolt against the Napoleonic regime in Italy similar to the insurrections which they had already helped to provoke in Spain and Portugal. In their efforts, the British agents were led by Lord William Bentinck,[21] the commander-in-chief of the British forces in the Mediterranean. Bentinck was a liberal Whig in opposition to the then existing conservative Tory Perceval and Liverpool ministries in England, and often acted contrary to the spirit of his instructions if not in open defiance of them. By means of fomenting a revolution, Bentinck evidently hoped to create in northern Italy an independent kingdom with a liberal governmental system copied after that of England and to make Great Britain the master of the Mediterranean.[22] England's political influence on Italy might be increased, and it was hoped that she might even get a monopoly on the trade of the whole peninsula.[23]

For several years Lord William Bentinck's headquarters in Sicily had been the center of considerable anti-French propa-

---

21 Previous to being sent to Italy, Bentinck had been head of one of the divisions of Sir Arthur Wellesley's army. From there he had been sent to Germany to organize a German legion to serve under his orders in Sicily and on the coast of Spain. In 1811 he was named ambassador to Sicily and commander-in-chief of the British troops stationed on that island. There he interfered much in the affairs of government and deprived the Bourbon monarch, Ferdinand IV, of most of his power. In April, 1814, he took Genoa, where he issued a proclamation that caused serious difficulties for his government. From there he returned to Palermo, from where he was driven in July, 1814, by the Sicilian king. As a result of his actions in Italy, Bentinck was now in disgrace with his government and without employment until 1821, when he was named governor-general of Bengal. He was soon forced to resign from this post on account of illness. He left India in May, 1836, and died at Paris, on January 17, 1839. Webster, Charles K., *The Foreign Policy of Castlereagh, 1812-1815; Britain and the Reconstruction of Europe* (London, 1931), 253-60.

22 Soriga, Renato, "Augusto Bozzi Granville e la Rivista 'L'Italico,'" *Bollettino* della Società pavese di storia patria, Anno XIV (1914), 270.

23 Capograssi, Antonio, "L'unità d'Italia nel pensiero di Lord William Bentinck," *Rassegna storica del Risorgimento*, Anno XXI (marzo-aprile 1934), 244-45; Luzio, Alessandro, *La Massoneria sotto il Regno italico e la restaurazione austriaca. Estratto dall'Archivio Storico Lombardo*, Anno XLIV, Fascicolo II (Milano, 1918), 53.

ganda. As early as 1811 the Piedmontese Marshal Vittorio Sallier de la Tour tried to convince Bentinck that the English government had an excellent opportunity to provoke an Italian national war against the French.[24] De la Tour, acting with the full support of the Austrian government, was in favor of a united Italian kingdom under the sovereignty of Francis of Este, Duke of Modena. Bentinck was only too glad to cooperate with de la Tour and the Austrians in this plot. Throughout 1812 and the early part of 1813, preparations were made to bring the plan to a successful conclusion.[25] In the summer of 1813, the Austrians, however, withdrew their encouragement of the project, and the scheme collapsed.

Bentinck's espousal of de la Tour's project, the liberal constitution which he gave the Sicilians in 1812,[26] and his well-known liberal convictions caused patriots of all descriptions to turn enthusiastically both to him and to the British Foreign Office. Many of them were " leading and influential Italians, who declared themselves ready to rise against " the " rulers of their fair but oppressed country provided England would aid them in their efforts." [27] To some of their proposals, such as the fantastic design of the megalomaniacal Carlo Francesco Comelli von Stuckenfeld to create a new Roman Empire in Italy,[28] the English turned a deaf ear. The projects of other

24 Capograssi, loc. cit., 246.

25 For a lengthy and complete account of this project, see Gallavresi, Giuseppe, e V. Sallier de la Tour de Cordon, Le Maréchal Sallier de la Tour. Mémoires et lettres (Torino, 1912). For a good short account, see Spadoni, Domenico, "Federazione e Re d'Italia mancati nel 1814-15," Nuova Rivista storica, Anno X (settembre-dicembre 1931), 407-10.

26 For an excellent description of Bentinck's activities in Sicily from 1811 to 1814, see Lackland, Miss H. M., "Lord William Bentinck in Sicily, 1811-12," The English Historical Review, XLII (July, 1927), 371-96, and her article on "The Failure of the Constitutional Experiment in Sicily, 1813-14," ibid., XLI (April, 1926), 210-35.

27 Bozzi Granville to Palmerston, August, 1848, Soriga, Renato, "Ugo Foscolo e il suo amico anglo-italo Augusto Bozzi Granville," La Lombardia nel Risorgimento italiano, Anno XIII (gennaio 1928), 130.

28 For an interesting account of Comelli von Stuckenfeld's fantastic mission, see Spadoni, Domenico, "Carlo Comelli de Stuckenfeld e il trono de'Cesari

Italian liberals, however, received the open aid and encouragement of the English government.

The British Foreign Office especially held out a helping hand to the two spirited and untiring propagandists, Vittorio Barzoni and Augusto Bozzi Granville. The former had penned clarion calls for the unification of Italy throughout the course of the Revolutionary and Napoleonic eras.[29] From the very beginning of the nineteenth century, Barzoni had secretly printed and distributed stirring appeals to the Sicilians and Maltese to revolt. After Napoleon's unfortunate Russian campaign, Barzoni's activities were redoubled. Working in conjunction with Lord Bentinck and the British Foreign Office, Barzoni succeeded in stirring up considerable anti-French feeling in Italy.[30]

Even more active and influential than Barzoni was the young ex-Milanese physician, Augusto Bozzi Granville. Born in Milan in 1783, and educated at the University of Pavia, Granville was made translator of Italian correspondence in the British Foreign Office in 1813, when his good friend William Hamilton was appointed under-secretary of state for foreign affairs.[31] At the time of Granville's appointment the English government was, in Italy as well as elsewhere, sedulously disseminating information intended to rouse people under the yoke of French military rule to revolt against their masters. Bulletins from the triumphant Peninsular armies were purposely translated and distributed in large numbers among the Italians to stimulate them to follow the example of the Spanish. After these bulletins

offerto a Casa Savoja nel 1814," *Rassegna storica del Risorgimento*, Anno XIV (ottobre-dicembre 1927), 593-656.

29 Soriga, Renato, "La passione italica di Vittorio Barzoni da Lonato (1767-1843)," *Rassegna storica del Risorgimento*, Anno XX (ottobre-dicembre 1933), 675-77. A good specimen of Barzoni's propaganda is in Rota, *op. cit.*, 214-17.

30 Soriga, "Augusto Bozzi Granville e la Rivista 'L'Italico,'" *loc. cit.*, 272; Spadoni, Domenico, "L'ultimo appello antinapoleonico del Barzoni," *La Lombardia nel Risorgimento italiano*, Anno XV (1930), 65-73.

31 Comandini, Alfredo, "Un Milanese per l'Italia a Londra nel 1814," *Il Secolo*, 10 aprile 1919 The writer saw a copy of this article in the *Biblioteca del Risorgimento italiano* of Milan.

were translated by Granville, they were printed and then distributed by special agents throughout the Italian peninsula.
These bulletins, along with other material, were also printed
in the *Italico,* an Italian propaganda journal begun in London
under Granville's editorship to organize the public opinion of
Granville's countrymen residing in London as well as that of
Italians in general.[32]

Early in the spring of 1814, Granville was charged as special
messenger to the British military and diplomatic commissioners
in Italy. Before leaving for his new post, he handed Hamilton
an appeal to Tsar Alexander of Russia which he had just
written.[33] This appeal called upon the Tsar to aid the Italians in
their struggle for liberty and unification. " Let the Hero of
Russia and of Europe," it went, " command the STANDARD
OF UNION to be unfurled in Italy," as he did in France.
" Let the powerful voice of Alexander recall Italy to the rank
of A NATION." [34] Italian resources and blood must no
longer be " squandered by whichever of the neighbouring
Potentates may again choose to become the terror of Europe." [35]
After so many centuries of division, the Italians could easily
be and must be united around the one remaining legitimate
prince, " in the veins of whose family runs the purest Italian
blood," the King of Sardinia.[36]

Granville was convinced that the views which he expressed
in the pamphlet represented those of Lord Castlereagh,[37] the

32 Granville, Paulina B. (edit.), *Autobiography of A. B. Granville, M.D.,
F.R.S.—being eighty-eight years of the life of a physician who practised his
profession in Italy, Greece, Turkey, Spain, Portugal, the West Indies, Russia,
Germany, France, and England* (London, 1874), I, 335; Soriga, "Augusto
Bozzi Granville e la Rivista ' L'Italico,' " *loc. cit.,* 274-79.

33 Granville, *op. cit.,* I, 347.

34 *Appello ad Alessandro, Imperatore e Autocrate di tutte le Russie, sul
destino dell'Italia.* Scritto nelle tre lingue [Italian, English, and French]
dall'editore dell'*Italico* (London, 1814), 13-14. An original copy of this appeal
is in the Milanese *Biblioteca del Risorgimento italiano.*

35 *Ibid.,* 22.

36 *Ibid.,* 25-6.

37 Granville, *op. cit.,* I, 348.

British minister of foreign affairs, and maintained that Lord Castlereagh approved of his " Appeal " and had assured him that it would have his support.[38] As late as the early spring of 1814, the British government was apparently still forwarding the cause of independence in Italy, as well as in Spain and Portugal.

Aided as they were by the British Foreign Office, Lord Bentinck and other British agents in Italy redoubled their efforts during the last days of the French regime to stir up liberal and national discontent in Italy. Count Mier, the Austrian representative at Naples, gave ample testimony as to the extent of their activities in his reports to the Austrian government. To Chancellor Metternich he wrote that it was necessary for the tranquillity of Italy " that Lord Bentinck change his conduct and cease all his secret schemes to revolutionize the country." Then, continuing, he declared : " The kind of tension that exists in Italy for liberty and for the unification of the whole country into one kingdom is only his work. I have heard people in his entourage say that for three years he has worked " to attain this aim in Italy and " that the English government has already dispensed much money for this object." [39] On March 15, 1814, Mier warned Count Bellegarde that throughout Italy all " the Jacobins and partisans of unification, who are very numerous," were gathering together around Bentinck.[40] Again, on April 6, he wrote Metternich that Lord Bentinck " foments a spirit of insurrection among the inhabitants,

38 *Ibid.*, 349. This contention of Granville's appears to be supported by the fact that about the time Granville wrote his appeal a plan of unifying at least a part of Italy under the hegemony of the King of Sardinia was being worked out in London by the Sardinian ambassador, the English liberal party, and important representatives of the British Foreign Office. Soriga, " Ugo Foscolo e il suo amico anglo-italo Augusto Bozzi Granville," *loc. cit.*, 135.

39 No date or place given, Weil, Maurice Henri, *Le prince Eugène et Murat 1813-1814; opérations militaires, négociations diplomatiques* (Paris, 1902), V, 121.

40 Sent from Reggio, *Staats-Archiv*, Vienna, *Staatskanzlei, Provinzen, Lombardei-Venedig*, Fasc. 3, Sect. 3, Fo. 91-2.

preaches the union of the Italians under a single chieftain, and promises them a constitution based on that of England." [41]

The activities of the British encouraged patriots, in the Kingdom of Italy as well as in the rest of the Apennine peninsula, to expect the powerful support of the English government in their endeavors to overthrow the Napoleonic regime and replace it with a national and constitutional government. The secret societies, the third group stirring up a liberal and national sentiment in Italy, as well as in other parts of Europe, on the other hand, gave the Italian patriots an energetic and well organized political instrument to use in attempting to carry their plans to a successful conclusion. Such societies as the Freemasons, the Guelfs, the Carbonari, and the Adelfi, played a portentous rôle in the dramatic but premature essays of Italian liberals to give the blessings of liberty and independence to their fellow countrymen.

The first of these four societies, the Freemasons, had probably first been introduced in Italy in 1733,[42] and flourished during the period just after the Kingdom of Italy had been established. Since Napoleon took the lodges under his personal protection and supervision, all sorts of individuals flocked into them.[43] Honors and favors of various kinds were showered upon the members of the organization, and some of them were appointed to the highest political positions in the land. By such measures, most of the Freemasons were completely won over to Napoleon.

A rather considerable number of Masons in Italy, nevertheless, still preserved their liberal tendencies and looked forward to the independence and unification of their country. They paid

41 Written at Bologna, Weil, *op. cit.,* V, 102.

42 The first Italian lodge is thought to have been opened at Florence. Redding, Moses W., *The Illustrated History of Free Masonry* (New York, 1907), 450; Marcolongo, Bianca, "La massoneria nel secolo XVIII," *Studi Storici,* XIX (1910), 409.

43 Dolce to Saurau, November, 1815, Luzio, Alessandro, *La Massoneria e il Risorgimento italiano. Saggio storico-critico. Con illustrazioni e molti documenti inediti* (Bologna, 1925), I, 117.

homage to the French Emperor because they found it necessary to do so, but at the same time they indulged in subterranean national and liberal propaganda.[44] Prominent among these Masons were the venerable and intrepid Professors Francesco Salfi [45] and Gian Domenico Romagnosi,[46] both of whom continually affirmed in their lectures the right of the Italians to form themselves into a united and independent nation, and proposed that the " new Italy " be a federation of constitutional states.[47] Salfi and Romagnosi prepared a reprint in Milan of the collection of Masonic verses published in the *Lira focense* of Abbé Antonio Ierocades. It was immediately confiscated because a committee formed to judge its Masonic orthodoxy considered that it was filled too much " with that democratic enthusiasm which has already led many men into error." [48]

Believing, after this rebuff, that the official Freemasonry, dominated as it was by the government, could never do more than chant paeans of praise to Napoleon, the two professors formed a new secret political society, whose aim was to throw off the yoke of despotism and to form Italy into an independent and united nation.[49] This action was indicative of what was

44 Soriga, Renato, " La ristampa milanese della ' Lira focense ' di Antonio Ierocades," *Rassegna storica del Risorgimento,* Anno V (ottobre-dicembre 1918), 732-33.

45 For a good account of the life of Salfi, see Nardi, Carlo, " La vita di Francesco Saverio Salfi (1759-1832)," *Rassegna storica del Risorgimento,* Anno VII (aprile-settembre 1920), 161-332.

46 For an account of Romagnosi's life and influence, see Monti, Antonio, " G. D. Romagnosi. Contributo Biografico," *Nuova Antologia. Rivista di lettere, scienze ed arti,* Anno LIII (1 maggio 1918), 41-50. Cesare Cantù, in his *Il Conciliatore e i Carbonari* (Milano, 1878), 125, says that Romagnosi " was chief of the Masonic lodges in the Kingdom of Italy."

47 Soriga, " La ristampa della ' Lira focense,' " *loc. cit.,* 734.

48 *Ibid.,* 735.

49 Pedrotti, Pietro, *Note autobiografiche del cospiratore trentino Gioacchino Prati, con annotazioni e commenti. Sulla base di documenti inediti d'archivio* (Rovereto, 1926), 31. Domenico Spadoni, in his " Le società segrete nella rivoluzione milanese dell'aprile 1814," *Nuova Antologia. Rivista di lettere, scienze ed arti,* Ser. VII, CCLXV (16 maggio 1929), 199, says that this society may have been either the Adelfi or the Centri.

happening with the whole organization. Italian Freemasonry by 1813 was rent with discontent and ever recurring disorders.[50] Some lodges, the Grand Orient of Italy, for example, were striving to reform their society along definite national lines, whereas others were still plodding along according to the traditional patterns. The French were losing their control over the lodges. Greatly perturbed, the viceroy hastened to decree that all Masonic lodges should be dissolved.[51]

Driven underground by the viceroy's order, the clandestine liberal agitation became more dangerous to the French. Now the dissentient Masonic groups, especially in Milan, collaborated with all kinds of liberal groups having the same general aims as theirs. By late 1813 and early 1814, the radical factions of Freemasonry were secretly but actively preparing to seize upon any favorable occasion to overthrow the Napoleonic government and to create in its place a united and independent Italy.[52] The hand of the Freemasons was clearly discernible in the events which finally led to the overthrow of the Kingdom of Italy.

The Guelf society also took part in the liberal intrigues which were carried on late in 1813 and in the opening months of 1814. The society appears to have been introduced into Italy by the English.[53] Its aim was to create an Italy united either under

50 Cipolla, C., "Un Documento Austriaco sui Massoni e sui Carbonari," *Rassegna Nazionale*, XXIV (1885), 483. This memoir was written by Pietro Dolce, a member of the Masonic organization who later became an informant of the Austrian government.

51 Soriga, "La ristampa della 'Lira focense,'" *loc. cit.*, 736.

52 Salfi, Francesco, *L'Italie au XIX siècle* (1821), as quoted in Spadoni, "Le società segrete nella rivoluzione milanese dell'aprile 1814," *loc. cit.*, 199.

53 The Guelf constitution of October 15, 1813, which Domenico Spadoni found in the Milanese archives and published in his "Gli Statuti della Guelfia in possesso della Polizia austriaca nel 1816," *Rassegna storica del Risorgimento*, Anno XI (1924), 704-38, definitely indicates that the English must have played a large part in organizing the Guelf society. Article 3 of the constitution asserts that the Guelfs put themselves "under the most valorous protection" of England. Article 4 states that as soon as this protection would be obtained, a member of the society was to be charged with keeping in constant contact with "H. E. L. W. B. [His Excellency Lord William

a republican form of government or under a government ruled by a prince from the English dynasty and with constitutional forms similar to those of England.[54] The evidence thus far brought to light on the early activities of the organization is extremely meager and sketchy, but it is of a nature that would lead us to believe that in late 1813 and early 1814 the Guelfs played no small rôle in fomenting the spirit of insurrection which finally brought Napoleon's northern Italian kingdom to an abrupt end.[55]

Much better known and perhaps more active than either the Freemasons or the Guelfs were the Carbonari. The society originated as an offshoot or reform of Freemasonry,[56] and

Bentinck], commander of the naval forces of H. B. M. [His Britannic Majesty] in the Mediterranean, to agree with him on the method of restoring Italian independence." In Article 43 "Lord W. Bentinck is declared Protector of the Order." Article 51 reveals that as soon as the hoped for revolution was carried to a successful conclusion, "the votes of the G. [Guelfs] to obtain a Prince" from the English house and dynasty, "in case the circumstances of the time did not permit the establishment of a Republic," would be manifested "to H. E. L. W. [His Excellency Lord William] Bentinck." It was to be understood "that the same Prince ought to rule all Italy with laws compatible with our principles and similar to those of the Parliament of England." "If England wishes to retain Sicily and Malta as compensation for its favor," Article 73 insists, "it is at least intended that the laws which are to fix the destinies of Italy should also become common to the inhabitants" of these two places. "As to the exclusive commerce which the English hope for in Italy, it is agreed," continues Article 74, "that it ought to be reconciled with reciprocal advantages relative to National honor."

54 See Article 51 in the preceding footnote.

55 In the Maroncelli trial after the 1820-21 revolutions, the Austrian judge, Salvotti, said that the Guelfs were scattered through Lombardy and Milan in 1814 under the title of the Society of the Centri. Spadoni, Domenico, *Milano e la congiura militare nel 1814 per l'indipendenza italiana: Il moto del 20 aprile e l'occupazione austriaca* (Modena, 1936), 278. Federico Confalonieri mentions in his memoirs that there existed at this time in Milan a society of the Guelfs, which was a sect quite distinct from the Masons and the Carbonari. *Ibid.* Also see *post*, 106-7.

56 Saint-Edme, M., *Constitution et organisation des Carbonari, ou documents exacts sur tout ce qui concerne l'existence, l'origine et le but de cette société secrète* (2nd ed., Paris, 1822), 7-8, points out the striking similarity between the rites and symbols of the Carbonari and the Freemasons. Other

during the early years of its history it had the strong encouragement and protection of Lord William Bentinck and other English officials.[57] The aim of the Carbonari was to establish

good works on the origins of the Carbonari which hold that the society emanated as a reform or offshoot of Freemasonry are: Dito, Oreste, *Massoneria, carboneria ed altre società segrete nella storia del Risorgimento italiano, con appendice ed illustrazioni* (Torino, 1905), 69-71; Ottolini, Angelo, *La carboneria dalle origini ai primi tentativi insurrezionali (1797-1817)* (Modena, 1936), 25-33; Leti, Giuseppe, *Carboneria e massoneria nel Risorgimento italiano. Saggio di critica storica* (2nd ed., Genova, 1926), 69-71; Cipolla, *loc. cit.*, 484; "L'origine e lo scopo della Carboneria secondo i costituti de'primi Carbonari e Guelfi," *La Civiltà cattolica*, Anno LXVI (19 giugno 1915), 654-55; Spadoni, Domenico, *Sette, cospirazioni e cospiratori nello stato pontificio all'indomani della restaurazione* (Torino, 1904), cv; Marcolongo, Bianca, "Le origini della Carboneria e le Società segrete nell'Italia Meridionale dal 1810 al 1820," *Studi Storici*, XX (1912), 305-6; and Gallavresi, Giuseppe, "La franc-maçonnerie et la formation de l'unité italienne," *Revue des questions historiques*, Année L (1er octobre 1922), 419. It should be pointed out, however, that Alessandro Luzio believes that, in spite of all similarities, the Carbonari and the Freemasons have always been distinct from one another. See his *La Massoneria e il Risorgimento italiano, op. cit.*, I, 170.

57 Colletta, Pietro, *Storia del reame di Napoli dal 1734 sino al 1825* (Firenze, 1848), II, 282, relates that the early emissaries of the Carbonari to Sicily were very well received "*by Lord Bentinck, who in this period designed still more vast plans.*" Marquis G. B. Canonici of Ferrara, when questioned in August, 1820, by the Austrian and papal authorities, informed them: "I have been told that the English have inspired the spirit of Italian unification in Sicily and also the society of the Carbonari." Quoted in "L'origine e lo scopo della Carboneria," *loc. cit.*, 642. Also very revealing is the report of Pietro Dolce, who wrote: "The English made use of the Illuminati [*sic?*] of Germany to create opposition to Napoleon; among the rulers and among the people they awakened sentiments of disdain against the feared author of the continental blockade. Wherever the English find monarchs, they turn to the populations by means of secret societies; and they made use of the Illuminati, who were not lacking in Naples, to organize Carbonari *vendite.*" Luzio, *La Massoneria e il Risorgimento italiano, op. cit.*, I, 162. On November 29, 1813, Minister Fontanelli sent to Luini, then director of the police of the Kingdom of Italy, a report of Senator Dandolo of Ancona, who asserted that the spread of the Carbonari was "*all the work of English gold.*" *Ibid.*, 165. And Pecchio, in his *Catechismo italiano*, published in Philadelphia in 1830, wrote: "Do you not know the origin of the Carbonari? They came to light toward 1807 in Sicily and had a Queen and a Cardinal for their protectors. The kind-hearted English undertook their education, and caressed, aroused, and encouraged them, because these gentle-

an independent and united Italy, with constitutional guarantees for the people, and with some form of national representation.[58]

Although stronger in southern Italy than in the other parts of the peninsula, the society spread rapidly to the North. In his trial in 1815, Cesare Giacomini of Ascoli said that he knew of the existence of Carbonari in Milan as early as 1811.[59] Various reports of the police of the Kingdom of Italy in 1813 indicated that Lombardy was being permeated with the propaganda of the Carbonari.[60] In his memoirs, Breganze says that, to the great perturbation of Prince Eugene, the name of Carbonari was reported in all quarters between the Adige and Po rivers.[61] And the ex-conspirator Pietro Dolce informed the Austrian police that by the spring of 1814 " all Milan was Carbonarized," and " Carbonarism was being propagandized in all the Lombard provinces." [62] By late 1813 and the spring of 1814, the Lombard Carbonari were ready to foment revolutionary machinations against their government.

By itself each of these societies—Freemason, Guelf, and Carbonaro—was in a position to be a real nuisance to the French regime. Organized together under a single directing hand, these societies could be truly dangerous. To form such a directing society for all the secret political sects was the aim of the Adelfia or Filadelfia society, which had been formed by independent Freemasons.[63] Banded together in national federa-

men occupying Sicily had need of the Carbonari to create and foment an Italian party against the French party." Quoted in *ibid.*, 165-66.

58 See the Social-Constitutional Pact of Ausonia, as printed in Saint-Edme, *op. cit*, 112-58; and the constitution of the Romagnese Carbonari, in Bandini, Gino, *Giornali e scritti politici clandestini della Carboneria romagnola (1819-21)* (Roma, 1908), 250-53.

59 Ottolini, *op. cit.*, 75-6.

60 *Ibid.*, 75.

61 *Ibid.*, 76.

62 Report of June 30, 1816, Luzio, *La Massoneria nel Regno italico, op. cit.*, 72.

63 Bersano, Arturo, "Adelfi, Federati e Carbonari. Contributo alla Storia delle Società segrete," *Atti* della R. Accademia delle Scienze di Torino, XLV (1909-1910), 413; Gallavresi, *loc. cit.*, 419.

tions, all its members took an oath to work to the best of their ability for the independence of their country. In Italy the chief centers of the society were in Bologna, Milan, and Turin. The international directing body of the sect, the *Gran Firmamento*, had its headquarters in Paris. From Paris the central directory hoped to penetrate all the European liberal societies and to govern them.[64] As early as 1814, the Adelfi strove to attain this unification,[65] and appear to have been at least partially successful in making themselves a revolutionary super-directory in the Kingdom of Italy.[66]

By 1813 and 1814, the adherents of the liberal and national factions had apparently made considerable headway in proselyting their ideas among the Italian populace. As early as November, 1813, Fouché, the French minister of police, wrote Napoleon from Rome: " Here as in all Italy, the word of independence has a magical virtue." [67] On December 12, 1813, Melzi admitted to Napoleon that there was a party in the Kingdom of Italy working for the independence of all Italy, and that, although its program was vague, it was gaining adherents every day.[68] About the same time Gabriele Pepe wrote: " The French are detested. People want liberty. The Austrians are feared. . . . Persons with good intentions want to see the *flag of a united and independent Italy* hoisted." [69]

A little later Sir Robert Wilson, the English attaché to the Austrian army in Italy, noted in his diary that the Italians were much alive to the "value of nationalisation." [70] The

64 Ottolini, *op. cit.*, 46-7.

65 Bersano, *loc. cit.*, 414.

66 See *post*, 107.

67 Cantù, Cesare (edit.), *Il principe Eugenio, memorie del Regno d'Italia* (Milano, 1880), VIII, 268. Also cited in Lemmi, *op. cit.*, 83-4.

68 Sent from Monza, Melzi d'Eril, Francesco, Duca di Lodi, *Memorie-documenti e lettere inedite di Napoleone I. e Beauharnais*. Raccolte e ordinate per cura di Giovanni Melzi (Milano, 1865), II, 283-85.

69 Weil, *op. cit.*, III, 580.

70 Under date of February 6, 1814, Wilson, Sir Robert, *Private Diary of Travels, Personal Services, and Public Events, during Mission and*

Austrian Baron Huegel asserted: "*There now exist in Italy a large number of persons in whom the idea of an Italian nation brought together in a large single state has taken root.*" [71] And on April 2, 1814, the Austrian Major General, Count Ficquelmont, wrote the Archduke Francis of Este that the only thing the Italians really liked and desired was a Kingdom of Italy. The idea of independence, he maintained, had taken very strong roots in the soil of Italy.[72]

The work of the patriotic writers, the English agents, and the secret societies had not been in vain. In various parts of Italy, and notably in Milan, there existed, particularly among the liberal upper and middle classes, a considerable amount of liberal and national sentiment. By the beginning of 1814, public opinion in the Kingdom of Italy, as well as in other countries under Napoleonic control, was permeated with anti-French feeling. Many people were ready to seize upon the first possible opportunity to overthrow the French regime. The opportunity came in the spring of 1814 when the Allied Powers, in the " War of Liberation " of 1813/14, finally succeeded in conquering the formidable military forces of France.

Employment with the European Armies in the Campaigns of 1812, 1813, 1814 (London, 1861), II, 306.

71 Weil, *op. cit.*, V, 99.

72 *Ibid.*, 123-24.

CHAPTER III

THE ITALIAN CAMPAIGN, 1813-1814

On August 12, 1813, Francis I, the Emperor of Austria, formally joined the seventh coalition by declaring war on Napoleon Bonaparte.[1] After having been at peace with the French Emperor since 1809, the Austrian government joined England, Russia, Prussia, and Sweden in their "War of Liberation" against him.

It was an auspicious time for the Austrians to take up the cudgel against the armies of the French Emperor. In the Iberian peninsula, English, Spanish, and Portuguese military forces had already won major victories over the French. Napoleon's former marshal, King Bernadotte of Sweden, had turned against him. Tens of thousands of Napoleon's troops had been left dead on the cold and barren plains of Russia, and Napoleon's military power appeared to have been largely spent. Prussia had joined Tsar Alexander in his war against the ubiquitous Gallic commander, and its king had issued spirited appeals to all Germans to join his country in a war of national independence. In spite of Napoleon's Pyrrhic victories over the Russians and Prussians at Lützen and Bautzen in May, 1813, it appeared that he was nearing the end of his career. Now was the time to drive him out of Central Europe.

To defeat the military forces of the French Emperor, the Allied sovereigns divided their forces, estimated at 512,000 men,[2] into several armies. The main army was to occupy Bohemia. In addition to it, there was the northern army under Bernadotte; and finally a Silesian army under Bluecher. The fundamental plan of strategy was that if the enemy attacked

1 A copy of this declaration can be found in *The British and Foreign State Papers*, I, Pt. 1, 810-22.

2 Caemmerer, Rudolf von, *Die Befreiungskriege, 1813-1815. Ein strategischer Ueberblick* (Berlin, 1907), 38.

any of these three armies with his main body, it should fall back while the other two advanced to the attack.

In addition to the main armies, several smaller forces were dispatched to dispose of the French forces in other parts of Europe. Among them was the so-called " Inner-Austrian " army of 70,000 men, under the command of General Hiller, which was sent to the southern boundary of Austria to attack the French armies in Italy.

To oppose the main armies of the Allied Powers in Central Europe, Napoleon had an army estimated at 440,000 men.[3] To oppose the Inner-Austrian army, Napoleon's viceroy in the Kingdom of Italy, Prince Eugene, was able to collect an army of between fifty-five and sixty thousand men.[4]

The first phase of the campaign of the main armies took place in Germany. In the Italian campaign,[5] it took place in Illyria,

3 *Ibid.*, 36.

4 *Précis historique des opérations militaires de l'armée d'Italie, en 1813 et 1814*, Par le Chef de l'État-Major-général de cette Armée (Paris, 1817), 31.

5 The best Austrian sources on the campaign written by men who actually took part in it are as follows: Welden, Ludwig Freiherr von, *Der Krieg der Oesterreicher in Italien gegen die Franzosen in den Jahren 1813 und 1814* (Graz, 1853) ; and Lemmi, Francesco, *La restaurazione in Italia nel 1814 nel diario del barone von Huegel (9 decembre 1813-25 mai 1814)* (Milano, 1910). (Copied from the original in the *Staats-Archiv*, Vienna, *Staatskanzlei, Provinzen, Lombardei-Venedig*, Fasc. 45, Sect. 1.) In future citations the latter of these two sources will be referred to as " Huegel Diary, *op. cit.*" Besides the *Précis historique, op. cit.*, the best contemporary French sources are: *Journal historique sur la campagne du Prince Eugène, en Italie, pendant les années 1813 et 1814.* Par L. D****, Capitaine attaché à l'État-major du Prince, et Chevalier de la Légion d'Honneur (Paris, 1817) ; and *Dernière campagne de l'armée franco-italienne, sous les ordres d'Eugène-Beauharnais, en 1813 et 1814, Suivie de Mémoires secrets sur la révolution de Milan, du 20 avril 1814, et les deux conjurations du 25 avril 1815; la campagne des Autrichiens contre Murat; sa mort tragique, et la situation politique actuelle des divers États d'Italie.* Par le chevalier S. J***, témoin oculaire (Paris, 1817). In addition to these contemporary records, the following studies should also be consulted: Holtz, Oberst Georg Freiherr vom, *Die inneroester-reichische Armee, 1813 und 1814* (Volume IV of Veltzé, Major Alois (edit.), *1813-1815. Oesterreich in den Befreiungskriegen*) (Wien, 1912) ; and Weil, *op. cit.*

NOTE.—The map on the opposite page has been taken from the *Journal historique sur la campagne du Prince Eugène, op. cit.*

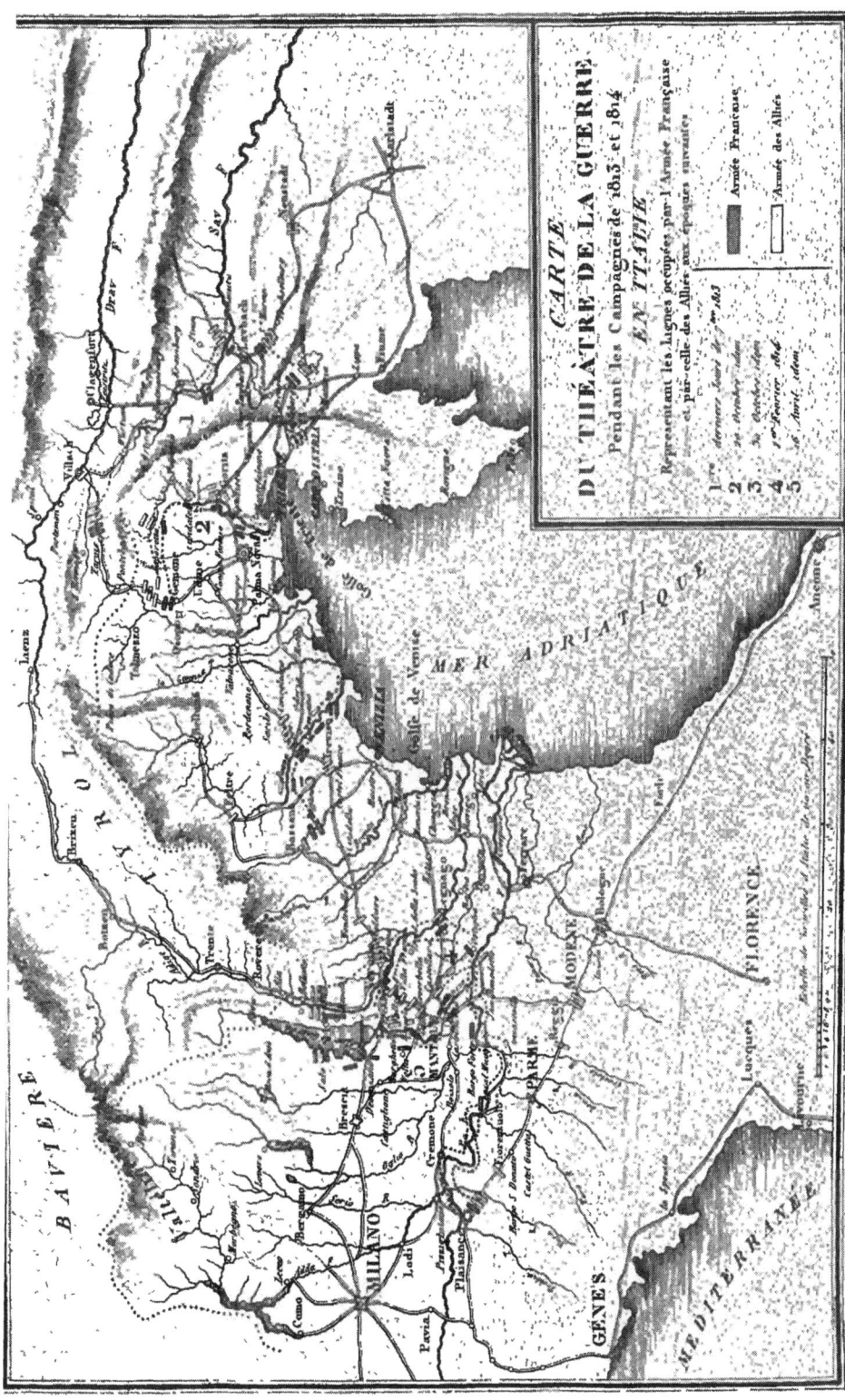

CARTE
DU THÉÂTRE DE LA GUERRE
Pendant les Campagnes de 1813 et 1814
EN ITALIE

Représentant les Lignes occupées par l'Armée Française
et par celle des Alliés aux époques suivantes

1er savoir bout le ... 1813
2 en décembre idem
3 en octobre idem
4 1er Février 1814
5 Avril idem

Armée Française
Armée des Alliés

BAVIERE

TYROL

MER ADRIATIQUE

Golfe de Venise

MILANO

GÊNES

PARME

MODÈNE

FLORENCE

Lucques

Ancône

MER MÉDITERRANÉE

which the Austrian army entered around the middle of August, 1813. The Illyrian phase of the campaign of the Inner-Austrian army was crowned with a succession of rapid victories. As soon as the Austrian forces entered the region, the Dalmatians and Croatians, who had long chafed under the burdens imposed upon them by their French masters, began an insurrection against the French. Habsburg troops were immediately sent to their aid. Assisted as they were by the revolt of the inhabitants, the Austrians advanced rapidly and took town after town from the French armies under Prince Eugene's command. Trieste and Laibach were soon captured without any formidable opposition, and later, on October 6, Goritz, on the Isonzo river, was taken. Illyria was now won by Austria. French power in the Adriatic had been broken up.

Along with the calamitous defeat in Illyria, Prince Eugene received other setbacks. On October 8, his father-in-law, King Maximilian of Bavaria, officially announced the abandonment of his alliance with Napoleon and his decision to cast his lot with the Allied Powers.[6] This was a double blow for Eugene. Not only was his wife's father now opposing him, but the Austrians were free to send against him the troops which had been stationed in western Austria to protect Habsburg territory from invasion from that direction. Less than a fortnight after Bavaria's defection came Napoleon's stunning defeat at Leipzig. If the viceroy had ever expected help from his stepfather in meeting the steady thrusts of the Habsburg army in Italy, he was now forced to abandon such hopes. Henceforth, it was obvious that Prince Eugene had to rely upon his own depleted resources to protect the French regime in the Apennine peninsula against its adversaries.

After Maximilian's desertion and the disaster at Leipzig, Hiller was free to hurl all his forces across the Tyrol into Italy. Under the new onslaught, the viceroy, with his insuffi-

6 On the same day the Bavarian king announced his decision to his son-in-law and advised him to follow the same procedure. Du Casse, op. cit., IX, 283-85.

cient and poorly trained troops, could do nothing but withdraw. On the 23rd of October, he was already in Udine; and by November 4, he was forced back to Verona, on the Adige.

While Beauharnais was rapidly withdrawing his troops to the Adige, Baron Hiller was not slow in advancing across the Alps with the main body of the Inner-Austrian army. By the 26th of October, he was at Trent. There he addressed the Italian people, informing them that he had entered the plains of Italy at the head of his army to free them from the tyranny oppressing them. In stirring words he exhorted them: " Arise, people of Italy! " " Remind your sons " that " the greatest glory is to fight under the Banner of the most just Monarch for the peace of the World and for the independence of the People." [7]

Later the Austrians issued other proclamations. After leaving Trent, General Hiller affirmed that Austria was not making war in order to aggrandize itself, but was, instead, fighting the oppressors of nations for the independence of the people. Again he urged the Italians to unite " with the defenders of religion and of the independence " of their country! [8] On December 10, the Austrian general, Nugent,[9] while in Ravenna, assured the Italian people that Austria was coming to bring them freedom and promised that they would have a fortunate future if they were " faithful to those who love and protect " them.[10] After Bellegarde took Hiller's place as commander of the Inner-Austrian army, the new general proclaimed to the inhabitants of the Apennine peninsula: " The Emperor has cast his fatherly glance upon the fields of Italy, which have always

7 *Archivio di Stato*, Venice, *Polizia*, V. A., Fo. 1138. A good German translation of this proclamation is in Holtz, *op. cit.*, 68-9.

8 Weil, *op. cit.*, II, 489.

9 Springer, Anton, *Geschichte Oesterreichs seit dem Wiener Frieden 1809* (Leipzig, 1863-65), I, 242, erroneously ascribes this proclamation to Hiller.

10 Weil, *op. cit.*, III, 212-13; Spadoni, *Il moto del 20 aprile, op. cit.*, 28-9; Cusani, *op. cit.*, VII, 47.

been so dear to him," and "assures you that the Alps are the proper boundary for Italy." [11]

The Italians, however, remained deaf to the voices of the Austrian generals. To win victory, instead of issuing propaganda to the people, the Austrians needed to strike the weakened French-Italian army a stunning blow. Unfortunately, General Hiller did not press the French-Italian army after its hurried retreat to the Adige, but contented himself with engaging in a few ineffective minor engagements. The Austrian commander's excessive prudence, singular hesitations, timidity, and abnormal slowness [12] were responsible for the loss of many opportunities to engage the enemy. These characteristics also lost him his position as commander-in-chief of the Inner-Austrian army. His irresoluteness and indolence were held accountable for the lack of success in Italy. After sharply reprimanding him, Emperor Francis supplanted him in his command [13] with Field Marshal Bellegarde,[14] who immediately left

11 Springer, *op. cit.*, I, 243.

12 Weil, *op. cit.*, II, 430.

13 Gentz to Caradja, Freiburg, December 19, 1813, Klinkowstroem, Alfons Freiherr von (edit.), *Oesterreichs Theilnahme an den Befreiungskriegen. Ein Beitrag zur Geschichte der Jahre 1813 bis 1815 nach Aufzeichnungen von Friedrich von Gentz, nebst einem Anhang: "Briefwechsel zwischen den Fuersten Schwarzenberg und Metternich"* (Wien, 1887), 143; Kerpen to Bellegarde, Vienne, December 14, 1813, cited in Weil, *op cit.*, III, 241; Kaiser Franz to Kerpen, Frankfurt, November 15, 1813, *Staats-Archiv*, Vienna, *Conferenz Akten*, Ser. a, 1813, No. 170.

14 Count Bellegarde, the son of a Saxon infantry general, was born at Dresden on August 29, 1756. In 1772, young Bellegarde passed into the service of Austria, holding the rank of a second-lieutenant. He was rapidly promoted in the Austrian army. In 1789 he was made a colonel, and in 1792 he was promoted to the rank of major-general. In 1799, he was given command of the Tyrolese army, and after the Battle of Marengo, was called to the command of the Italian army. At the end of the 1809 campaign, the Emperor named Bellegarde field marshal, and called him, in April, 1810, to the presidency of the *Hof-Kriegs-Rath*, to direct the reorganization of the Austrian army. In December, 1813, he was again given the command of the Italian army, and the next year was made imperial commissioner for the newly reacquired Italian provinces. In 1815, he was made grand master of the court of the hereditary archduke, and, in 1820, was called for a second time to

for Italy and arrived at the Austrian headquarters at Vicenza on December 15, 1813.[15]

While the military campaign was dragging on at a lumbering gait, and while the command of the Inner-Austrian army was being changed, the Allies made a concerted effort to induce Prince Eugene and Joachim Murat, the King of Naples, to desert Napoleon for their own cause. As early as October 8, 1813, Eugene's father-in-law, King Maximilian, had tried to induce him to join the Allies.[16] Again, on the evening of November 22, Prince Thurn und Taxis, presented himself at Eugene's headquarters with another communication from the Bavarian king, promising Eugene that if he abandoned the French Emperor he would receive a kingship in Italy.[17] Around the middle of January, Marshal Bellegarde himself tried to seduce the viceroy with promises to make the Adige river the boundary between Eugene's and Austrian territory.[18] Somewhat later the proposals were again renewed when, on February 18, a certain Poggi [Poni?],[19] a Bavarian general, appeared at the viceroy's headquarters. All these attempts to win Eugene over to the Allied cause were rebuffed by Napo-

the presidency of the *Hof-Kriegs-Rath*. In 1825, he retired from active service, and twenty years later he died in Vienna. Weil, *op. cit*, III, 571.

15 Huegel Diary, *op. cit.*, December 15, 1813, 3.

16 Du Casse, *op. cit.*, IX, 283-85.

17 Zanoli, Alessandro, *Sulla milizia cisalpino-italiana. Cenni storico-statistici dal 1796 al 1814* (Milano, 1845), II, 269-70; La Tour et Taxis to the Duchesse de Leuchtemberg, Munich, November 15, 1836, Du Casse, *op cit*, IX, 300-7; Eugene to King of Bavaria, Verona, 8.00 P. M., November 22, 1813, *ibid.*, 308; Eugene to Napoleon, Verona, 11.00 P. M., November 22, 1813, *ibid.*, 308-12; Cusani, *op. cit.*, VII, 39-42; Lemmi, *La restaurazione austriaca, op. cit.*, 65-7.

18 Eugene to Melzi, Verona, January 18, 1814, Cantù, *Il principe Eugenio, op. cit*, IX, 71-2; Eugene to Augusta Amelia, January 17, 1814, Du Casse, *op. cit.*, IX, 317. Also see Lemmi, *La restaurazione austriaca, op. cit.*, 67.

19 Huegel Diary, *op cit*, February 18, 20, 26, 1814, 32-4, 39-40, refers to this emissary as Poggi. In a letter which the viceroy wrote his wife at Volta on February 21, 1814 (Cantù, *Il principe Eugenio, op. cit.*, IX, 97-8), on the other hand, he is called Poni. Also see Lemmi, *La restaurazione austriaca, op. cit.*, 67.

leon's self-willed stepson. Eugene remained unchangeable in his loyalty to his stepfather. He was one of the few favorites of Napoleon who remained faithful to the very end.

Joachim Murat, the King of Naples, however, did not remain as true to his brother-in-law and benefactor as did the devoted viceroy of the Kingdom of Italy. Murat had long been displeased with Napoleon, and after the latter's return from Russia in the last weeks of 1812, the former brewed a vast political scheme. Murat, feeling convinced that the French Empire would soon fall to pieces, hoped that all Italy, from the Alps to Sicily, might be united into a single state with himself as ruler. In November, 1813, he requested his brother-in-law, Napoleon, to proclaim the independence of Italy.[20] At the same time, he began sending troops to northern Italy and holding numerous conferences with various malcontents on the way to assure them that he was marching north as the champion of independence.[21]

The French Emperor's disastrous check at Leipzig convinced Joachim that his brother-in-law would soon be defeated. He knew that he dared remain no longer on the Napoleonic bandwagon. Loyalty to a defeated Napoleon would not only frustrate his plans to make himself sovereign of a united kingdom of Italy, but also would make him another princeling without a kingdom. To prevent such a catastrophe, he must come at once to terms with the British and the Austrians. With such thoughts in mind, Murat immediately approached Count Mier, the Austrian minister at the Neapolitan capital, with definite proposals of an alliance, decreed the abolition of the continental system in the Kingdom of Naples, and sent the Marquis de St. Elie to Bentinck and Prince Cariati to negotiate with the authorities at Vienna.[22] Bentinck, who had long been more or

20 Johnston, R. M., *The Napoleonic Empire in Southern Italy and the Rise of the Secret Societies* (London, 1904), I, 270-72.

21 Melzi to Napoleon, Monza, December 12, 1813, Melzi d'Eril, *op. cit.*, II, 283-85.

22 Koch, Christophe G de, et Friedrich Schoell, *Histoire abrégée des traités de paix entre les puissances de l'Europe depuis la paix de Westphalie* (Paris, 1817-18), X, 457-58.

less hostile to Murat, gave no encouragement to his proposals of alliance, but the Austrian Emperor accepted them cheerfully and sent Count Neipperg to conclude a treaty with Murat.[23]

With Neipperg in Naples, satisfactory terms were speedily agreed upon, and on January 11, 1814, a treaty of alliance was signed. Murat was to enter the seventh coalition against Napoleon and to keep an army of at least 30,000 men in the field against the French. The Austrian government, for its part, guaranteed the crown of Naples to Joachim, promised to keep at least 60,000 soldiers in Italy during the war, and, in secret articles appended to the treaty, guaranteed Murat an addition of 400,000 people, to be taken from the papal states.[24]

With great reluctance, Bentinck also made peace with King Joachim, and, on February 3, he signed a convention with him, providing for an armistice between the English and the Neapolitans whereby hostilities were not to begin again until at least three months after a rupture was announced by one of the two parties.[25]

While these negotiations with King Joachim were going on, the battle front in northern Italy was almost entirely quiet. The strengthening of the French-Italian forces behind the Adige had momentarily checked the progress of the Habsburg army, while the heavy snow greatly hampered the movements of both armies. The chief reason, however, for the lull in the campaign was that Bellegarde was waiting for Murat's army to make a junction with his own forces before proceeding against the viceroy's troops.

23 Metternich to Mier, Francfort-sur-le-Mein, December 10, 1813, Weil, *op. cit.*, III, 562; Huegel Diary, *op. cit.*, December 19, 1813, 4.

24 Orloff, Comte Grégoire, *Mémoires historiques, politiques, et littéraires sur le royaume de Naples* (Paris, 1819-21), II, 432-38. Also see Mier to Metternich, Naples, January 16, 1814, Helfert, Josef Alexander Freiherr von, *Joachim Murat, seine letzten Kaempfe und sein Ende* (Wien, 1878), 138-41.

25 Martens, Geo. Fréd., et Charles Martens, *Nouveau recueil de traités d'alliance, de paix, de trève, de neutralité, de commerce, de limites, d'échange, etc. et de plusieurs autres actes servant à la connaissance des rélations étrangères des puissances et états de l'Europe* (Gottingue, 1817-42), V, 31-2; Weil, *op. cit.*, III, 643-44.

In the latter part of January, Count Bellegarde had grounds for believing that the Neapolitan forces would soon join his own, for Murat's army was on the march northward. On January 16, the Neapolitans took possession of Rome, on the 18th, they entered Ferrara and Bologna, and on the 31st, they took possession of Florence. But then they halted their march, while various of Murat's officials occupied themselves with making appeals to the Italian people by issuing spirited propaganda proclamations.

A proclamation made by Carascosa at Rimini on January 31,[26] and another one made by General Lechi at Florence on February 5 or 6,[27] assured the Italians that Murat's sole intention in engaging in his present activities was to prepare the way for the re-establishment of their freedom. Still another proclamation, posted in Modena on February 1, under Carascosa's name, promised that Murat and the other Allied sovereigns would bring the Italian people a durable peace and the independence which they had always desired.[28] Again, on February 9, a fourth appeal, made in Bologna by the Neapolitan commissioner Poerio, informed the inhabitants of the Apennine peninsula of Murat's treaty with Austria and his armistice with England, and entreated them to second "the projects of His Majesty and of the Allied Powers" with all the resources at their command.[29]

While King Murat's lieutenants were posting these liberal appeals, the Austrians resumed their propaganda campaign. On

26 *Staats-Archiv*, Vienna, *Staatskanzlei, Provinzen, Lombardei-Venedig*, Fasc. 3, Sect. 3, Fo. 45. Weil, *op. cit.*, III, 635, contains an Italian copy of the same document, but it is represented as having been proclaimed at Modena. The above, however, is the only copy of the proclamation which I have been able to find in the *Staats-Archiv*.

27 Weil, *op cit.*, V, 3, says this proclamation was made on February 5. The *Oesterreichisch-Kaiserliche privilegirte Wiener-Zeitung nebst Amtsblatt*, February 26, 1814, 230, on the other hand, says that it was given on February 6 In future references the latter will be cited as "*Wiener Zeitung*."

28 Weil, *op cit*, III, 635.

29 *Ibid*, 635-36.

February 4, two hours after the viceroy had deserted it, Belle-garde entered Verona.[30] Here he issued two proclamations, one addressed to the army, and the other, to the Italian people. In the first, he asserted that the army would rapidly decide the fate of Italy, and assured the people that the Austrians had come to deliver their friends, " the people of Italy, . . . from foreign oppression." [31] In the proclamation to " the people of Italy," Bellegarde guaranteed the population that the Austrian armies had entered their country under the banner of freedom. " See in us," he continued, " your liberators who demand nothing that is not indispensable for our sustenance. We come to protect well-founded rights and to re-establish what force and ambition have destroyed." [32] Somewhat later, the Austrian General Nugent published another proclamation, directed to the Italian troops and calling on them to fight for " national independence, the most sacred cause of your rights." " Soldiers, and you to whom Italy is entrusted," he went on, " show your-selves worthy of your name, and of the memory of your Fathers. Remember that a people can flatter itself with its independence only when its united and armed brave display a determined attitude, under the guidance and command of national Leaders. Without union, without arms, you have no country, no civil liberty, no rights, but instead, can only be a nation which must expect the slavery and despotism of foreigners." [33]

Prince Eugene took action against these proclamations, designed as they were to provoke the Italians to revolt against the French, with proclamations of his own. On February 1, as soon as he heard of Murat's treason, Eugene published two

30 Huegel Diary, op. cit., 18 ftn.

31 *Staats-Archiv*, Vienna, *Staatskanzlei, Provinzen, Lombardei-Venedig,* Fasc. 3, Sect. 3, Fo. 54.

32 Weil, op. cit., III, 647-48.

33 Quoted in Spadoni, *Il moto del 20 aprile, op. cit*, 30-1 ; and in Cusani, *op. cit.*, VII, 48-9. Spadoni relates that the proclamation was published at Parma, on February 17. Cusani, on the other hand, says that the proclamation was given at Modena on February 25.

proclamations at Verona, one addressed to the " soldiers of the Italian army," [34] and the other to the " people of the Kingdom of Italy." [35] In them he announced Joachim's desertion of Napoleon and urged the Italians to continue to resist the Allies as valorously as they had in the past. On the 3rd, the viceroy published still another proclamation urging the Italian people always to be loyal to him and to the Emperor and to assist them in their cause.[36]

These appeals were made at a time when both Napoleon's and the viceroy's position appeared to be hopeless. On the other side of the Alps, the Allied armies had already pushed their way across the Rhine to French soil. All Germany, even the entire Rhenish Confederation, was arrayed against Napoleon, and the Dutch had revolted against him. In the Iberian peninsula, the Spanish national war had resulted in new successes over the French. Napoleon's armies had been so nearly annihilated that the losses they had suffered could be made good only with extreme difficulty.

In Italy itself the troops under Eugene's own command were wavering, and Murat's defection had made the viceroy's position on the Adige an extremely critical one. There was nothing left for the viceroy to do but withdraw his forces from the Adige to the Mincio. This he did on February 4. He was followed a few days later by the Austrians, who, on the 8th attempted to cross the Mincio to attack him. The viceroy ordered his men to prevent their crossing, and the so-called " Battle of the Mincio "—one of the biggest and bloodiest battles of the whole campaign—was fought. The Austrians were prevented from crossing the river, but the losses in men and

34 Beauharnais Archives, Princeton University, Fasc. 23, No. 123; *Wiener Zeitung*, February 22, 1814, 215; Weil, *op. cit.*, III, 636-37.

35 Beauharnais Archives, Princeton University, Fasc. 23, No. 122; *Wiener Zeitung*, February 20, 1814, 207; Weil, *op. cit.*, III, 637-38.

36 Beauharnais Archives, Princeton University, Fasc. 23, No. 124; Weil, *op. cit.*, III, 656.

material to Eugene's already badly weakened army were terrific.[37]

A certain and quick defeat for Prince Eugene seemed very near. An almost immediate end to the war was averted only because Marshal Bellegarde failed to continue the pursuit of Eugene's forces and because two of the viceroy's opponents, King Joachim and Lord Bentinck, practically gave up the campaign to engage in quarreling between themselves. Instead of hurriedly pressing the French-Italian forces, Bellegarde remained inactive for weeks after the Battle of the Mincio.[38] Part of Bellegarde's hesitancy was due to poor weather conditions. Most of his inertia, however, was due to the fact that Murat did not bring his troops north to cooperate with the Habsburg armies but kept them in Tuscany to protect his own personal interests against Lord Bentinck. The squabble between Joachim and Lord William over the occupation of Tuscany gave the French-Italian army a few more weeks of grace before its final extinction.

The quarrel over Tuscany began almost immediately after Bentinck's arrival at Leghorn from Sicily on March 7, with 9,000 Sicilian and British troops. Bentinck's first move at Leghorn was to publish a proclamation, on the 14th, stating the arrival of British troops on the Italian mainland and announc-

---

37 *Précis historique, op. cit*, 117-32; Smola, Karl Freiherrn von, *Das Leben des Feldmarschalls Heinrich Grafen von Bellegarde* (Wien, 1837), 238-47.

38 Because of Bellegarde's hesitancy to pursue the French forces, all kinds of murmurs of discontent were heard against him. He was accused of indecision and lack of energy, and it was said that his inactivity was beginning to affect the morale of the whole Austrian army. Anonymous letter to Emperor Francis, Verona, March 4, 1814, *Kriegs-Archiv*, Vienna, *Feld Akten (Italien)*, 1814, Fasc. 3, No. 42½; Bentinck to Castlereagh, Verona, March 27, 1814, Vane, Charles W., *Correspondence, Despatches and other Papers of Viscount Castlereagh, Second Marquess of Londonderry* (London, 1851-53), IX, 400-1. In future references the latter source will be cited as " Castlereagh Correspondence, *op. cit.*"

ing: " Warriors of Italy, you are not asked to come to us, but you are asked to assert your rights and your liberty." [39]

After making this announcement, Bentinck, contrary to his instructions,[40] went, on March 15, to Reggio to demand that the King of Naples immediately evacuate Tuscany on the ground that it was necessary as a base to begin the English attack on Genoa which Bellegarde had requested him to make.[41] Murat, whose officials were already in control of all Tuscany and a large part of the papal states and were everywhere proclaiming the approaching independence of Italy under the King of Naples,[42] refused to accede to Lord William's request. He suggested, however, that a compromise be reached whereby the military occupation of Tuscany should be left to him until Lord Castlereagh would decide its fate. The querulous Bentinck obstinately refused, threatening that if Murat did not first give Tuscany to him, " he would chase the Neapolitans out of the country, revolutionize the country," take his army to Naples,

39 Hansard, T. C., *The Parliamentary Debates from the Year 1803 to the Present Time*, XXIX (November 8, 1814—March 3, 1815), 727. Bellegarde was very much displeased over this proclamation, saying that it was nothing else but an attempt " to announce to the Italians the liberal views of England." Letter to Metternich, Verona, March 21, 1814, *Staats-Archiv*, Vienna, *Staatskanzlei, Provinzen, Lombardei-Venedig*, Fasc. 3, Sect. 3, Fo. 102-3.

40 On February 21, 1814, Castlereagh had written Bentinck from Châtillon to advise him that at this time the most important thing was to secure the effective cooperation of the Neapolitans, "whose active assistance appears indispensable to give to the allies the rapid and commanding success which may speedily decide the fate of Italy." Castlereagh Correspondence, *op. cit.,* IX, 285.

41 As early as February 8, Bellegarde had written Murat that he had invited Bentinck to divert an expedition from Sicily to Genoa. Letter cited in Weil, *op cit.,* IV, 103 Bentinck's own government had ordered him to attack Genoa as early as December 28, 1813. Hansard, *op. cit ,* XXX (March 6 to May 1, 1815), 387-88.

42 Bellegarde to Metternich, Verona, March 21, 1814, *Staats-Archiv*, Vienna, *Staatskanzlei, Provinzen, Lombardei-Venedig*, Fasc. 3, Sect. 3, Fo. 89-106.

and then proclaim Ferdinand, the former sovereign of the country, king of Naples.[43]

Bentinck's intransigeance both irritated and perturbed Murat. Fearing that Bentinck might effectively check all his vast ambitions to carve out a large kingdom for himself, Joachim intensified the negotiations which he had been conducting with Prince Eugene and other French officials ever since he had signed the treaty of alliance with Austria.[44] On March 18, he sent a letter to the Duc d'Otrante [45] and another one to Prince Eugene, [46] professing his desire for a reconciliation with the French. At the same time, he sent General Carascosa to negotiate directly with the viceroy. Fortunately for the Allied cause, these negotiations ended in a deadlock, and Murat's attempted *rapprochement* with the French came to naught.[47]

While Joachim was having these flirtations with the French, pressure was brought to bear on Lord William to give up his cantankerous opposition to the ambitious Neapolitan king. In several interviews with the British commander, Bellegarde tried to convince him of the puerility of his claims to Tuscany. Lord Castlereagh also dispatched two strong letters to Bentinck, admonishing him that he was to consider his troops only as auxiliary forces subject to Bellegarde's command and that he was to refrain from further actions that would serve to antagonize Murat.[48] Thereafter, Bentinck assumed a more con-

43 Mier to Metternich, Reggio, March 20, 1814, Weil, *op. cit.*, IV, 393, Helfert, *Murat, op. cit.*, 151-53.

44 For an account of these negotiations, see Weil, C., "Les négociations secrètes entre Joachim Murat et le prince Eugène (février-mars 1814)," *Revue d'histoire moderne et contemporaine*, VII (1905-6), 509-23.

45 Du Casse, *op. cit.*, X, 225-26.

46 Weil, *Eugène et Murat, op. cit.*, IV, 401-2.

47 Eugene to Napoleon, Mantova, March 23, 1814, Bianchi, Nicomede, *Storia documentata della diplomazia europea in Italia dall'anno 1814 all'anno 1861* (Torino, 1865-72), I, 337-38.

48 Letters of March 30, and April 3, 1814, Castlereagh Correspondence, *op. cit.*, IX, 409-10, 427-28. On April 4, Bentinck was also relieved of his diplomatic functions at the Sicilian Court. Weil, Maurice Henri, *Joachim Murat, roi de Naples, la dérnière année de régne (mai 1814-mai 1815)* (Paris, 1909-10), I, 41.

ciliatory attitude, and in the early part of April the Austrian field marshal succeeded in effecting a reconciliation between his two allies at Rovera. Bentinck agreed to evacuate Tuscany and to direct an expedition against Genoa. Murat promised to cross the Taro to take Piacenza and then to make a forced march across the Po to cooperate with Marshal Bellegarde in an attempt to compel the viceroy to evacuate Lombardy.[49]

As soon as the dissidence between the English commander-in-chief and the Neapolitan king had been satisfactorily settled, a concerted drive against the French-Italian army was begun. Bentinck departed for Genoa, attacked the city, and forced the French to permit the English to take it over.[50] Once in the city, Bentinck arranged for the establishment of a provisional government, and, on April 26, again acting contrary to his instructions,[51] he issued a proclamation announcing that, with a few modifications, the Genoese state, as it had existed in 1797, was to be re-established.[52]

On April 13, Murat, in accordance with the Rovera agreement, passed the Taro. Two days later his forces drove the French out of Piacenza. At the same time, the main body of the Austrian army was preparing to resume its attack on the viceroy's forces. Now Prince Eugene's cause was definitely hopeless. The enemy was in control of all the Kingdom of Italy east of the Mincio and south of the Po. On the other side

49 Koch et Schoell, *op. cit.*, X, 471-72.

50 Intelligence from Genoa, April 28, 1814, *The London Times*, May 7, 1814.

51 When Castlereagh had heard of Bentinck's Leghorn proclamation of March 14, he had admonished Bentinck that, " surrounded as your lordship must be by individuals who wish for another system to be established in Italy," it was very necessary " not to afford any plausible occasion or pretext for umbrage to those with whom we are acting, but with whom our relations may not be such as at once to generate confidence." Letter of April 3, 1814, from Dijon, Castlereagh Correspondence, *op. cit.*, IX, 434. It should be noted that in the spring of 1814, as the campaign was drawing to a close, the British Foreign Office reversed its previous policy of attempting to stir up the Italian people to revolt against Napoleon by appealing to their liberal and national sensibilities.

52 Hansard, *op. cit.*, XXIX, 729-30.

of the Alps, the Allied armies had entered Paris on March 30, and Eugene's stepfather had, on April 11, renounced his rights to the throne of France in the Treaty of Fontainebleau. Realizing that Napoleon's cause in both Italy and France was irretrievably lost, the viceroy, on April 16, formally gave up the struggle by signing the Convention of Schiarino-Rizzino.

According to the terms of this convention, the French troops under the viceroy's command were immediately to withdraw beyond the Alps. The fortresses of Osoppo, Palmanova, Legnago, and Venice were to be handed over to the Austrians on April 20. The Italian soldiers under the viceroy's command, however, were to continue to hold the other parts of the Kingdom of Italy not yet occupied by the Allies. The fate of the Kingdom of Italy was to be decided by the Allied Powers, but " a deputation of the Kingdom of Italy " was to have permission to go to the general Allied headquarters to present the views of the people in regard to their future.[53]

On the morning of the 20th, in accordance with the stipulations at Schiarino-Rizzino, the Austrians entered Legnago, Palmanova, Osoppo, and Venice. Then a revolution staged in Milan on the same day[54] gave Bellegarde a pretext to demand the cession of the entire kingdom. On the 23rd, General Ficquelmont was sent to the viceroy to represent to him that it was necessary for Austrian troops to occupy the whole kingdom in order to restore tranquillity. There was nothing left for Eugene to do but to comply with this request; accordingly, on the same day, another convention was signed at Mantua. This so-called " Convention of Mantua " stipulated that Peschiera would be handed over to the Allies on April 24 and Mantua on May 1, or twenty-four hours after Eugene's departure, if he left before that date. The remaining places and fortresses in the kingdom would be given to the first Austrian troops that arrived.[55]

53 Weil, *Eugène et Murat, op. cit.*, V, 133-35.
54 See Chapter VII.
55 *The British and Foreign State Papers*, I, Pt. 2, 1014-15.

With the signing of the Convention of Mantua, the long Italian campaign was over. It had not been a creditable one. Inefficiency, lack of ability, mutual distrust and suspicion, and subterranean intrigues and manipulations had characterized many of the activities on both sides. If the issue had not been decided in the battlefields of Germany and France, the Italian campaign might have dragged on indefinitely. Nevertheless, the Allied Powers were the victors in Italy, as well as in the rest of Europe, and were confronted with the task of organizing the government of the occupied provinces in the Apennine peninsula.

CHAPTER IV
THE AUSTRIAN PROVISIONAL GOVERNMENT IN VENETIA,
1813-1814

WHEN Austrian soldiers first marched into the Venetian departments in October, 1813, the inhabitants hailed them as their liberators and friends. The Venetians felt certain that the day of their liberation from the yoke of despotism was at hand. They believed that the hated continental system, the burdensome taxation, and the oppressive military levies would no longer destroy the possibility of orderly economic progress and prosperity.[1] A new Saturnian age of affluence, they assured themselves, would inevitably ensue.

Although welcomed by the populace with encomiastic " Hallelujah choruses," the Habsburgs, nevertheless, were faced with the onerous task of providing the citizens of the conquered parts of the Kingdom of Italy—nearly all the Venetian departments—with a provisional government. In performing this duty, the Austrians did not tarry. On November 8, 1813, less than a fortnight after his arrival on Italian soil, the commander-in-chief of the Austrian forces, General Hiller, issued a proclamation informing the people of the outlines of the provisional government which was to be established in all Italian territories already occupied or which would be occupied by Austrian arms.[2]

On the 9th, Baron Antonio Marenzi was dispatched to the capitals of each of the occupied departments to make arrangements for the stipulations of the proclamation to be put into

1 Wiedemann-Warnhelm, Adolf von, *Die Wiederherstellung der oesterreichischen Vorherrschaft in Italien (1813-1815)* (Wien, 1912), 34-5.

2 *Collezione di leggi e regolamenti pubblicati dall'imp. regio governo delle province venete* (Venezia, 1814), 1813-14, I, 3-16.

effect as quickly as possible.[3] At the same time, Prince Reuss-Plauen was named military governor of all territory occupied in Italy by the Habsburg military forces,[4] and Baron Rossetti and Count Thurn were appointed his assistants.[5]

The new governor was instructed to consider all territories under his administration as being merely under military occupation. He was to conserve the existing government as much as possible, and was to leave at their posts all state employees not culpable of malfeasances or of being ardent supporters of the French. Immediately after his arrival in Italy, Reuss was to take possession of all state property in Emperor Francis's name, and to arrange for the collection of the existing taxes and imposts. He was to aid in the provisioning of all the Austrian military forces in the peninsula, and to make detailed reports on the conditions of the land and its inhabitants. He was, in particular, to do all in his power to keep Italian public opinion in favor of Austria.[6]

Prince Reuss-Plauen arrived in Vicenza to take over his new post on the morning of December 18.[7] At the same time, Baron von Roschmann was placed in charge of the civil administration of " the conquered Italian and Illyrian parts of the Tyrol," [8] and Baron Rossetti was made Marshal Bellegarde's general assistant, with the task of promptly procuring for Bellegarde's troops all necessary money and supplies. Baron Hingenau succeeded Rossetti as Reuss-Plauen's assistant.[9]

3 Hiller to Marenzi, Trento, November 9, 1813, *Archivio di Stato*, Venice, 1813, *Atti Hiller*, No 1.

4 Kaiser Franz to Reuss, Jena, October 25, 1813, *Archivio di Stato*, Venice, *Organizzazione*, 1813, Fasc. IV-V, enclosed in No. 16/F.

5 Kaiser Franz to Zichy, Jena, October 25, 1813, *Staats-Archiv*, Vienna, *Conferenz Akten*, Ser. b, 1813, No. 650.

6 Kaiser Franz to Reuss, Frankfurt, November 9, 1813, *ibid.*, No. 789.

7 Thurn to Prefect of Bacchiglione, Vicenza, December 18, 1813, *Archivio di Stato*, Venice, *Organizzazione*, 1814, No. 936.

8 Kaiser Franz to Baldacci, Frankfurt, December 10, 1813, *Staats-Archiv*, Vienna, *Conferenz Akten*, Ser. b, 1813, No. 893.

9 Kaiser Franz to Zichy, Freyburg, December 21, 1813, *ibid*, No. 925; Reuss to Zichy, January 26, 1814, *ibid.*, 1814, No. 354.

With the appointment of Reuss-Plauen, Rossetti, Hingenau, and Thurn, a central directory to govern the occupied parts of the peninsula was created. There was, however, much more that had to be done. Efficient police and judicial systems had to be established and the government of the municipalities regulated. Necessary rules for the civil service had to be devised, and provision had to be made to take care of deserters from the French-Italian army. The question of whether or not Austrian paper money was to be circulated in the Venetian departments had to be solved, and taxes and military requisitions had to be collected.

Especially pressing was the necessity of providing the country with an efficient police force. To meet this need, the Habsburg government decreed that all police employees who were at their respective posts at the time of the occupation of any district by the Austrian army were to continue their work. They were to act in conjunction with the army commanders of their respective districts in discharging their various duties, and were empowered to arrest soldiers and officers for disturbing the public peace or security. In such cases they were immediately to report the arrest to the military commander of their particular district. If they apprehended people on charges of spreading seditious writings, acting as spies, corresponding with the enemy, or trying to create disorders for their own personal profit, they were to consult with the military commander of their district before bringing such malefactors up for judicial prosecution.[10]

The police at first remained, as had been the case in the Kingdom of Italy, under the control of the prefects of the various provinces.[11] The imperial police administration, however, was not satisfied with this arrangement, and insisted that the Italian police be directly responsible to officials appointed

10 Instructions to the police, November 24, 1813, *Collezione di leggi venete, op. cit.*, 1813-14, I, 19-26.

11 Reuss to Ugarte, Udine, February 11, 1814, *Staats-Archiv*, Vienna, *Kaiser Franz Akten*, Fasc. 27, Sect. 1, Fo. 19-20.

by its central office in Vienna. Emperor Francis approved this view, and a central police directory was created, with Antonio von Raab as director, and Barons von Maurizio, Ehrenheim, Stocca, and Emberg as police commissioners, to direct police activities in all the occupied Italian provinces.[12]

To aid the police, the Italian constabulary (the so-called *Satellizio*) was conserved. Its head in each department was to be an inspector, whose immediate superior was to be the prefect of his department. The constabulary was charged with executing all commissions demanded of it by the courts of justice and the justices of the peace, mayors, and police commissioners, and was to make provision to put down effectively all disorders and insurrections.[13]

The necessity of providing the occupied territories with a new judicial system was almost as urgent as that of creating an effective police system. Under the Kingdom of Italy, there had been in the territory between the Isonzo and the Adige rivers a court of cassation and five courts of appeals, the latter dependent upon the supreme court of appeals in Venice. In each important town there had been a civil and criminal court, and a tribunal of first instance to handle minor civil and criminal cases. In each canton there had been a justice of the peace. Special courts had handled singular criminal cases.[14] Now that the French government no longer existed in the Venetian territory, a substitute for these courts had to be established.

Immediately after the arrival of Austrian troops in Italy, it was ordered that all these courts except the court of cassation, the courts of appeals, and the special courts were to be

12 *Staats-Conferenz* to President of the Aulic Police Department, December 2, 1813, *Staats-Archiv*, Vienna, *Conferenz Akten*, Ser. b, 1813, No. 766; Hager to Reuss, Wien, January 16, 1814, *Archivio di Stato*, Venice, *Organizzazione*, 1814, Rub. 2, No. 3116.

13 Regulation of December 14, 1813, *Collezione di leggi venete, op. cit.*, 1813-14, I, 27-37.

14 Reuss to Ugarte, Udine, February 11, 1814, *Staats-Archiv*, Vienna, *Kaiser Franz Akten*, Fasc. 27, Sect. 1, Fo. 22; Proclamation, January 9, 1814, *Collezione di leggi venete, op. cit.*, 1813-14, I, 66-7.

preserved, and that, in addition, all the existing criminal, civil, and commercial laws, as well as all decrees and special regulations, were to continue in force.[15] To arrange for the handling of appeals, it was provided that, beginning on February 1, 1814, the courts of justice of the departments occupied by the imperial army were provisionally to judge such cases.[16] After the capture of the city of Venice on April 20, this function of the departmental courts was suspended, and the court of appeals in this city was again made court of appeals for all the Venetian provinces.[17]

In January, 1814, the Emperor ordered that the Austrian law books should be translated into Italian.[18] Two months later, Baron von Plenciz, who had previously been appointed special commissioner to effectuate changes in the Illyrian judiciary, was sent to Italy to reorganize the judicial system of the occupied Venetian departments.[19] In April, Baron Hager was charged with providing for the Viennese Council of Justice a description of the abilities, character, political opinions, and experience of all judicial officials in the occupied provinces.[20]

In the winter of 1813/14 and the spring of 1814, the Austrians created a provisional judicial system and laid the groundwork for the establishment of a permanent judicial system in the Venetian departments. They also changed the existing form of municipal administration. The former French subdivisions

15 Proclamation, General Hiller, Trento, November 8, 1813, *Collezione di leggi venete, op. cit.*, 1813-14, I, 10-12; Proclamation of January 9, 1814, *ibid.*, 66-7; Proclamation, Count Porcia, Padova, November 8, 1813, *Archivio di Stato*, Venice, *Polizia*, 1813-14, Fasc. VI, A, No. 1138/5.

16 Decree of January 21, 1814, *Collezione di leggi venete, op. cit.*, 1813-14, I, 78-80.

17 Decree, May 5, 1814, *ibid.*, 232-34; *Staats-Conferenz* to Reuss, Wien, May 7, 1814, *Staats-Archiv*, Vienna, *Conferenz Akten*, Ser. b, 1814, No. 932.

18 Helfert, *Kaiser Franz, op. cit.*, 8.

19 Protocol, *Staats-Conferenz*, March 15, 1814, *Staats-Archiv*, Vienna, *Conferenz Akten*, Ser. b, 1814, No. 618.

20 *Staats-Conferenz* to Hager, Wien, April 13, 1814, *ibid.*, No. 762.

of both cantons and communes were abolished, and all the communes in a former canton were grouped together in a single unit, called the commune. Each commune was given the name of its capital, and was to be governed by a communal council of forty members, a mayor, six so-called "learned men," a communal agent, and a chief of the police court.[21]

Judging from the lack of complaints in various documents in the Venetian and Austrian state archives, one can conclude that the creation of the police and judicial systems and the changes wrought in the municipal government gave no particular ground for dissatisfaction among the populace. A considerable amount of discontent, however, was expressed over other administrative measures, and over most of the military and economic policies of the Habsburg government. Displeasure over some of these measures of the Habsburgs in Italy came immediately after General Hiller announced, on November 8, 1813, that with certain minor exceptions, the existing French form of administration was temporarily to be continued.[22] At least a part of the Venetian population was highly displeased with this proclamation.[23] Thoroughly disgusted with the French, these people wanted a complete overthrow of all vestiges of the hated French regime. When this was not done, many of them grumbled. The Austrians had miscalculated the feelings of the populace.

The conduct of many government officials also caused complaints. When their armies first entered Italy, the Austrians adopted the policy of conserving in their positions all the officials of the former Kingdom of Italy who had not abandoned their posts and who would give an oath of allegiance to the

21 Decree of February 19, 1814, *Collezione di leggi venete, op. cit.,* 1813-14, I, 94-111.

22 *Collezione di leggi venete, op cit.,* 1813-14, I, 4-5.

23 See *Staats-Kabinet* Reports of January 3, March 1, March 25, April 5, and April 6, 1814, *Staats-Archiv,* Vienna, *Kabinets-Akten,* 1814, Nos. 957, 1193, 1320, 1371, and 1385.

Austrian Emperor.[24] Some of these employees hastened to ingratiate themselves with their new masters, protesting at every turn their continued loyalty to the Habsburgs. Many went too far and indirectly injured the Austrian cause thereby. Others proved to be unfaithful to their new masters, and were accused of conducting their administration in a manner which would incite the people against the Austrians. Still others acted in such an arbitrary and officious manner that they exasperated the inhabitants. Of the few officials sent to Italy from Austria, some were denounced by the inhabitants because they could not speak Italian.[25] The protests of the inhabitants over the demeanor of the officials were so numerous that the Austrian Emperor was finally constrained to order that exceptional care should be taken to insure that only faithful officials, of good moral character, who did not irritate the sensibilities of the inhabitants should be kept in their posts.[26]

In filling vacancies in the Italian civil service, the Austrian Emperor specified that preference was to be given to Austrian officials who had served in the Lombard and Venetian administrations before these provinces had been taken over by the French.[27] Other persons might be considered, but the Viennese State Conference was to examine their qualifications very carefully before appointing them to any positions.[28] In particular,

24 Hiller Proclamation, Trento, November 8, 1813, *Collezione di leggi venete, op. cit*, 1813-14, I, 5.

25 Hager Report, January 11, 1814, *Staats-Archiv*, Vienna, *Conferenz Akten*, Ser. b, 1814, No. 38; Hingenau to Zichy, Padua, February 24, 1814, *ibid.*, No. 507; *Staats-Kabinet* Reports of February 6, and March 1, 1814, *Staats-Archiv*, Vienna, *Kabinets-Akten*, 1814, Nos 1077, and 1193; Prefectural Council of Piave to Porcia, Belluno, November 16, 1813, *Archivio di Stato*, Venice, 1813, *Atti Hiller*, No. 11.

26 Kaiser Franz to Zichy, Paris, April 25, 1814, *Staats-Archiv*, Vienna, *Conferenz Akten*, Ser. b, 1814, No. 873

27 On December 4, 1813, and February 24, 1814, Emperor Francis asked the State Conference to send him reliable information about all such persons. Kaiser Franz to Zichy, Frankfurt, December 4, 1813, *ibid*, 1813, No. 818; Kaiser Franz to Zichy, Vendeuvre, February 24, 1814, *ibid.*, 1814, No. 486.

28 Kaiser Franz to Zichy, Frankfurt, December 4, 1813, *ibid.*, 1813, No 818.

was no person to be appointed who had ever expressed himself in any hostile manner toward the Austrian government or political interests, or who belonged to any dangerous secret societies.[29]

Emperor Francis was particularly insistent that none of his officials in Italy belong to secret political societies. Francis had been inimical to organizations of this kind from the first days of his rule, and, on April 23, 1801, had ordered that all secret societies or brotherhoods were to be abolished in his Empire.[30] In Italy, where many of the former officials of the Kingdom of Italy who were provisionally kept in their posts still continued their membership in Masonic lodges,[31] it was decided that they might be permitted to continue in their employment only if they immediately withdrew from any secret society with which they were connected and promised under oath that they would never again join one.[32]

Another worry to both the inhabitants of the conquered districts and the Austrian governing officials was the conduct of the soldiers, Italian as well as Austrian. Deserters from the French-Italian army gathered together in formidable bands and ravaged the countryside.[33] Austrian soldiers, on the other hand, forced the population to accept Austrian paper money at exorbitant rates of exchange, spent considerable time in riotous drinking and brawling, and even insulted and attacked

29 Imperial Resolution, Chaumont, March 9, 1814, *Staats-Archiv*, Vienna, *Kabinets-Akten*, 1814, No. 1262.

30 Beidtel, Ignaz, *Geschichte der oesterreichischen Staatsverwaltung, 1740-1848* (Innsbruck, 1896-98), II, 96.

31 Hager to *Staats-Conferenz*, January 5, 1814, *Staats-Archiv*, Vienna, *Conferenz Akten*, Ser. b, 1814, No. 51.

32 Hager to Baron von Lattermann, Prince Reuss, and General von Tomassich, Vienna, March 20, 1814, Helfert, *La caduta, op. cit.*, Appendix I, 233-34. A copy of the oath which all employees took is included in Reuss to Ugarte, Padova, April 11, 1814, *Staats-Archiv*, Vienna, *Conferenz Akten*, Ser. b, 1814, No 952.

33 *Oesterreichischer Beobachter*, 1814, No. 32 (February 1, 1814), 185.

the inhabitants.[34] So crude were the offenses of some of these soldiers that the populace was vociferous in its clamor against them.[35]

To induce the deserters from the French-Italian army to stop their depredations, the Austrians named two battalions of the Austrian army " Battalions of Italian Volunteers " and invited all Italian soldiers who wished to fight against their former French masters to join them.[36] To check the excesses of the Austrian soldiers, Emperor Francis personally intervened to command first Bellegarde and then the *Hofkriegsrath* to punish severely all soldiers who perpetrated abuses and to stop at no measures necessary to restore the discipline of the armed forces in Italy.[37] The Emperor was seriously aggrieved at the conduct of his army, but apparently he did not have effective control over its discipline. For this weakness the Emperor had to pay dearly in lack of affection from many inhabitants of his Venetian provinces.

Much more difficult than the problem of checking the excesses of the soldiers, however, was the task of financing the Italian campaign. Austrian state finances had been on an unsound foundation ever since the beginning of the Revolutionary wars. Since 1792 the increased administrative and military expenses necessitated by the war had been met by levying higher taxes, by receiving subsidies from England, by increasing the public debt, by exacting compulsory loans, and by increasing the amount of bank notes in circulation.[38] Measures such as these met the daily needs of the treasury, but they did not stave

34 Hager Report of January 3, 1814, and *Staats-Kabinet* Report of January 17, 1814, *Staats-Archiv*, Vienna, *Kabinets-Akten*, 1814, No. 957.

35 Sardegna to Kaiser Franz, Verona, April 2, 1814, *Kriegs-Archiv*, Vienna, *Feld Akten (Italien)*, 1814, Fasc. 4, No. 23 2/4.

36 Proclamation, Reuss-Plauen, Udine, January 8, 1814, *Staats-Archiv*, Vienna, *Conferenz Akten*, Ser. b, 1814, No. 357.

37 Imperial Resolution, Kaiser Franz, Freyburg, January 2, 1814, *ibid.*, No. 104; Imperial Resolutions of March 27 and April 6, 1814, *Staats-Archiv*, Vienna, *Kabinets-Akten*, 1814, Nos. 1320 and 1371.

38 Beidtel, *op. cit.*, II, 173-77.

off inflation. Soon the amount of bank notes in circulation was hopelessly out of proportion with the amount of gold and silver available to redeem them, and their value fell to such a point that in 1810 one florin in gold was worth 12.40 florins in bank notes.[39]

To save the Austrian state finances from utter collapse, in February, 1811, a new paper currency—the so-called " redemption notes " (Einloesungsscheine)—was substituted for the old bank notes. The new notes were to have the same value as gold and silver coins of a similar denomination, and the older notes were to be redeemable in the new currency at the rate of five to one. This was tantamount to a repudiation of four-fifths of the face value of all existing paper money.[40]

Austrian financial difficulties, however, did not end with the substitution of the redemption notes for the old bank notes. The redemption notes, like the former bank notes, did not have sufficient gold and silver coverage to guarantee their value, and quickly depreciated. It was soon necessary to issue more currency. On April 16, 1813, so-called " anticipation notes " (Anticipationsscheine), which were to be backed by the future proceeds of the land tax, were issued. These were to be limited in amount to 45,000,000 florins, and, beginning in 1814, 3,750,000 florins of them were to be withdrawn from circulation each year. The amount proved to be insufficient. Within a few months, 100,000,000 florins more were put into circulation. In 1814, this amount was increased by 150,000,000; and in 1815, by 155,000,000 florins.[41] Naturally, paper currency, thus inflated, was circulated below par through the years 1812, 1813, and 1814. In October, 1812, one gold florin was worth

39 Ibid., 190; Bermann, Moriz, Oesterreich-Ungarn im neunzehnten Jahrhundert. Mit besonderer Beruecksichtigung aller wichtigen Vorfaelle in der Geschichte, Wissenschaft, Kunst, Industrie, und dem Volksleben (Wien, 1884), 230-31.

40 Beidtel, op. cit, II, 192-93; Bibl, Viktor, Kaiser Franz und sein Erbe (Volume I of his Der Zerfall Oesterreichs) (Wien, 1922), 197-99.

41 Beer, Adolf, Die Finanzen Oesterreichs im XIX. Jahrhundert. Nach archivalischen Quellen (Prag, 1877), 82-5.

1.39 in paper; in October, 1813, 1.69; and in April, 1814, 2.38.[42]

In 1813/14 there were thus three different kinds of money existing in Austria: gold and silver, redeemable at par; and redemption and anticipation notes, the value of which fluctuated considerably but was always much below par. As the Austrian government was extremely hard pressed for money, the soldiers and officers fighting in Italy were paid in the depreciated paper money, and it was decreed that the inhabitants had to accept the redemption and anticipation notes at their full nominal value in payment for such articles as salt and tobacco. Taxes, however, for the time being, were to be paid only in gold or silver money.[43]

Since the acceptance of paper money in exchange for certain commodities was thus forced upon the inhabitants, the soldiers used all possible means to have their paper currency, with which their salaries were paid, changed into gold and silver money. Their actions, along with the fact that the tax authorities would not accept paper money, resulted in a still greater depreciation in the value of the redemption and anticipation notes in Italy.[44] It is no wonder that many persons in the Venetian provinces were furious [45] and that Marshal Bellegarde and Governor Reuss-Plauen hastened to exhort their government to put an end to compulsory circulation of depreciated paper money in Italy.[46]

42 Beidtel, op. cit., II, 197.

43 Hiller Proclamation, Vicenza, November 17, 1813, Archivio di Stato, Venice, 1813, Atti Hiller, no number given.

44 Wiedemann-Warnhelm, op cit., 14-15; Reuss to Ugarte, Udine, January 9, 1814, Staats-Archiv, Vienna, Kaiser Franz Akten, Fasc. 27, Sect. 1, Fo. 8-15.

45 Kaiser Franz to Zichy, Frankfurt, November 12, 1813, Staats-Archiv, Vienna, Conferenz Akten, Ser. b, 1813, No. 703; Staats-Kabinet Report, January 17, 1814, Staats-Archiv, Vienna, Kabinets-Akten, 1814, No. 957.

46 Bellegarde to Metternich, Vicence, December 18, 1813, Staats-Archiv, Vienna, Staatskanzlei, Provinzen, Lombardei-Venedig, Fasc. 3, Sect. 3, Fo. 4-7; Bellegarde to Metternich, Vicence, December 21, 1813, ibid., Fo. 1-3; Bellegarde to Metternich, Vicence, January 3, 1814, ibid., Fo. 11-12; Reuss

When he became fully aware of the situation, Emperor Francis, who along with all his faults possessed many attributes of a benevolent despot, personally intervened to repair the mischief done in Italy by the use of the redemption and anticipation notes. On January 6, 1814, although the State Conference had admonished him that the Austrian finances were not stable enough to warrant it,[47] he issued a patent ordering that the sum of 500,000 florins be sent to Bellegarde and Reuss every month to be used by them in paying for necessary military expenditures, and that arrangements be immediately initiated to pay the military forces in metallic money and to abolish the forced circulation of Austrian currency in Italy.[48] Strict measures were to be taken to insure that members of the Austrian army would not abuse their position to force the inhabitants to accept depreciated Austrian paper money,[49] and to guarantee that the existing redemption and anticipation notes would be withdrawn from circulation in Italy.[50] This decision of the Habsburg government was announced to the inhabitants of the occupied Italian provinces in a proclamation which Governor Reuss-Plauen made on January 29, 1814.[51] One of the most obnoxious grievances of the Venetian people was thus repaired, but, before the Austrian bureaucracy had been able to obviate the causes for their dissatisfaction, irreparable injury was done to Austrian prestige.

to Kaiser Franz, Udine, January 9, 1814, *Staats-Archiv*, Vienna, *Kaiser Franz Akten*, Fasc. 27, Sect. 1, Fo. 7; Reuss to Ugarte, Udine, January 9, 1814, *ibid.*, Fo. 8-15.

47 Imperial Resolution, Kaiser Franz, Frankfurt, December 9, 1813, *Staats-Archiv*, Vienna, *Conferenz Akten*, Ser. b, 1813, No. 856.

48 Issued at Freyburg, *ibid*, 1813, No. 857.

49 *Staats-Conferenz* to Bellegarde, Wien, January 25, 1814, *ibid.*, 1814, No. 104; Army order, Vicenza, February 1, 1814, *Kriegs-Archiv*, Vienna, *Feld Akten (Italien)*, 1814, Fasc. 2, No. 1.

50 Ugarte to Reuss, Wien, January 29, 1814, *Staats-Archiv*, Vienna, *Conferenz Akten*, Ser. b, 1814, No. 291.

51 Given at Udine, *Staats-Archiv*, Vienna, *Staatskanzlei, Provinzen, Lombardei-Venedig*, Fasc. 18, Sect. 1, Fo. 2; *Wiener Zeitung*, February 22, 1814, 215.

Maddening as the paper money was to the residents of the occupied provinces, the weighty taxes and requisitions levied by the conquerors were even more exacerbating. As many of the inhabitants were exhausted and impoverished in the latter part of 1813, the Habsburgs, if they had been in a position to be wise and prudent, should have sent their armies into Italy bearing wagon trains laden with food and should have promised to reduce taxes and to dispense with all extraordinary military requisitions. Unfortunately, the Austrians were almost as desperately in need of money as the French had been. Since Austria's own finances were tottering on the brink of disaster, the Austrian army in Italy found it necessary to rely largely upon the taxes paid by the inhabitants to obtain the funds and supplies necessary for its military operations, and much as General Hiller, Marshal Bellegarde, and Governor Reuss-Plauen deplored weighing down the residents of the occupied territories with obnoxious and oppressive burdens, they were in no position to do otherwise.

Soon after the Habsburg army entered Italy, Emperor Francis ordered his officials to take over all possible sources of revenue that they could find in the Apennine peninsula and to use them to the best advantage of the state.[52] Governor Reuss-Plauen was advised that the existing taxes and imposts could be lowered only in decidedly exceptional cases, and then only if incontrovertible evidence of unequivocally gross injustice was produced.[53] In addition, he was urged to take all measures necessary to insure that all taxes due the government were collected[54] and that the costs of the civil administration in the Venetian provinces were reduced to the lowest possible level.[55]

52 Imperial Resolution, Kaiser Franz, Frankfurt, December 9, 1813, *Staats-Archiv*, Vienna, *Conferenz Akten*, Ser. b, 1813, No. 856.

53 Ugarte to Reuss, Wien, December 11, 1813, *Archivio di Stato*, Venice, *Organizzazione*, 1813, Fasc. IV-V, enclosed in Fo. 16/F.

54 Zichy to Reuss, Wien, December 16, 1813, *Archivio di Stato*, Venice, *Finanze*, 1813, Busta I-II, Rub. 1, No. 1164.

55 Ugarte to Reuss, Wien, January 21, 1814, *Staats-Archiv*, Vienna,

There was thus to be, temporarily at least, no relief from the repressive sy̆stem of taxation which had been saddled upon the populace by the preceding French regime. The taxes were not to be lowered, in spite of the fact that scores of entreaties and reports describing the wretched conditions in various communities and beseeching the authorities to lower various oppressive and obnoxious taxes were sent to the Austrian authorities by local officials.[56] In sheer desperation, many Venetians turned to violence, and by early January, 1814, Governor Reuss-Plauen was forced to admit to the Viennese authorities that the tax collectors were so strenuously resisted in numerous parts of the Venetian territory that the taxes could be collected only with military aid.[57]

The attempted collection of the hated sales tax, which was levied upon such necessities as food and fuel, especially caused spirited opposition and even open rebellion in various districts, particularly in the mountain valleys. In the Venetian State Archives, there are many reports of popular uprisings against the tax. At Gemona, near Udine, in the district of Asiago, in numerous villages in the district of Schio, and in the communes of Posina and Valdagno, revolts occurred which were put down only with the greatest difficulty after several days of tumult and disorder.[58] In the commune of Castelfranco, the inhabitants were so sullen that the intendant of finance of the department

Conferenz Akten, Ser. b, 1814, No. 283; Staats-Conferenz Report, February 8, 1814, ibid., No. 290.

56 For good examples of these entreaties, see Archivio di Stato, Venice, Atti Hiller, 1813; Imposte, 1814, Busta XXXII; Polizia, 1814, Busta XXXIX; and Pubblico Politico, 1813 and 1814.

57 Report of January 10, 1814, Staats-Archiv, Vienna, Kabinets-Akten, 1814, No. 1006.

58 Prefectural Council of the Department of Passariano to Marenzi, Udine, November 20, 1813, Archivio di Stato, Venice, Finanze, 1813, Busta I-II, Rub. 5, No. 18,714; Prefect of Bacchiglione Report, Vicenza, January 10, 1814, Archivio di Stato, Venice, Polizia, 1814, Busta XXXIX, Fasc. 11, No. 451; Prefect of Bacchiglione to Reuss, Vicenza, February 28, 1814, Archivio di Stato, Venice, Imposte, 1814, Busta XXXII, Fasc. 47, No. 4249.

of Bacchiglione recommended that no one should venture to collect the sales tax.[59] And in the district of Cadore, the inhabitants absolutely refused to pay the tax.[60]

Just as strenuous was the opposition to the tax collectors, who, being held personally responsible for all losses, frequently acted in a very inconsiderate and harsh manner.[61] The collectors every now and then were so relentless in fulfilling their duties that the inhabitants in protest refused to pay taxes, and, in some places, they even began popular rebellions against them. At Pozzale, Forzenighe, Bragherezza, Dozra, and Igne, armed mobs of women, accompanied by a few men, forcibly prevented the communal authorities from sequestering the belongings of villagers owing taxes to the government.[62] In the communes of Cavasso and Castegnamoro, the enraged citizens attacked the tax collectors while they were holding proceedings against tax delinquents and forced them to flee for safety.[63] And at Cadore, minor insurrections prevented the tax receiver from impounding goods for back taxes during the whole month of February and even threatened his personal safety.[64]

These and many other examples which we have not cited show what a bad taste the taxation policies of the Austrians

59 Letter to the Central Government, Vicenza, March 6, 1814, *Archivio di Stato*, Venice, *Dazi Consumo*, 1814, Fasc. XIX-XX, Rub. 1, No. 1422.

60 Prefect of Piave to Reuss, Belluno, January 5, 1814, *ibid.*, No. 2126.

61 *Staats-Kabinet* Report, Wien, March 1, 1814, *Staats-Archiv*, Vienna, *Kabinets-Akten*, 1814, No. 1193. In the Venetian archives there are many letters complaining about the undue harshness of this or that tax collector. See especially *Atti Hiller*, 1813; *Polizia*, 1814, Busta XXXIX; and *Imposte*, 1814, Busta XXXII.

62 Prefect of Piave to Central Government, Udine, January 26, 1814, *Archivio di Stato*, Venice, *Polizia*, 1814, Busta XXXIX, Fasc. 68, No. 3067; Prefect of Piave to Reuss, Belluno, January 15, 1814, *ibid.*, Fasc. 55, No. 73/74.

63 Prefect of Bacchiglione to Central Government, Vicenza, February 1, 1814, *Archivio di Stato*, Venice, *Imposte*, 1814, Busta XXXII, Fasc. 53, No. 1983.

64 Prefect of Piave to Central Government, Belluno, March 14, 1814, *ibid.*, Fasc. 190, No. 240b.

left in the mouths of the inhabitants of the conquered territories. Taxes, however, formed only a portion of the oppressive exactions levied by the Austrian authorities upon the inhabitants of the Venetian provinces. Forced contributions of various sorts also bore down heavily upon them. Troops were quartered upon the inhabitants, and the people living in the sections occupied by Austrian arms had to provide the troops not only with board and room but often with such items as clothing, shoes, and transportation.[65] Furthermore, extraordinary financial levies were frequently exacted from the inhabitants of the districts in which the military forces were quartered.[66] Soon many parts of the conquered territory were full of vociferous lamentations and bitter complaints about the harsh and unfair military requisitions, and people begged for mercy.[67]

Realizing that the requisitions were affecting Venetian public opinion in a deleterious manner, Governor Reuss-Plauen suggested to the central authorities in Vienna that all forced contributions should be abolished and that a loan should be floated among the financial, land-owning, and commercial classes of the occupied provinces to procure funds to pay in cash for all the supplies needed by the army.[68] This recommendation was

65 Wiedemann-Warnhelm, *op. cit.*, 35.

66 Between December 1, 1813, and the last of March, 1814, for example, at least four special extraordinary taxes were levied upon the inhabitants of the department of Bacchiglione. Prefect of Bacchiglione to Central Government, Vicenza, March 23, 1814, *Archivio di Stato*, Venice, *Imposte*, 1814, Busta XXXII, Fasc. 226, No. 5664. Again, in Verona a single extraordinary levy of 2,000,000 florins was saddled upon the people. Other towns in the Venetian territory had to pay a proportional sum. Huegel Diary, *op. cit*, March 1, 1814, 44.

67 Huegel Diary, *op. cit.*, March 1, 1814, 44; Reuss to Ugarte, Udine, February 11, 1814, *Staats-Archiv*, Vienna, *Kaiser Franz Akten*, Fasc. 27, Sect. 1, Fo. 24

68 Ugarte to Reuss, Wien, January 21, 1814, *Staats-Archiv*, Vienna, *Conferenz Akten*, Ser. b, 1814, No. 283.

eventually approved,[69] and a loan of 1,200,000 florins [70] was floated to provide money for the purchase of supplies.[71] Governor Reuss was empowered to compel the property and money holding classes to subscribe to this loan if they did not do so voluntarily. The very fact that the loan was compulsory, however, made it very unpopular and gave ground for opposition among the Italians.[72] Again the actions of the Austrian government, although they were made with the best of intentions, served to make enemies rather than friends among the Italian population.

The bitter discontent expressed in the occupied Venetian departments over the fiscal policies of the Austrian government shows that there had been a great change in the public opinion of the Venetian populace during the winter of 1813/14 and the spring of 1814. The same Italians who at the outset, when Austrian troops had first entered the Apennine peninsula, had been so joyful and expectant, became so disillusioned and sullen that in February, 1814, they expressed open jubilation over the reverses of the Austrian military forces on the Mincio.[73] Several things were responsible for this tremendous change in public feeling. The snail-like progress of the Austrian army in its campaign against the forces of Prince Eugene and the reten-

---

69 Imperial Resolution, Kaiser Franz, Chaumont, February 28, 1814, *Staats-Archiv*, Vienna, *Kabinets-Akten*, 1814, No. 1204.

70 Wiedemann-Warnhelm, *op. cit.*, 35, states that this loan amounted to 800,000 florins. In the Imperial Resolution given at Chaumont on February 28, 1814, and cited above, the amount of the loan was given as 1,200,000 florins. A report of the *Staats-Kabinet*, bearing the date of March 26, 1814 (*Staats-Archiv*, Vienna, *Kabinets-Akten*, 1814, No. 1331), and a report sent by police president, Baron Hager, on April 16, 1814, to the *Staats-Conferenz* (*Staats-Archiv*, Vienna, *Conferenz Akten*, Ser. b, 1814, No. 917) also confirm the 1,200,000 figure.

71 *Staats-Kabinet* Report, March 26, 1814, *Staats-Archiv*, Vienna, *Kabinets-Akten*, 1814, No. 1331.

72 Hager to *Staats-Conferenz*, April 16, 1814, *Staats-Archiv*, Vienna, *Conferenz Akten*, Ser. b, 1814, No. 917.

73 Hager Report, as summarized by the *Staats-Kabinet* Report of April 5, 1814, *Staats-Archiv*, Vienna, *Kabinets-Akten*, 1814, No. 1371.

tion of the French administrative system annoyed many Italians. The refusal of the Austrians to dismiss all the officials of the former Kingdom of Italy and the ill-mannered behavior of the Austrian soldiers irritated many a person who might otherwise have been in a mood to forgive and forget. But it was the Austrian paper money, the high taxes, and the forced contributions, in a time of general poverty, which really drove most of the populace to despair.[74] Economic oppression, hunger, and misery, and not such actions as the thwarting of national feeling, the political and military repression of the inhabitants, and the alleged restoration of the *status quo* of the pre-Revolutionary era, were the paramount factors in causing many Venetians to be dissatisfied with the Austrian government in the spring of 1814.

It is obvious that the Habsburg government had no intention of deliberately exasperating the Venetian people. As we have already seen, Emperor Francis frequently ordered that changes be made in the occupied provinces which served to relieve the inhabitants of their burdens and grievances. He, however, was in no position to do away with the forced contributions and to lower taxes, for the state of Austrian finances demanded that additional revenue be sought in every section of the conquered area. Governor Reuss-Plauen was ordered to make no changes in the tax structure that would in any way endanger the needs of the army or the ability of the inhabitants to pay increased taxation [75] until " the glowing period when peace will have been attained." [76]

Moreover, the clumsiness and unwieldiness of the Austrian bureaucracy hampered the Emperor at every turn. The Austrian administrative system was too highly centralized to move

---

74 All the documents which the writer has examined in the Venetian and Viennese archives demonstrate that economic factors played the predominant rôle in determining the opinion which the Venetians had toward their new Austrian government.

75 Ugarte to Reuss, Wien, January 29, 1814, *Staats-Archiv*, Vienna, *Conferenz Akten*, Ser. b, 1814, 291.

76 Ugarte to Reuss, Wien, January 21, 1814, *ibid.*, No. 283.

rapidly. Subordinates were given no authority to make important decisions of their own, but, on the contrary, had to obtain the consent of the high state officials, and even that of the Emperor, in Vienna, before they could initiate any important policies. Months usually intervened between the time that urgent requests were sent to Vienna by the local authorities and the time that approval or disapproval was received by them. This state of affairs had a particularly pernicious effect in Italy, where the quick alleviation of many grievances was essential if the good will of the inhabitants was to be retained. The Austrians paid for their inefficiency in the disaffection of Venetian public opinion.

CHAPTER V

THE PRELUDE TO A CRISIS IN THE UNCONQUERED PART OF THE KINGDOM OF ITALY

On April 16, 1814, when the Convention of Schiarino-Rizzino ended the Italian campaign, the whole French edifice in the Kingdom of Italy crumbled. The South Tyrol and the Venetian departments, as we have seen, had already been governed as part of the Habsburg domains for several months. In the departments of Panaro and Crostolo, which represented the former Duchy of Modena, the Austrian Count Nugent had established a provisional military government for Archduke Francis IV of Austria-Este. Those portions of the kingdom which had originally comprised part of the Patrimony of St. Peter were temporarily in the hands of the Austrians and the Neapolitans. Only the territory west of the Mincio and north of the Po remained unconquered and under French-Italian domination. Even there Napoleon was no longer the legal sovereign, for, in the Treaty of Fontainebleau, of April 11, 1814, he had given up his rights to the throne of France and its dependencies.

In early April, 1814, many conflicting desires and emotions moved the inhabitants of this unconquered part of the Kingdom of Italy. Class prejudices, private ambitions, personal hatreds, intense patriotism, and bitter resentment over the exactions caused by the vicissitudes of almost perpetual warfare and by the stringencies of the continental system all showed their hand in crystallizing in certain well-defined channels the views of various inhabitants. The activities of the secret societies and of sundry liberal propagandists stirred the imaginations of many. The stimulus which the French had given to Italian national pride, and the intrigues and propaganda of English, Austrian, and Neapolitan agents swayed the emotions and intensified the expectations of a large throng, especially the middle classes. Hope for personal gain, a pressing desire to do anything to overthrow the last vestiges of the most vexatious oppressions of the French, and the fanciful imaginations of both the old and the young played a significant rôle in influencing public opinion.

Various, and often conflicting, emotions and stimuli prompted many persons to join the ranks of the different parties which intrigued and conspired to fashion a kingdom in accordance with their principles. These parties have usually been termed French, Austrian, and "pure Italian." This division is not exact, and the line between the parties was often extremely confused and irregular. Men frequently passed from the ranks of one into those of another. Nevertheless, this traditional grouping of French, Austrian, and " pure Italian " is perhaps the clearest and most distinct that can be made.

The French or Beauharnais party was small in numbers, but strong because of the power that its members possessed. It was composed chiefly of personal friends of the viceroy, " of high officials, and of the majority of the state employees; in short, of all those who had something to lose in a change of government." [1] The larger part of the army, who saw Eugene as the chieftain who had led them to victories, and a few liberal bourgeoisie, who desired to conserve the existing institutions, also adhered to this faction. Their aim was the creation of an independent Kingdom of Italy with the same boundaries as those of the existing one and with Eugene Beauharnais as king. Prominent among their ranks were such officials as Melzi, the chancellor of the kingdom; Vaccari, the minister of interior; Paradisi, the vice-president of the senate; Méjean, Eugene's counsellor of state; Darnay, the director of the posts; and Prina, the hated minister of finance. The actions of the members of this party in trying to convince the Allied Powers that the inhabitants of the kingdom were solidly behind Eugene Beauharnais in his ambitions to become king of Italy

1 Wiedemann-Warnhelm, *op. cit.*, 19.

provoked the adherents of the other factions to bring about the Milanese revolution of April 20, 1814.

Another party was the so-called Austrian party, many of the members of which desired a direct return to the mild Austrian rule which had existed prior to 1796. " During the period of the French domination in Italy, hatred of the new order " and " fond memories of the benign " reigns of Maria Theresa and Joseph II never ceased,[2] and dissatisfied persons from all classes rallied to the support of Austria. The most numerous of these were the old Lombard nobility, whose titles and coats of arms had been abolished by the French government, and those men who had been punished in some manner by the Napoleonic regime. But there were still others. The clergy chafed under the restrictions placed upon them, and longed for the more dignified and dominating position which they had held under the preceding regime. Many among the proletariat and peasant classes, exhausted by the vicissitudes of warfare, the burdensome exactions of men and money, and the continued disturbances which lessened their chances to make a livelihood, turned to look toward the tranquillity and security of olden times under Habsburg domination. Even some of the middle classes—those very classes toward the improvement of which much of the French legislation had been directed—expressed themselves in favor of their Habsburg neighbors. By April, 1814, the ranks of the Austrian party had swollen to formidable proportions.

The members of the Austrian party, however, were not at all united. Those who wanted a complete return of all the features of the pre-Revolutionary Austrian regime appear to have been few.[3] Some Austrian partisans wanted the support of the powerful military and diplomatic resources of the Habsburgs only to further a regime that would be conformable with their

2 Lemmi, *La restaurazione austriaca, op. cit.*, 115.

3 See Ceria, Luigi, *L'eccidio del Prina e gli ultimi giorni del regno italico (1814)* (Milano, 1937), 153; and Lemmi, *La restaurazione austriaca, op. cit.*, 119-20.

own individual wishes. A much larger faction, influenced by the various propaganda proclamations of Generals Hiller and Nugent, and Marshal Bellegarde, hoped even to obtain independence through Austrian efforts. They aspired to obtain an independent kingdom closely connected with the Habsburgs by calling an Austrian archduke to the throne.[4] In short, the longings of the Austrian partisans were both confused and variegated.

Equally divided and confused were the ranks of the so-called " pure Italian " party. In the party " ambitious and dissatisfied members of the military, equally ambitious members of the Milanese aristocracy," a number of exalted and dreamy souls who " aspired to speak the language of Alfieri's heroes," and persons " of that agitated and restless mind to whom that which is not always appears beautiful "[5] were combined with sagacious, honest, experienced, and sincere men, whose only concern was the well-being of their country.

All the adherents of the party wanted independence, but they could by no means agree as to the future government of the new state which they desired to create and the best program by which to carry out their plans. Some of the " pure Italians," such as General Mazzucchelli, Marquis Fagnani, Giacomo Luini, Ugo Foscolo, and the haughty, petulant, and ambitious

4 General Bellegarde bore witness to the strength of this last group when he wrote Metternich: "The Austrian party which is the most numerous demands an Austrian archduke, and preferably the Archduke Francis, born in Milan, but it demands him as sovereign, for all the parties are united in desiring the conservation and independence of the capital." Letter written at Verona on April 26, 1814, *Staats-Archiv*, Vienna, *Staatskanzlei, Provinzen, Lombardei-Venedig*, Fasc. 3, Sect. 3, Fo. 173. This letter has been published by Lemmi in his *La restaurazione austriaca, op. cit.*, Appendix XIV, 412-17.

5 *Studi intorno alla storia della Lombardia negli ultimi trent'anni e delle cagioni del difetto d'energia dei Lombardi* (Parigi, 1847), 33-4. This work, prohibited by the Austrian censorship, was published in Paris without the name of either the author or of the publisher given It was commonly known, however, that Princess Cristina Belgiojoso-Trivulzio wrote it. In future references the book will be cited as " *Studi intorno*."

General Domenico Pino,[6] supported the pretensions of Joachim Murat to become king of a united Italy. Others, like Antonio Durini, the mayor of Milan, Benigno Bossi, Giovanni Trivulzio, Luigi Porro Lambertenghi, and Carlo Castiglioni, visualized a powerful independent kingdom under the protection of Austria and thought of an Austrian prince, perhaps the Archduke Francis of Austria-Este, as a possible ruler. Their views differed from those of some of the more liberal members of the Austrian party only in that they laid a much greater emphasis upon liberty and independence. Another group, affirming that since England was a constitutional monarchy she would always uphold the cause of freedom, looked to the Duke of Clarence, the third son of King George III of England, for the sovereign in whom the chief governmental authority was to be vested. Still others of the "pure Italians," led by the young Count Federico Confalonieri, were undecided about whom they wished to call upon to assume the kingship of the new independent Italian state which they aspired to bring into being. They concerned themselves only with the attainment of liberty and independence, and were willing to cooperate with any faction which desired to accomplish this end.

Thus far we have spoken of the politically active sections of

6 General Domenico Pino was born in Milan on October 1, 1767. When the French armies marched into Italy, young Pino became one of Napoleon's most ardent supporters. Disgusted after a little while because Bonaparte kept Italy subservient to the French rule, Pino joined General Lahoz in 1799 in his attempted conspiracy to bring about an independent Italian kingdom. After this attempt failed ignominiously, General Pino again entered the service of the French, and rose rapidly in rank and position. In 1804, he was appointed minister of war of the Kingdom of Italy. For a time he was one of Napoleon's most trusted Italian generals. During the Russian campaign, General Pino, however, broke with Napoleon and with Prince Eugene. He bitterly reproached the latter for showing an offensive partiality to the French. Thereafter, relations between Pino and Eugene were very much strained, although General Pino still continued to serve in the French-Italian army. With the beginning of the 1813-14 campaign, the relations between the two men became even worse, and Prince Eugene demoted Pino to a command of secondary importance. General Pino was deeply offended and retired to private life, where he began intriguing to bring about Prince Eugene's overthrow. Lemmi, *La restaurazione austriaca, op. cit.,* 107-11.

the population, and have found that in a general way they tended to divide themselves into French, Austrian, and " pure Italian " parties. These groups were composed of the nobility, the state employees, the officials of the army, the intellectuals, most of the bourgeoisie, and people from a few other strata of society, but, on the whole, they did not include the great masses of the population. As a general rule, the masses took little interest in high political affairs and concerned themselves only with such phases as had a direct and immediate effect upon them. Being almost totally exhausted, they prayed for one thing : peace ! Since the French were held responsible for their desperate plight, many of the proletariat desired their complete overthrow. They concerned themselves with little more, and did not especially care what type of government was established if they secured their ardently longed for peace.

With the Kingdom of Italy practically exhausted, with the enemy in occupation of a considerable portion of its territory, and with foreign agents, secret societies, and important sections of the population actively intriguing to bring about a change in the government of the country, it was only natural that there was little economic and political stability left. Robbers and brigands infested the countryside, and many disorders broke out in various parts of the kingdom.[7] The economic and political structure of the kingdom was crumbling. The end was rapidly drawing near. It was only a question of whether that end would be slow and orderly, as it had been in the Venetian departments, or abrupt and violent.

While the kingdom was thus slowly disintegrating, there was great consternation in the circles of Prince Eugene and of the loyal Italian officers and soldiers in Mantua. On April 13, Marshal Bellegarde had sent to Prince Eugene official documents of the entry of the Allied Powers into Paris and of the

---

7 Report from Milan, April 10, 1814, *Wiener Zeitung*, April 25, 1814, 462; Melzi to Eugene, Milano, April 8, 1814, Melzi d'Eril, *op. cit.*, II, 427-28; *Mantovani Diario politico-ecclesiastico di Milano*, April 2, 1814, V, 246 The last of these sources is found in manuscript form in the Ambrosiana Library of Milan under the signature of M. S. IV. 5.

installation of a provisional government in France, and asked him to declare what his attitude toward the Allied Powers would be in the light of this evidence.[8] On the 15th, Lieutenant-General Wartenberg, *aide-de-camp* of the King of Bavaria, accompanied by the Austrian Count Neipperg, presented himself to Eugene with a letter written by his father-in-law, King Maximilian,[9] imploring Eugene for the sake of his wife and children to profit by the good will of the Allied Powers and sever his connections with the French immediately.[10]

Free from his obligations to Napoleon, the viceroy could now think of his own future and that of his family. To continue to resist Austria was futile. He could either give up his position as viceroy and leave the kingdom forever, or, supported by the vote of his people, he could call upon the Allied Powers to confer the crown of the Kingdom of Italy upon him. Eugene chose the second alternative. On April 16, a military convention was signed at Schiarino-Rizzino providing that all French troops in the viceroy's army were to be sent back to France immediately and that a deputation of the Kingdom of Italy was to go to the general headquarters of the Allies.[11]

It was now necessary for the viceroy to insure that deputies favorable to his candidacy would be sent to the Allied headquarters. To win the favor of the army, Prince Eugene took occasion to announce as the French soldiers were dispatched on their way home: " A loyal, generous, and good people has claim to the rest of my life, which I have dedicated to them for ten years. As long as I have the pleasure of occupying myself with their well-being, which has long been the dearest occupation of my life, I will ask no other calling for myself." [12]

8 In a letter written at Verona, Lemmi, *La restaurazione austriaca, op cit.,* Appendix I, 395.

9 Weil, *Eugène et Murat, op. cit.,* IV, 527.

10 Letter written at Munich on April 11, 1814, Du Casse, *op. cit.,* X, 236-37.

11 See *ante,* 60.

12 Proclamation, Eugene to the French soldiers, April 17, 1814, *Oesterreichischer Beobachter,* 1814, No. 125 (May 5, 1814), 679. A correspondent

General Lechi, of the Italian army, replied with these words: " We, independent and guided by Eugene, will be great, honored, felicitous, respected, and, in the shadow of an illustrious throne and a secure and lasting peace, we shall enjoy those benefits for the attainment of which fifteen years of uninterrupted fatigue have been directed." [13]

The viceroy accepted Lechi's words as representing the army's approval of his scheme to make himself king of an independent Kingdom of Italy and chose General Achille Fontanelli, then minister of war, and General Antonio Bertoletti to express these sentiments, in the name of the Italian army, to the Allies at Paris. On April 20, Fontanelli and Bertoletti left Mantua to go to Munich to await the arrival of deputies selected by the senate of the kingdom and accompany them to Paris.[14] The viceroy's plan was progressing very smoothly. If deputies favorable to him were also chosen to represent the people and dispatched to Paris, so Eugene thought, the crown of the kingdom would virtually be his.

Since his trusted chancellor, Melzi, had already suggested to him that the electoral colleges, if convoked, " would undoubtedly proclaim with enthusiasm the independence of the country " and invite " Your Highness to take the crown," [15] Prince Eugene thought first of calling that body into session

of the May 10, 1814, issue of the *Oesterreichischer Beobachter* (No. 130, 707), in commenting on the above proclamation, said: " In a proclamation of the 17th, when the viceroy sent the French to their home land, he used expressions which gave the impression that he already looked upon himself as King of Italy."

13 Proclamation to the soldiers of the royal guard, April 19, 1814, Pellini, Silvio, *Il General Pino e la morte del Ministro Prina* (Novara, 1905), 18. This book consists almost entirely of documents which are very important for the study of the events which took place during the period of the Milanese revolution of April 20, 1814.

14 Proclamation, Eugene, Mantova, April 20, 1814, Cantù, *Il principe Eugenio, op. cit.*, IX, 129; *Studi intorno, op. cit.*, 49.

15 Melzi to Eugene, Milano, April 11, 1814, Cantù, *Il principe Eugenio, op. cit.*, VIII, 279. Also see Cusani, *op. cit.*, VII, 85-7.

and urging it immediately to choose such men as Prina, Fontanelli, or Testi to represent the people of the kingdom before the Allies.[16] A little later, however, the viceroy felt that the immediate choice of the deputies who were to go to Paris was so urgent that it would be very unwise to wait the fifteen days that his chancellor deemed necessary for the assembling of the electoral colleges. He decided, therefore, to call upon the senate, which could be speedily convoked, to choose the delegates to be dispatched to the Allied Powers, and sent his secretary and counsellor of state, Méjean, from Mantua to Milan to prepare the ground for the opening of the senate meeting.[17]

On the evening of April 16, Chancellor Melzi sent messages to the senators to come together the next day for an extraordinary sitting,[18] without revealing what the purpose of

16 Eugene to Melzi, Mantova, April 15, 1814, Melzi d'Eril, *op cit*, II, 431-32.

17 "A message from the prince Viceroy in the person of Monsieur Méjean arrived here on the 16th current treating with the sitting of the senate for the unanimous vote to promulgate the regency in Italy." Anonymous to Hager, Milano, April 29, 1814, Lemmi, *La restaurazione austriaca, op cit*, 133 ftn. "On the 15th, Méjan hurried here to the officials and dignitaries to induce Melzi, with his colleagues, to propose Eugene as our king in the Senate." Borda to Gallotta, Milano, April 20, 1814, Fiorani, G., "L'eccidio del Ministro Prina," *Rendiconti* del Reale Istituto lombardo di scienze e lettere, Ser. II, XXVIII (1895), 424. "At the same time, the viceroy made use of Monsieur Melzi d'Eril, the arch-chancellor and president of the senate, to engage this body to demand solemnly of the Allies that Eugene have the Kingdom of Italy.... The secretary of the cabinet, Méjan, was secretly sent to Milan to arrange with Melzi what was to be done under the actual circumstances." *Dernière campagne de l'armée franco-italienne, op. cit*, 82. It should be noted that although Eugene's secretary is referred to as "Méjan" in two of the above sources, the most common spelling of the name is "Méjean."

18 On May 1, 1814, Melzi wrote the president of the provisional regency that, following the viceroy's advice, he convoked the senate because he believed that the Allies were inclined to favor such a project, because he thought that Prince Eugene, more than any other monarch who might be chosen, would rule according to constitutional principles and according to the wishes of the inhabitants, and because he thought that Eugene was much more popular with the Lombards than the revolution of April 20 proved him to be. Gallavresi, Giuseppe, "Ricerche intorno alla rivoluzione

the assembly was to be.[19] The next day the senators gathered together in the extraordinary session for which they had been summoned. They were in ignorance as to the possible motives for their convocation, especially since they had been informed on the morning of the 16th that an ordinary sitting of the senate would be held on the 20th.[20] The president of the senate, Count Veneri, opened the sitting by reading several letters which Chancellor Melzi had given him to present

milanese del 1814," *Rendiconti* del Reale Istituto lombardo di scienze e lettere, Ser. II, XL (1907), Appendix II, 414-15.

19 Bonfadini, *op. cit.*, 80; Ceria, *op. cit.*, 103. In his relation, Senator Verri said · " It was on the evening of the 16th April, 1814, when I, being in the company of various persons, . . . received a letter of advice that on the following morning the Senate would meet in an extraordinary sitting." Verri, Conte Carlo, *Sugli avvenimenti di Milano 17-20 aprile 1814*, 103. This valuable and enlightening source on the causes and events of the Milanese revolution of April 20, 1814, was written by Senator Verri in Nice in the winter of 1817, and was reprinted by Tommaso Casini in his *La rivoluzione di Milano dell'aprile 1814. Relazioni storiche di Leopoldo Armaroli e Carlo Verri, Senatori del Regno italico*, as Volume I, No. 3, of the *Biblioteca storica del Risorgimento italiano*, edited by T. Casini and V. Fiorini, and published by the Società editrice Dante Alighieri This particular work was published in 1897. All the writer's references from this work will be cited from this edition, and will be cited as " Verri, *op. cit.*" Cusani, *op cit.*, VII, 91-3, 101, 106, 117, 119-24, quotes certain parts of Verri's relation. His citations, however, differ in certain details from those in the account reprinted by Casini. Also see Lemmi, *La restaurazione austriaca, op. cit.*, 130 ftn.

20 Relation of the sitting of the senate of the Kingdom of Italy, held on April 17, 1814, *Sulla rivoluzione di Milano seguita nel giorno 20 aprile 1814, sul primo suo governo provvisorio e sulle quivi tenute adunanze de'collegi elettorali. Memoria storica con documenti* (Parigi, Novembre 1814), Appendix I, 43. A printed copy of this work is in the Ambrosiana Library of Milan, under the signature of S. C. V. V., 26, No. 5. In 1822, M. Saint-Edme published a French translation of this anonymous work in Paris under the following title: *Relation historique de la révolution du royaume d'Italie en 1814*, par le Conte Guicciardi, ex-Chancelier du Sénat. Thereafter the authorship of the book was erroneously attributed to Guicciardi for more than half a century. In 1897, Tommaso Casini, reprinted the work in his *La rivoluzione di Milano dell'aprile 1814, op. cit.*, and definitely proved that the author of this relation was not Senator Guicciardi but Senator Leopoldo Armaroli. *Ibid.*, vii-xviii. In all future references this work will be cited as "Armaroli, *op cit.*," and the page references which have been given above and which will be given in the future will refer to those of the Casini edition.

to the senate.[21] In them the chancellor proposed that the senators send without delay a deputation to the Austrian Emperor to implore him to use his powerful influence on the other Allied Powers to insure the conservation of an independent and undivided Kingdom of Italy, with " a free and independent king, notably Prince Eugene, who, through his virtues, his knowledge, and his honorable conduct, both during peace and during war, has merited the love, recognition, and fidelity of the people of the Kingdom of Italy, and the esteem of all Europe." [22]

21 Later, during the course of the Milanese revolution, when several persons threatened to go to Melzi's house to attack him, General Pino, in an effort to deter them, erroneously proclaimed that the above letters were not sent to the senate by Melzi, but were signed with his name by an amanuensis and drafted by persons other than him. Proclamation to the Milanese, Milano, April 21, 1814, Pellini, *op. cit.*, 21-2. There is no basis in fact for the general's assertions. Senator Verri said that the documents were signed in the following manner : " *Secretary Villa, by the express commission of His Excellency, the Duke of Lodi, prevented because of gout.*" Verri, *op cit.*, 110. When a senatorial commission was sent to Melzi to question him about his proposed project, he assumed full responsibility for it. Gallavresi, " Ricerche intorno alla rivoluzione milanese del 1814," *loc. cit.*, 413. In his letter of May 1, 1814, to the president of the provisional regency, Melzi asserted in a very positive manner that the letters were " signed by my order and with my name." *Ibid.*, Appendix II, 414. It can not legitimately be denied that the real author of the project was Melzi

22 Project for the deliberation of the senate joined to the message of the Duke of Lodi, Milano, April 17, 1814, Armaroli, *op. cit*, Appendix I, B, 50-2, Cusani, *op cit.*, VII, 96-8. It should be noted that the " Relations of the Provisional Regency on the events of April 17-21," found in the *Staats-Archiv*, Vienna, *Staatskanzlei, Provinzen, Lombardei-Venedig*, Fasc. 3, Sect. 3, Fo. 179-80, and printed in Lemmi, *La restaurazione austriaca, op cit*, Appendix III, 397-400, differs in minor respects from the original letter sent to the senate by Melzi and included in Armaroli's and Cusani's accounts. It related that the senate, according to the project of Melzi's decree, was to name " a deputation, which was to go to the High Allied Powers to demand

" 1. The total cessation of hostilities.

" 2. The conservation of the Kingdom of Italy with a constitution founded upon the liberal principles proclaimed by the said High Powers to tranquilize Europe.

" 3. To manifest with indirect means to the said High Powers the public vote to obtain as sovereign a personage whom the people do not wish."

The members of the provisional regency, which was established on April 21,

As soon as President Veneri finished reading the chancellor's message, Senator Guicciardi, an ardent partisan of Austria, jumped up to demand that an investigation of the legality of this extraordinary convocation of the senate immediately be started.[23] Senator Dandolo suggested that a special committee should be appointed and given at least two days to investigate the whole project thoroughly. Count Paradisi, President Veneri, and the minister of interior, Count Vaccari, objected strenuously. It was both preposterous and suicidal, they insisted, to lose two days of precious time in critical and urgent circumstances, particularly since the proposed business was beyond the shadow of a doubt both legitimate and constitutional. Veneri proposed that if a majority of the senate believed that the matter at hand must be examined, it should be done by a secret committee, instructed to present its conclusions posthaste to the full senate. Guicciardi maintained that such an act was both impractical and unconstitutional, but his objections were overruled by the majority of the senators.

A committee of seven members was finally chosen to examine the question under debate, and three members of this committee, Senators Guicciardi, Verri, and Dandolo, went to Chancellor Melzi to relate what had happened in the senate and to secure further advice from him.[24] Melzi justified his convocation of the senate by showing the three members of the committee an old decree of the king which, in the absence of the viceroy, conferred upon him ample power to convoke the

belonged to the anti-Eugene factions, and no doubt colored their account in order to give their personal viewpoint.

23 Verri, *op. cit.*, 108.

24 Relation of the sitting of the senate of the Kingdom of Italy, held on April 17, 1814, Armaroli, *op. cit.*, Appendix I, 44-6; *Studi intorno, op. cit.*, 50-1; Fabi, Massimo, *Milano e il ministro Prina Narrazione storica del Regno d'Italia (aprile 1814). Tratta da documenti editi ed inediti* (Novara, 1860), 17-20. In regard to the last book, Cantù, in his *Cronistoria, op cit.*, I, 869 ftn , has written the following: " This is the work of Counsellor Carlo Castiglia, who exhibited it to me and several others before selling it to Fabi, who printed it as his own work." Also see Cusani, *op. cit.*, VII, 98-100.

senate, and in vain tried to convince them of the necessity of elevating Eugene to the kingship.[25]

After Guicciardi, Verri, and Dandolo left Melzi's home, they and the other four members of the committee drew up a new project for the consideration of the senate.[26] This new plan differed from the one which Melzi had originally proposed in that it did not specifically ask for Prince Eugene as king, but limited itself to charging the deputation to inform the Allied Powers that " the Senate seizes this opportunity to renew to His Imperial Excellency, Prince Eugene, the sentiments of its high esteem and its most sincere attachment." [27]

At eight o'clock in the evening, the sitting of the senate was resumed. The report of the committee was read. When it was learned that the committee advised against the proposed deputation's being charged with asking for Eugene as king, several adherents of the Beauharnais faction raised a great commotion. Paradisi and Vaccari, in particular, emphatically insisted that this omission be repaired, and Veneri and Prina jumped into

25 After the three members of the committee left, Melzi hastened to write Eugene: " The Commission of Senators has been at my home. It is impossible to appraise the infinite quantity of difficulties which they have made. They insist on naming the deputies by themselves; thus the nomination of Fontanelli which I wished to make can not take place, unless Your Excellency finds the means to have him nominated by the army or in some other manner. According to the voting and the debates which have taken place here, I am convinced that these heads are in an inconceivable confusion and are entirely incapable of putting themselves on the level of circumstances Even those who wished to aid have contributed rather to spoil things." Letter of April 17, 1814, Melzi d'Eril, *op. cit.*, II, 435.

26 Verri, *op. cit.*, 110-11; Relation of the sitting of the senate of the Kingdom of Italy, held on April 17, 1814, Armaroli, *op cit.*, Appendix I, 46.

27 Relation of the sitting of the senate of the Kingdom of Italy, held on April 17, 1814, Armaroli, *op. cit.*, Appendix I, 46. The account of Senator Verri, *op. cit*, 111-12, differs considerably from this, but from the general nature of the debates which followed and from the decree which was finally adopted by the senate, it can be deduced that in this instance Verri's account is incorrect. Princess Belgiojoso-Trivulzio, in her *Studi intorno, op. cit.*, 51; Lemmi, *La restaurazione austriaca, op. cit*, 138; Ceria, *op. cit.*, 105; and Helfert, *La caduta, op. cit*, 45, all describe recommendations exactly like those contained in the appendix of Armaroli's account.

the fray to support them. With countless arguments, they sought to induce the senate to accept Melzi's plan in its original form. Guicciardi, Dandolo, Massari, Verri, and Castiglioni, along with several other senators, sprang to the defense of the committee. Both sides disputed fast and furiously, rejecting argument after argument with counter contentions.[28]

A veritable deadlock ensued, which was not terminated until long after midnight, when Count Moscati proposed in way of compromise that the objectionable statement in reference to Prince Eugene be changed to the following: " The deputies will be charged with presenting on this occasion to the Allied Powers the sentiments of admiration of the Senate for the virtues of the viceroy and Prince, and of its enthusiastic recognition of his government." [29] This suggestion was finally adopted, and the report of the committee was amended to include this change.[30]

When the time came for the selection of the deputies who were to be sent to Paris, several nominations were made, and Castiglioni, Testi, and Guicciardi were finally chosen for the mission. Both Testi and Guicciardi begged to be released from the charge conferred upon them, but, since everyone was exhausted from the long night of tedious argumentation, this request was refused and President Veneri declared the sitting adjourned.[31] Later Testi again voiced his protests, this time to Chancellor Melzi. In spite of his entreaties, Melzi could not persuade the refractory Testi to leave Milan, and had to con-

28 Relation of the sitting of the senate of the Kingdom of Italy, held on April 17, 1814, Armaroli, *op. cit.*, Appendix I, 47-8; Fabi, *op. cit.*, 21-4; Cusani, *op. cit*, VII, 103-5.

29 Relation of the sitting of the senate of the Kingdom of Italy, held on April 17, 1814, Armaroli, *op. cit.*, 48.

30 For the text of the decree of the senate which officially put into effect the results of the day's sitting, see Beauharnais Archives, Princeton University, Fasc. 62, no number given. A copy of the text is also included in Armaroli, *op. cit.*, Appendix I, C, 52-3; and in Fabi, *op cit.*, Appendix III, 94-6.

31 Relation of the sitting of the senate of the Kingdom of Italy, held on April 17, 1814, Armaroli, *op. cit.*, Appendix I, 48-9.

tent himself with sending only Castiglioni and Guicciardi on the mission.[32] On April 18 the two senators received their instructions [33] and departed for Mantua, which they left on April 21 for Paris.

The extraordinary meeting of the senate served to arouse popular opinion to a high pitch of excitement, and to increase the acrid discord among the "pure Italian," Austrian, and French factions.[34] Although the deliberations of the senate were supposed to have been secret, sufficient news concerning what took place leaked out to provoke a lamentable confusion of public opinion. Some of the agitated and excited inhabitants proclaimed that the senate had elected the hated viceroy king.[35] Others fulminated against the convocation of the senate and insisted that the electoral colleges should have been called. Still others hurled dire threats and imprecations against the partisans of the viceroy.[36] " We do not want as King him who as Viceroy has broken and despoiled Italy ! " they cried.[37]

On the 18th and the 19th the uncertainty and anger of the Milanese populace increased by leaps and bounds. The various contradictory notices and reports which had been spread among the people the previous day were multiplied. Most people occupied themselves with little besides the question of the future fate of their kingdom. When the news arrived in the city of the negotiations at Schiarino-Rizzino and of Napoleon's abdication at Fontainebleau,[38] it was received with jubilation. On the

32 Melzi to Eugene, Milano, April 19, 1814, Cantù, *Il principe Eugenio, op. cit.,* IX, 127.

33 A copy of these instructions is in Armaroli, *op. cit*, Appendix II, 54-5.

34 Melzi to Eugene, Milano, April 19, 1814, Cantù, *Il principe Eugenio, op. cit.,* IX, 128.

35 Relations of the provisional regency on the events of April 17-21, Lemmi, *La restaurazione austriaca, op. cit*, Appendix III, 398.

36 Director of the Police to Eugene, Milano, April 20, 1814, Beauharnais Archives, Princeton University, Fasc. 62, No. 4.

37 Weil, *Eugène et Murat, op. cit*, IV, 554; Lemmi, *La restaurazione austriaca, op. cit*, 141.

38 On April 19, the *Giornale italiano* published the text of the Convention of Schiarino-Rizzino. Fabi, *op. cit.,* 28, Cusani, *op. cit.,* VII, 111. According

other hand, the rumors that Eugene had addressed himself to
the departing French army in a way which indicated that he
considered himself sovereign of the kingdom profoundly irritated and vexed the viceroy's opponents, some of whom were
prepared to begin a popular uprising.[39]

Large numbers of people were particularly insistent that the
electoral colleges be called to deliberate on the fate of the
Kingdom of Italy, maintaining that they alone adequately
represented the popular will.[40] On April 19, some of the men
who were of this opinion circulated a petition demanding the
immediate convocation of the electoral colleges.[41] By the morning of April 20, there were considerably over a hundred names
appended to it, some of them of the most illustrious citizens of
Milan. The petition was to be presented to the senate on April
20, when it was scheduled to meet in ordinary session.[42]

to Federico Confalonieri, the news of Napoleon's abdication first arrived in
Milan on April 18. Casati, Gabrio, *Federico Confalonieri, Memorie e lettere*
(Milano, 1889), I, 81.

39 " On the 19th current there began to manifest themselves here signs
of insubordination, with libels posted in several parts of the city and with
such radical discourses as to make one fear that disorders were imminent "
Prefect of Police to Eugene, Milano, April 21, 1814, Beauharnais Archives,
Princeton University, Fasc. 62, No. 10.

40 The prefect of the Milanese police wrote Eugene that " several Senators
and many members of the Electoral Colleges distinguished themselves " in
insisting on this. Letter of April 20, 1814, Beauharnais Archives, Princeton
University, Fasc. 62, No. 4.

41 The text of the petition reads as follows: "After the sitting of the
Senate on the 16th [*sic*] of the current month, nothing of the deliberations
of which was ever communicated to the public, it is the universal opinion that
at it were proposed, discussed, and defined an affair of the greatest importance for our Kingdom. If in the present extraordinary vicissitudes, it is
necessary to invoke extraordinary remedies, the undersigned think that according to the principles of the constitution it is indispensable that the
Electoral Colleges, in which alone resides the legitimate representation of the
nation, should be convoked." An original copy of this petition is in the
Carte del Giacomo Beccaria, in the *Museo del Risorgimento Nazionale* of
Milan, Busta I, Carte 8, Fasc. I, Pezza 6, A. A copy of this petition is
also in Fabi, *op. cit.*, Appendix VIII, 110-15.

42 Gallavresi, Giuseppe, " I ricordi ed il carteggio del conte Ludovico
Giovio," *Periodico* della Società storica per la Provincia e antica Diocesi
di Como, XVII-XVIII (1906-8), Appendix A, 245.

The senate, however, was destined never to consider the petition. Persons walking down the streets of Milan on the evening of April 19, tarrying in the Piazza del Duomo, the Piazza della Scala, or any other popular resort of the Milanese, must have sensed that something unusual was afoot. In all the squares, cafés, and public lodgings they could not help seeing many strange and tense looking faces, which seemed to presage disaster for some enemy. They must have heard some of the excited arguments and heated discussions about the dire intrigues of Eugene's partisans or the unconstitutionality of the actions of the senate.[43] They were witnessing only the natural results of years of military and financial exactions and of days of confused and mingled hopes, fears, loves, and excitement. They were living through an historic moment, for they were hearing the rumblings of one of the most tumultuous and bloody Milanese revolutions in half a century.

43 See *ibid.*, 245-46, for a short but vivid depiction of the atmosphere in Milan on the evening of the 19th.

CHAPTER VI

PLOTTING A REVOLUTION

WHEN the senate of the Kingdom of Italy met in regular session at noon on April 20, 1814, the storm clouds which had been gathering for several days burst, leaving in their trail a deluge of disorder and confusion, wrecked homes, razed palaces, terrified officials, and a dead minister of finance. For days the streets of Milan had been crowded with throngs of confused and uneasy people, ready to spring on a moment's notice at a real or imaginary enemy within the gates of the city. Nerves were taut; feelings were at fever pitch. Mobs were at the beck and call of any group of individuals who had the temerity to use these excited people to their own advantage in the name of patriotism and of vengeance against the hated French.

In the ranks of the Austrian and Italian parties and of the secret political societies were persons who were willing to utilize the mob, with all its mingled hates, jealousies, ambitions, longings, and fears, to bring about a forcible and violent end to the Kingdom of Italy. Members of all three of these opposition groups, both honorable and depraved, joined a cabal to foment a revolution in order to prevent the creation of an independent Kingdom of Italy with Eugene Beauharnais as king.

Contemporary writers have named several of the ringleaders of this conspiracy. The anonymous author of the bitter and vehement " Lamentations or the Nights of General Pino, with interesting Notes on the Milanese Revolution of April 20, 1814," [1] accused some of the most prominent citizens of the kingdom of taking a significant part in the unfortunate acts

1 *Le Lamentazioni ossiano le notti del Gle. Pino con note interessanti la Rivoluzione di Milano del 20 Aple. 1814.* A handwritten copy of this curious document is in the Ambrosiana Library of Milan, under the signature of S. C. V. V. 26, No. 10. The complete text is printed in Pellini, *op. cit.*, 114-50. The part entitled "Notte III. L'ingratitudine" (Pellini, *op. cit.*, 128-40) is particularly interesting. Because of its much greater accessibility, the writer's page references to this memoir will be to the copy printed in Pellini.

happening on April 20. Fagnani and the Cicogna brothers were reproached with personally helping the assassins who attacked the senatorial palace and murdered Minister Prina. Confalonieri, jealous because Prince Eugene may have had an amorous intrigue with his wife Teresa, " conceived the idea of taking vengeance on the aforesaid Prince." Ciani paid back the viceroy for all the titles and honors which he had showered upon him " by associating himself with the rank of the seditious and the revolters." Ballabio and Bossi were responsible for letting a crowd of miserable malefactors penetrate the palace of the senate. Crivelli, Porro, Serbelloni, Borromeo, Fossati, and " Castiglione " [sic?] all aided in the conspiracy in the hope of finding personal gain. The " impudent females Triulzi, Decapitani, and Crivelli," the author continued, meditated the massacre of several prominent personages.[2] And General Domenico Pino, against whom the main accusation of this diatribe is directed, was charged with using the sum of 50,000 lire which Prince Eugene had given him to pay his debts to organize the revolution of April 20 against the same prince.[3]

It is difficult to believe the veracity of the scurrilous charges made by the anonymous author of the " Lamentations," but it must be noted that many of the intriguers attacked in this work are also singled out in other contemporary accounts as having taken an especially prominent part in organizing the Milanese revolution. The names of Ciani, Confalonieri,[4] and Bossi are

2 *Ibid.*, 132-38.

3 This is the gist of the accusation made against General Pino. For the charges made against him, see the whole text, as printed in *ibid.*, 114-50, or as found in the original manuscript in the Ambrosiana Library.

4 Federico Confalonieri emphatically denied that he had any complicity in fomenting the Milanese revolution. Letter to a friend, Milano, March 15, 1815, Casati, *op. cit.*, I, 253-73. His good friend, Silvio Pellico, supported him in his disavowal, and attributed these charges to the fact that Confalonieri had made too many enemies. To Stanislao Marchisio, July, 1815, Chiattone, Domenico, " Nuovi documenti su Federico Confalonieri e per le sue relazioni intime e patriottiche prima del processo," *Archivo Storico Lombardo*, Anno XXXIII (1906), 51-2. Confalonieri's biographers have also come to his rescue. Bonfadini has asserted that young Federico played " a vivacious,

mentioned by Botta,[5] Armaroli,[6] and Princess Belgiojoso-
Trivulzio,[7] as well as by the author of the " Lamentations," as
being among the chief fomenters of the plot. Castiglioni, Serbelloni, the Cicogna brothers, and Fagnani are named by
Armaroli and Botta. Princess Belgiojoso-Trivulzio stresses the
fact that Porro played a significant rôle, and Botta asserts that
several prominent women, particularly Lady De Capitani and
a Marchioness Oppozoni, took an active part. Botta, Armaroli,
and Belgiojoso-Trivulzio in their relations all indicated that
they were mentioning the names of only a few of those im-
plicated in directing the revolution, and that other prominent
Milanese took part in it. Perhaps Fossati, Borromeo, Crivelli,
and Ballabio, and the Signore Crivelli and Triulzi were some
of these other prominent Milanese. And General Domenico
Pino, against whom the main indictment of the " Lamentations " is hurled, is mentioned by so many sources as having
taken an active part in the intrigue that his complicity appears
undeniable.[8]

passionate, perhaps imprudent," but never " culpable " part in the Milanese
revolution. He insisted that Confalonieri's character was entirely too noble
for him to have committed the various things ascribed to him. Bonfadini, R.,
" Federico Confalonieri," *Nuova Antologia di scienze, lettere ed arti*, Ser. IV,
CLVI (1897), 673. D'Ancona, in denying the imputations, asked: " Can
anyone imagine Count Confalonieri in the act of brandishing furniture,
chairs, and pictures, and hurling them out of windows? " D'Ancona,
Alessandro, *Federico Confalonieri. Su documenti inediti di archivj pubblici
e privati* (Milano, 1898), 7. These writers have, however, cited no specific
proof of Confalonieri's innocence, and have merely rested their case upon
the assertion that Federico was of too noble and fine a character to commit
the transgressions of which he was accused. The most recent biography of
Confalonieri, Ricarda Huch's *Das Leben des Grafen Federigo Confalonieri*
(Leipzig, 1934), does not discuss Confalonieri's part in the Milanese
revolution.

5 Botta, Carlo, *Storia d'Italia dal 1789 al 1814* (Paris, 1824), X, 256-57.
This book was also translated into English under the following title: *History
of Italy during the Consulate and Empire of Napoleon Buonaparte* (London,
1828). In the English edition, the above citation is in Volume II, 442-43.

6 Armaroli, *op cit.*, 15

7 *Studi intorno, op. cit.*, 59.

8 General Pino denied that he took an active part in organizing the
Milanese revolution of April 20, and wrote two tracts in an attempt to prove

At least some of these conspirators made plans to provoke an uprising at a series of secret meetings which were held in Milan. Ugo Foscolo, himself accused of being one of the conspirators, asserted that these meetings were " held in the house of a very rich person, and were presided over by his own wife, who was one of those adulteresses rewarded with celebrity." [9] Without doubt he referred to the Milanese house of Countess Traversa, the wife of the nefarious lawyer Traversa, who had accumulated vast riches and large estates in the district between the Sesia and the Ticino and who was a bitter enemy of both Prince Eugene and Minister Prina.[10] Other meetings were also said to have taken place at the homes of Bianca Milesi,[11] and Councillor Freganeschi.[12]

Traversa was accused of having proposed to his confederates at these conferences that a large number of resolute and determined men be brought to Milan from the Novarese—the section in which Traversa had his largest landholdings—to provoke sedition, menace the government, and even assassinate

his innocence. The first, penned in answer to Senator Armaroli's anonymous account of the Milanese revolution, was the *Osservazioni del Generale Pino sopra alcune asserzioni dell'autore dell'opuscolo che ha per titolo: ' Sulla rivoluzione di Milano, seguita il 20 aprile 1814, ec. Parigi in novembre Italia, 1815.'* A printed copy of this memoir is in the Ambrosiana Library of Milan, under the signature of S. C. V. V. 26, No. 7. The complete text is also published in Pellini, *op. cit.,* 96-112. The second, written in refutation of the "Lamentations," was his *Schiarimenti sopra alcuni articoli esistenti nel libello intitolato: ' Le quattro notti del Generale PINO, stampato in Italia.' Il restante delle insussistenti infernali invenzioni non meritando osservazione, può solo eccitare orrore e disprezzo.* A copy of this is in Pellini, *op. cit.,* 152-60. Pino's conduct during this time and the fact that contemporaries of all types and descriptions mentioned him as one of the ringleaders of the conspiracy, however, must discredit his protestations of innocence.

9 " Lettera Apologetica," in *Opere complete di Ugo Foscolo* (Napoli, 1860), I, 698.

10 *Studi intorno, op. cit* , 59; Ceria, *op cit.,* 162-63.

11 *Studi intorno, op. cit.,* 59.

12 Lemmi, *La restaurazione austriaca, op cit.,* 149 Fabi, *op cit,* 33 ftn , says: " Even other congresses were held in the houses of Cicogna, Confalonieri, Castiglioni, Silva, etc."

persons at the bidding of the conspirators.[13] It was even charged that these hired assassins were ordered " to kill some important personage or several," and that " each was promised six lire per day for the whole time that he was absent from home." The one who succeeded in killing Minister Prina would, in addition, receive "a large sum of money " from Traversa's friend, Baron Gambarana.[14]

Some of the plotters of the rebellion, such as Gambarana, Borromeo, and Freganeschi, belonged to the Austrian party. They desired to profit by the existing uneasiness and confusion to cause disturbances in Milan which would make the intervention of the Austrian army inevitable. Others, such as the Cicogna brothers, Traversa, Confalonieri, Bossi, Fagnani, and Pino, were leaders of one or another of the " pure Italian " factions, who, incensed because the senate had refused to sustain their program, in their blindness hoped that through revolt might come the ultimate triumph of their party.[15] " Pure

13 *Studi intorno, op. cit*, 59-60. Senator Verri even went so far as to assert emphatically that the principal actors in the assassination of Minister Prina and in the razing of his house were not Milanese citizens but people from the region around Lago Maggiore. Verri, *op. cit.*, 144-45. It is also significant to note that citizens from the province of Novara, in which part of the Lago Maggiore district is located, and other surrounding districts arrived in large numbers in Milan on the afternoon and evening of April 19 and on the morning of April 20.

14 *Studi intorno, op. cit.*, 60. In his memoirs, Ludovico Giovio related that when, on April 20, he walked through the mob which was sacking Minister Prina's house, he said to himself: "Ordered crime—hired executioners—,... since I heard more than once from the rabble, that to obtain the promised recompense, they were here to insult and kill, and to demolish the House of the Minister." *Memoria di Lodovico Giovio intorno all'opuscolo intitolato: 'Sulla rivoluzione di Milano seguita nel giorno 20 aprile, e nei successivi 1814. Li 7 febbrajo 1815.'* A handwritten copy of the memoir is in the Ambrosiana Library of Milan, under the signature of S. C. V. V. 26, No. 6, and a printed copy in Pellini, *op. cit.*, 81-94. In the printed copy in Pellini, the above quotation is on page 87 ftn. It should be noted that although Giovio's first name is spelled "Lodovico" in the above title, in all other places that the writer has seen it, it is spelled "Ludovico." Also see Lemmi, *La restaurazione austriaca, op. cit.*, 150 ftn.

15 Bonfadini, *op. cit.*, 94-5.

Italians" with all sorts of differing predilections for their desired future ruler, as well as Austrian partisans, were intriguing to overthrow Prince Eugene's government, but the most active of them appeared to be those "pure Italians" who, headed by General Pino, wanted to place Joachim Murat on the throne of Italy.

The suspicions of both French-Italian and Austrian officials were aroused in regard to the intrigues of this group of men around General Pino. On the morning of April 20, just before the revolt actually broke out, Chancellor Melzi hastened to recommend to the viceroy that since "the traces of the Neapolitan intrigue" were becoming more obvious, and since it was certain that "General Pino and Chamberlain Fagnani" were taking "a distinguished part in the whole movement," it might be well if both of these gentlemen, and particularly Pino, were called away from Milan on some pretext.[16] The Austrians, too, were wary of the intentions of Murat's supporters. They knew that King Joachim was greatly perturbed when he heard of the signing of the Convention of Schiarino-Rizzino,[17] and when Murat tried to approach the city of Milan by way of Piacenza, they hurriedly, but not without difficulty, prevented this move.[18] They became especially uneasy when they learned that the Neapolitan "General Livron was in Milan" on April 20, and that in the "midst of the revolution several voices pronounced the name of the King of Naples."[19] Their anxiety was justified, for there was in the kingdom an ambitious coterie of men, headed by Giacomo Luini, General Mazzucchelli, General Dembowsky, Ugo Foscolo, Fagnani, and, above all, the haughty Domenico Pino, actively at work

16 Beauharnais Archives, Princeton University, Fasc. 62, No. 6. Also printed in Melzi d'Eril, *op. cit.*, II, 439-40.

17 Weil, *Eugène et Murat, op. cit.*, IV, 535.

18 *Studi intorno, op. cit.*, 76; Ceria, *op. cit.*, 178; Lemmi, *La restaurazione austriaca, op. cit.*, 149.

19 Bellegarde to Metternich, Verona, April 26, 1814, Lemmi, *La restaurazione austriaca, op. cit.*, Appendix XIV, 414.

to second Murat's conspiracy to make himself king of a united Italy.[20]

Various persons from the ranks of the " pure Italians " thus collaborated with persons desiring a return of Austrian hegemony in northern Italy. Freemasons, Carbonari, Guelfs, and Adelfi appear to have cooperated with both groups to accomplish a violent overthrow of the kingdom, in the hope that in the ensuing confusion they could in some way or other establish an independent and unified Italy.

The evidence concerning the activities of the secret societies in the spring of 1814 is, indeed, very scant, but it is of such a nature as to lead one to suspect that these societies must have played no small part in plotting the Milanese revolution. In regard to the first of these societies—the Freemasons—it can be said that several prominent conspirators of the uprising appear to have been active members of the Masonic organization. In the list of officials of the Grand Orient lodge of Italy discovered by Renato Soriga, there are included the names of Luini, Ciani, Mazzucchelli, and Pino.[21] This list contains officials of only one of several Masonic organizations in the kingdom. Very probably—at least circumstantial evidence points in this direction—others of the conspirators were also members of other Masonic lodges.

The fact that Luini, Mazzucchelli, and Pino were active partisans of Murat, as well as officers of the Grand Orient, would indicate that the Freemasons actively championed King Joachim's candidacy to make himself king of a united Italy. Other evidence supports this contention. Chancellor Melzi asserted that police director Luini belonged to a party which was fused with the Masons and which was disposed to second the

20 Ceria, *op. cit*, 177-78.

21 Printed in Soriga, Renato, *Il primo Grande Oriente d'Italia*. Estratto dal *Bollettino* della Società Pavese di Storia Patria, Anno XVII (Pavia, 1917), 10-18.

Neapolitans in their attempts to form an independent Italy.[22] Baron Hager, the Austrian police president, went so far as to maintain that the Italian Masons seconded Murat's intrigues and that they even addressed him as the " Great King of the Italian Empire." [23] But of much greater significance in pointing toward the possible involvement of the Freemasons in the conspiracy to overthrow the Kingdom of Italy is the revelation which Giovanni Soveri Latuada, the good friend and secret agent of General Pino, made to the Austrian authorities on December 10, 1814, when on trial for his complicity in the Brescian-Milanese military conspiracy of the fall of 1814. There he revealed that " all the projects made around the 20th of April and immediately before and after to assure the independence of Italy were concerted under the Masonic secret." [24] Perhaps this is an exaggeration, but it seems probable that some of the Freemasons cooperated in plotting the insurrection of the 20th of April in the hope of bringing about a united and independent Italy under the scepter of King Joachim Murat.

It appears that the Carbonari, too, might have had a hand in perpetrating the Milanese revolution. The Carbonari were well intrenched in Lombardy by 1813 and early 1814.[25] It is known that General Pino and several of his friends were members of the society and made no mystery about it, and that Milan was the principal center of the society in Lombardy.[26] That General Pino and his friends might have been acting under the instructions of the Carbonari in plotting the

22 Letter to Eugene, January 22, 1814, Melzi d'Eril, *op. cit.*, II, 415-16. Also see Lemmi, *La restaurazione austriaca, op. cit.*, 105-6, for hints of collaboration between the Freemasons and partisans of King Murat.

23 Letter to Bellegarde, Wien, July 5, 1814, *Archivio di Stato*, Milan, *Atti segreti*, 1814, Busta I, No. 65.

24 Quoted in Spadoni, Domenico, " Le società segrete nella rivoluzione milanese dell'aprile 1814," *loc. cit.*, 200-1; and in Spadoni, Domenico, *Milano e la congiura militare nel 1814 per l'indipendenza italiana: La congiura militare e il suo processo* (Modena, 1937), 154.

25 See *ante*, 42.

26 Ottolini, *op. cit.*, 77, 81.

revolution is hinted at in the memoirs of Giacomo Breganze, an active member of the Carbonari world of the time. In his memoirs, Breganze said: " Several Officials and Generals affected by Carbonarism and *in agreement with the society of Milan,* after the viceroy's proclamation of April 17, 1814, when he dismissed the French troops in Mantua, wanted a provision different from the majority of the army officers, who professed themselves as favorable to recognizing the viceroy as Prince." [27] It is clear that General Pino and his friends were among the chief fomenters of the revolution. If they acted " in agreement with the society of Milan," it is evident that the Carbonari as an organization took part in the conspiracy in order to prevent the consummation of the plan of Eugene's partisans to make him sovereign of an independent Kingdom of Italy.

In addition to the Freemasons and the Carbonari, the Guelf and Adelfia societies were apparently also involved in instigating the events of April 20. It is significant that Article 42 of the Guelf constitution of October, 1813, reads as follows: " Prina, nefarious Minister of Finance of the Kingdom of Italy, who dissuaded Napoleon from separating Italy from France, *is abandoned to the G.* [Guelf] *vendetta.*" [28] Just a few days after the drafting of the constitution, some unknown person posted on the door of Minister Prina's house a card on which was written: " Prina! Prina! The day is drawing near! " A week later it was followed by another card reading: " House for rent. Address Doctor Scappa [Flight]." Still later, while Prina was staying in Monza, stones were thrown through the windows of the room in which he lived, and just a few days

27 Giacomo Breganze Memoirs, in the *Museo del Risorgimento* of Milan, as quoted in *ibid.,* 82. The italics are mine.

28 Spadoni, " Gli Statuti della Guelfia," *loc. cit.,* 720. The italics are mine. In his report of November 15, 1816, Pietro Dolce related that he met Frediano, the member of the Austrian secret police who had discovered this Guelf constitution, who showed him the constitution. " In Article 42, made towards the end of 1813," Dolce said, " the massacre of Minister Prina was determined." Luzio, *La Massoneria sotto il Regno italico, op. cit.,* 88-9.

before April 20, 1814, a note was given to him exhorting him to leave Milan immediately.[29] There must have been a connection between these warnings and the article in the Guelf constitution alluding to Prina's death.

In thus deciding upon Minister Prina's death, the Guelfs were apparently acting in close collaboration with another society. Gioacchino Prati, a member of both the Masonic and Adelfia societies, related in his memoirs that as early as 1811 and 1812 the more radical Freemasons had taken out membership in another secret society, and that Minister Prina's death was already determined in 1812 by the secret tribunal of the *Gran Firmamento,* or the directing council of the Adelfia society.[30] The society of the Adelfi, which aimed at becoming a super-directory of all the secret political organizations, was evidently fairly active in directing the Italian secret societies as early as the spring of 1814.[31] The constitution of the Guelfs indicates that there was a close relationship between the Guelfs and the Adelfi.[32] Very probably the connections between the Adelfi and the Carbonari and the radical dissentient Freemasons were also close. It is possible that the *Gran Firmamento* of the Adelfia society might have been responsible for the giving orders which prompted members of the secret societies to cause Minister Prina's assassination and to cooperate in the other disturbances which took place in Milan on April 20.[33]

Partisans of Austria, members of the "pure Italian" factions, and persons from the ranks of the secret societies all

29 Ottolini, *op. cit.*, 85.

30 Pedrotti, *op. cit.*, 33-4.

31 Bersano, *loc. cit.*, 414, 417-18; Spadoni, *Il moto del 20 aprile, op. cit.*, 278.

32 According to Article 25 of the Guelf constitution, the supreme council of the Guelf society was to maintain close relations with various other political societies in other European countries. Listed in the constitution among these other secret societies is the name of the Filadelfi or Adelfi. Spadoni, "Gli Statuti della Guelfia," *loc. cit.*, 718.

33 Domenico Spadoni maintains that the *Gran Firmamento* was responsible for giving the orders which led to Minister Prina's assassination. Spadoni, "Le società segrete nella rivoluzione milanese dell'aprile 1814," *loc. cit.*, 209-11.

cooperated in bringing to Milan a large number of people to do their bidding. On the afternoon and evening of April 19 and on the morning of April 20, a large crowd of persons from the province of Novara and other surrounding districts arrived in Milan.[34] There was already a mob of restless and excited people in the city. If the armed forces within the capital could be sent to some other place or controlled in such a manner as to render them ineffective, it seemed almost certain that the plans of the conspirators could easily be carried out without opposition.

That the task of rendering the armed forces unusable was performed in a thorough and efficient manner was apparent. At the beginning of the first signs of disorder on April 20, the prefect of the police, Giovanni Villa, went directly to the acting minister of war, Bianchi d'Adda,[35] to demand from him enough soldiers to maintain order.[36] At the same time, he ordered Colonel Patroni to proceed quickly to the arsenal to prevent the conspirators from getting the guns and ammunition stored in it, and sent Luigi Vercellon, the head of a battalion of royal light-infantry, and Major Giuseppe De Felici to collect soldiers and horses in the various barracks and to command them to prepare for action. When they set out on their mission to assemble the military, Vercellon and De Felici received a rude shock. Very few soldiers were in Milan. When they made inquiries about this strange lack of troops, they learned that on the previous evening Giacomo Luini, the director of the police and the accomplice of General Pino in his intrigues to make Joachim Murat king of Italy, had sent two detachments of soldiers out of the city. One of these was commissioned to go to Varese, under the pretext of putting down

---

34 *Studi intorno, op. cit.,* 59-60.

35 General Fontanelli, the minister of war, was in Mantua awaiting instructions to go to Paris to demand from the Allied Powers an independent Kingdom of Italy with Eugene as possible king. In his absence, Bianchi d'Adda directed the affairs of the ministry.

36 Prefect of police to Eugene, Milano, April 21, 1814, Beauharnais Archives, Princeton University, Fasc. 62, No. 10; Zanoli, *op. cit.,* II, 308.

a seditious movement in that place, and the other, to Sesto Calende to defend the Ticino.[37]

When the acting minister of war, Bianchi d'Adda, was asked for troops, he replied: " My instructions do not permit me to put my men at your disposition; for such an end address yourselves to a superior official, as, for example, General Pino." [38] That General Pino would not permit the loyal portion of the Milanese police to use troops to interfere with his plans was clear. Prefect Villa actually attempted to do his duty with the few troops which his subordinates could muster. He ordered Vercellon, with only forty light-infantry troops, and Bosisio, with a still smaller detachment of twenty-eight mounted dragoons, to repair to the police prefecture on Santa Margherita street to get ready for action. This attempt was wholly unsuccessful. These troops had hardly arrived at their destination when Luigi Cima, Pino's assistant, appeared and ordered the troops to return immediately to their quarters.[39] The conspirators were then able to proceed as they wished. It was impossible to prevent them from overthrowing the government of the kingdom.

All sorts of people cooperated in bringing the Kingdom of Italy to an abrupt and violent end. Leaders of the Austrian party intrigued on equal terms with the supporters of the King of Naples and those members of the " pure Italian " faction who desired an independent kingdom under the kingship of either Francis of Austria-Este or the Duke of Clarence. The Freemasons, the Carbonari, the Guelfs, and the Adelfi drew from all kinds of discontented individuals support for their attempts to establish a " liberal, independent, and constitutional regime." The rogue and the prostitute cooperated with eminent

37 Zanoli, *op. cit.*, II, 308-9; *Studi intorno, op. cit.*, 61.

38 *Studi intorno, op. cit* , 61.

39 Prefect of police to Eugene, Milano, April 21, 1814, Beauharnais Archives, Princeton University, Fasc. 62, No. 10; Prefect of police to Eugene, Milano, April 20, 1814, *ibid.*, No. 8; Zanoli, *op. cit.*, II, 309; Lemmi, *La restaurazione austriaca, op. cit.*, 162-63.

ladies and gentlemen of the Milanese aristocracy. Lowly pro-
letarians rubbed shoulders with haughty Lombard nobles. In
short, Milanese opposition politics in April, 1814, drew together into one camp an extremely strange assemblage of persons. All worked together in the hope of accomplishing their
own individual aims. Their united efforts produced the Milanese
revolution of April 20, 1814.

CHAPTER VII

THE MILANESE REVOLUTION OF APRIL 20, 1814 [1]

THE regular meeting of the senate of the Kingdom of Italy was scheduled for 1.00 P. M. on Wednesday, April 20, 1814. The day was dreary and gloomy, as if to forecast the sad events which were to follow before nightfall. Most of the time it was raining hard; the rest of the time it was drizzling. Large crowds of people were wandering hither and thither, with many carrying umbrellas to protect themselves against the rain.

A few perspicacious individuals had a premonition of what might occur. Chancellor Melzi, in particular, was worried. On the day before the fateful meeting of the senate, he wrote the viceroy: " At Milan spirits are rather excited." It would be " convenient " if " some forces " could be sent to Milan.[2] Councillor of State, Ludovico Giovio, was also full of misgivings, and thought that it was very strange that the senate " would venture to meet while the squares, the clubs, the cafés, and all the public places were loud with imprecations against " it.[3] Even the director of the police, Giacomo Luini, perhaps fearing that the conspiracy which he had helped to plot might get out of hand, went on the morning of April 20 to Melzi and Veneri and advised them to suspend the sitting.[4]

Towards noon, when the senators began to arrive at the senatorial palace, they found their meeting place surrounded by a small group of men, all of whom were using silk umbrellas as

1 Lemmi, *La restaurazione austriaca, op. cit.,* Helfert, *La caduta, op. cit ,* and Ceria, *op. cit.,* all give good accounts of the Milanese revolution The writer found all three of these works, and particularly Lemmi, very useful.

2 Letter of April 19, 1814, Cantù, *Il principe Eugenio, op. cit.,* IX, 128

3 *Memoria di Giovio,* in Pellini, *op. cit.,* 85. Also cited in Lemmi, *La restaurazione austriaca, op. cit.,* 154.

4 Ceria, *op. cit.,* 191 ; Director of the police to Eugene, Milano, April 20, 1814, Beauharnais Archives, Princeton University, Fasc. 62, No. 4.

protection from the rain.[5] Near the principal entrance to the palace stood a tall man,[6] who, when each of the senators arrived, made a certain sign indicating whether or not he was a partisan of the government. If he was, the crowd hissed at him as he passed through the entrance; if he was not, he was given a spirited ovation.[7]

As soon as the sitting of the senate began, President Veneri read to the senators the petition requesting the immediate convocation of the electoral colleges, which had been circulated for signature on April 19 and 20, and which had been presented to him. Hardly had he finished when Benigno Bossi, one of the ringleaders of the conspiracy to overthrow the viceroy's government, entered the chamber to inform the senators that the officers of the civic guard wished to have the opportunity to defend them in place of the regular troops. President Veneri felt compelled to accede to the request, whereupon the civic guard immediately drove away the few loyal soldiers who were guarding the palace. The way was now open for the conspirators to accomplish whatever they wished.[8]

The regular troops had hardly been withdrawn when a body of men of low and vicious appearance joined the crowd of

5 Senator Verri estimated that this group consisted of about twenty persons. Verri, *op. cit.*, 123.

6 Fabi, *op. cit.*, 34 ftn., says that this man was one of Count Castiglioni's servants. Helfert, *La caduta, op. cit.*, 53, relates that Carlo Verri wrote in his memoirs that " he had recognized the Count F. C. (Federico Confalonieri) as one of those who gave the signals." The writer has been unable to find such a statement in Verri's account, either as reprinted in Casini or as quoted in Cusani, *op. cit.*, VII, 117. Furthermore, Count Confalonieri not only denied that he gave signals, but emphatically asserted that he was not even among the persons before the senatorial palace before the meeting of the senate began. In his letter to a friend, written on March 15, 1815, he said that he remained in the municipal palace until 1.30 P. M., when he left it to go to the senate. He maintained that when he arrived there, " the largest part of the senators had already entered." Then he continued: " No person will be able to assert that he saw me take part in the clamors, whether of applause or of disapproval, in which many of them participated." Casati, *op. cit.*, I, 267.

7 Armaroli, *op. cit.*, 15-16.

8 Armaroli, *op. cit.*, 17-18; Helfert, *La caduta, op. cit.*, 53-4.

dandies with their silk umbrellas and the great number of curiosity seekers, always present at disturbances, in the street in front of the palace. Under the pretext of sheltering themselves from the rain, they obtained the permission of the civic guard to crowd into the very entrance of the palace.[9] With their arrival, the mob became much more intrepid and clamorous. There was so much confusion that it was difficult for the senate to transact business.

Noticing the mob at the very doors of the palace, Senator Verri offered to go down to quiet them. When he arrived at the front entrance, he was very much surprised to learn that the whole character of the crowd had changed. Instead of finding " citizens all of the same social condition and all with silk umbrellas," as he had upon his arrival at the senate, he now saw " only individuals of the lowest classes," who " seemed to be made for sacking and rapine." [10]

Definitely worried at the rough appearance of the crowd, Verri turned toward them, exhorted them to remain tranquil, and assured them that the senate would act only in conformity with public interest. Then, seeing that everyone was absolutely calm, he returned to the senate. He had just arrived there when several ushers hurried up to announce that the throng was increasing to formidable and menacing proportions. Again Verri, this time accompanied by Senators Massari and Felici, went down to expostulate with the mob. All three senators mixed with the people, exhorting them to remain quiet and assuring them of the good intentions of the senate. Instead of remaining immobile and quiet as they had before, the crowd began to advance slowly against the three. Fearing for their lives and realizing that their attempt had resulted in a complete fiasco, they hurried back to the senate chamber.[11]

As Verri, Massari, and Felici returned to the second floor, they noticed that several ushers, pallid with fright, were loudly

9 *Studi intorno, op. cit.,* 66.
10 Verri, *op. cit.,* 126.
11 *Ibid.,* 126-29.

pounding on the door of the senate chamber and shouting that the crowd had increased to perilous proportions. With the consent of the other senators, Verri descended the stairs for a third time to exhort the people to behave. By now the uproar was so terrific that it was useless for him to try to talk. At that juncture, Count Confalonieri approached him, commanded the people to be silent, and demanded that the rebels reveal their intentions. A loud voice asked what the senate had decreed on the 17th. Verri replied: " Two good things has the Senate decreed. It has nominated a Deputation to the High Allied Powers, first, to demand not only an armistice, but the full cessation of hostilities, . . . and, secondly, to demand . . . that the independence of the State, with an independent king acceptable to the nation, be established." [12]

The crowd applauded, but only for a moment. After a few minutes of hesitation, some of the more spirited revolutionaries insisted that the senate revoke the decree which had ordered the deputation to go to the Allied Powers. With this demand, a deafening roar again resounded through the lower portico of the palace. By this time, every possibility of restraining the agitated horde had vanished. Verri again started back to the senate chamber. On the way he looked around and saw the resolute and tumultuous mob slowly advancing towards him. Thoroughly frightened, he turned around and rushed into the chamber, shouting: " Senators, you have only a few minutes of safety. Immediately decree the recall of the Deputation, or we are lost! " [13]

These words fell like a bombshell upon the senate. Immediately everything in the chamber was in utmost confusion. In spite of Verri's entreaties, President Veneri remained motionless and irresolute, as if he were petrified. Several senators who had not entirely lost their wits hurried up to the president's table. One of them grabbed a pen and started writing: " The

---

12 *Ibid.*, 130-32. Also see Lemmi, *La restaurazione austriaca, op. cit.*, 158-59; Helfert, *La caduta, op. cit.*, 54-6; and Cusani, *op. cit.*, VII, 119-20.

13 Verri, 133-34.

deputation is recalled, the Electoral Colleges are convoked, and the sitting of the Senate is adjourned." [14] Verri commanded the president to sign the note, and he acceded to this request almost mechanically. Several other senators then busied themselves with copying the decree on other sheets of paper so that it could be scattered among the mob.[15] In such a manner more than thirty copies were made by the senators and signed by the president.[16]

Before the senators completed their task, the mob surged into the room. There was great confusion and a general uproar. Many of the senators, in sheer desperation, crouched against the wall to make a final stand. Fortunately for them, the minds of the people were turned to objects of plunder, and all the senators managed to escape without injury.

As soon as the crowd entered the room, they began to plunder and destroy everything that was within reach. Imperial emblems, chairs, tables, mirrors, stoves, shades, and doors were smashed to pieces and thrown out of the window. Tapestries, window panes, and books suffered the same fate. Count Confalonieri, accused of being one of the most active of the plunderers, according to report, even poked his umbrella through a picture of Napoleon, which had been painted by the famous artist, Appiani, and threw it out of the window.[17]

14 Copies of this note, bearing the signature of President Veneri and the date of 2.30 P. M., April 20, 1814, can be found in the *Wiener Zeitung, 1814* (May 6, 1814), 506; Fabi, *op. cit.*, Appendix IX, 115; and Pellini, *op. cit.*, 18.

15 Verri, *op. cit.*, 134-35.

16 Armaroli, *op. cit.*, 20.

17 Both Armaroli, *op. cit*, 20; and *Studi intorno, op. cit.*, 69, relate that Confalonieri did this. Lemmi, *La restaurazione austriaca, op. cit.*, 160; and Helfert, *La caduta, op. cit.*, 58, repeat this accusation as if they thought it were true, and Ceria, *op. cit.*, 203, does not deny it. In his letter to a friend, written in Milan on March 15, 1815, Confalonieri, however, emphatically denied the accusation. Casati, *op. cit.*, I, 253-73. Giovanni de Castro, in his " I ricordi autobiografici inediti del Marchese Benigno Bossi," *Archivio Storico Lombardo*, Anno XVII (1890), 907, says in regard to this accusation: " It is most definitely proved that he [Confalonieri] not only did not commit it, but that he was not capable of committing it."

Soon the interior of the senate palace was almost demolished.[18] Then there was a moment of indecision about what was to be done next. Verri related that he heard at that time somebody suggest that the crowd proceed to Porto Nuova, where Chancellor Melzi lived, but " Count F. Confalonieri, who was in the crowd, cried out that it would be better for them to go towards San Fedele, where the house of Minister Prina was." [19] It has never been definitely proved whether it was Confalonieri or some other person who uttered these fateful words, but that is inconsequential. The important thing is that this suggestion served to incite the infuriated mob to take revenge for all the odious taxation of the Napoleonic regime upon the unfortunate minister of finance.[20] In throngs

18 When Chancellor Melzi learned of what had transpired in the senate, he wrote Prince Eugene. "Monseigneur, I no longer know the people of Milan. They are in a state of effervescence which is inexplicable." Beauharnais Archives, Princeton University, Fasc. 62, No. 6.

19 Verri, *op. cit.*, 140-41. This statement of Senator Verri's has given occasion for a battle royal between the friends and enemies of Count Confalonieri All the various statements which have been written on whether or not it was Confalonieri who suggested that the mob go to San Fedele are well summarized in D'Ancona, *op cit*, 11-29; and Ceria, *op. cit*, 204-10. Whether Confalonieri expressed these words or not, it should be noted that they probably saved Chancellor Melzi's life. If the angry mob had gone to his house, there is no telling what might have happened to him.

20 The minister of finance, Giuseppe Prina, was born in Novara on July 19, 1766. He was educated at the Jesuit college at Monza and at the University of Pavia, and then went to Turin, where he soon became a recognized authority in political economy. Having fled from Turin to Novara when Napoleon's army arrived in Sardinia in 1796, Prina became a citizen of the Cisalpine Republic when this district was assigned to it. Prina's unusual ability in public economy aroused Napoleon's interest in him, and after the Italian Republic was created, Napoleon appointed him as its minister of finance. When the republic became the Kingdom of Italy, Prina still continued in his position. Prina was always very loyal to Napoleon, and always managed to devise the taxes necessary to meet the increasing demands which Napoleon made from the Kingdom of Italy. His acts made him odious in the eyes of the people, who began to hold him personally responsible for all the vexatious taxes which were levied. By April, 1814, he had become the most hated official in the Kingdom of Italy. Fabi, *op. cit.*, 41-4; Castro, *Principio di secolo, op. cit.*, 100-6.

of hundreds the crowd immediately hastened to the square in front of Prina's residence.

In a very short time, the angry and agitated horde [21] forced its way into the building. The palace was soon infested by a turbulent, savage, and destructive mob, bent upon dashing into bits anything which they might stumble upon. The looting was deplorable. Decorations, chairs, desks, money, and manuscripts were hurled out of the window. Even fireplaces and window frames were torn from the walls and broken up, window panes were shattered, and beds were completely destroyed.[22]

While most of the rioters were pillaging and ransacking the place for objects of plunder, others went through every nook and cranny of the palace to search for the unfortunate minister. One of these managed to find Prina's hiding place. As soon as he was found, the crowd forgot their plundering, rushed up to the unlucky man, showered a volley of blows upon him, and threw him out of an open window to the people waiting in the street below.

The mob in the square grabbed the minister's body. Rejecting Prina's pleas for mercy, some of his persecutors turned ferociously upon the miserable wretch and beat him almost to death, while others picked him up and dragged him through the streets. When the procession arrived in front of a church

21 One observer estimated the crowd at 7,000 persons. Gallone to Bianchini, Milano, April 20, 1814, Pellini, S, "La sommossa di Milano del 20 aprile 1814 e la morte del Prina secondo un testimonio oculare," *Rivista mensile di lettere, di storia e d'arte*, Anno I (1900), 7. Domenico Giovanelli wrote an unknown friend from Milan, on May 7, 1814, that there were 20,000 people in front of Prina's house. Pellini, *Pino, op. cit.*, 47.

22 *Mantovani Diario, op. cit.*, April 21, 1814 (This particular entry in the diary is printed in Pellini, *Pino, op. cit.*, 5-8.); Prefect of police to Eugene, Milano, April 21, 1814, Beauharnais Archives, Princeton University, Fasc. 62, No. 10; Cusani, *op. cit.*, VII, 133. Borda wrote Battista on April 20, 1814, that even the minister's carriages, and the hay and horses in his stable were not spared. Gallavresi, Giuseppe, *Il carteggio intimo di Andrea Borda.* Estratto dall'*Archivio Storico Lombardo*, Anno XLVII (Milano, 1921), 35. Also see Lemmi, *La restaurazione austriaca, op. cit.*, 171-72; and Helfert, *La caduta, op cit.*, 64.

near-by, Prina, realizing that the end was near, implored his oppressors to send for a priest to give him confession. The mob refused, shouting: " No, let him go to Hell with all his sins! " Stunned by this rebuff, Prina fell against the corner of the church, and a handful of resourceful and intrepid men profited by this moment to carry him quickly into a neighboring wine shop.[23]

It was not until this moment that a small military force came to the finance minister's rescue.[24] General Peyri, the leader of the group, however, was immediately attacked by a large number of infuriated ruffians, and would probably have been beaten to death if General Pino had not suddenly arrived with fifty men and taken him under his personal protection.[25]

23 I am relying chiefly upon the following sources for my description of Minister Prina's assassination: Lemmi, *La restaurazione austriaca, op. cit*, 172-78; Helfert, *La caduta, op. cit.*, 64-70; *Studi intorno, op. cit.*, 73; and Cusani, *op cit*, VII, 133-41.

24 General Pino later asserted that he had asked General Peyri to make this move. *Osservazioni del Generale Pino, op cit.* In the printed copy in the Ambrosiana Library of Milan the above statement is on page 8; in the copy reprinted in Pellini, *Pino, op cit.*, it is on page 102. General Pino's assertion, however, is not supported by other evidence. When, earlier in the day, Confalonieri and Mayor Durini had tried to persuade General Pino, who had just been put in command of all the armed forces in the city, to go with the dozen armed civic guards who were available to save Prina, Pino refused, asserting that such a move would be ineffective and would result only in needless spilling of blood Confalonieri to a friend, Milano, March 15, 1815, Casati, *op cit*, I, 270-71. Likewise, when the intendant of finance, Frigerio, who had a body of two hundred customs guards at his disposal near the scene of the disturbances, went to General Pino to ask for permission to use them, General Pino refused to reply to his request. Bonfadini, *Mezzo secolo di patriotismo, op cit*, 116. General Pino's actions until late in the afternoon indicate that he did everything he possibly could to prevent anyone from putting down the rebellion.

25 Later General Pino wrote in regard to this action· " General Pino did not hesitate, although wholly without forces, to go to Peyri's aid, ordering the battalion chieftain Foscolo, whom the general saw in the distance, and who was the nearest, ... to go to the aid of General Peyri, whom after many hours he succeeded in taking from the hands of the madmen, who thought that Peyri was the disguised Minister and who were in the neighborhood to massacre him " *Osservazioni del Generale Pino, op. cit*, 8 Also see Pellini,

When General Pino had succeeded in rescuing Peyri, the mob concentrated upon breaking into the wine shop and tearing Minister Prina from his friends. Shouts of fire and death were echoing through the streets when the minister, to save his protectors, voluntarily left his hiding place, opened the door, and with the words, "Vent your wrath solely upon me and at least make me your only victim," surrendered to his persecutors.[26]

Count Prina was then dragged through the streets of Milan to the stamp office, while his assassins beat, pushed, and poked him with their umbrellas.[27] By the time the crowd reached their destination, the unlucky man was dead. His corpse was propped up against one of the walls of the building, and preparations were being made to burn his body and the stamp office when several divisions of the national guard arrived on the scene.[28]

By this time, Mayor Durini had ordered published and posted in the streets of Milan two proclamations inviting the citizens to go home and remain peaceful, informing them that General Pino had been appointed to command all the armed forces in the city, and promising that the electoral colleges would be convoked to meet in Milan by April 22 at the latest.[29]

Pino, op. cit., 102-3. Luigi Fassò has pointed out that the pronoun "he" in the above quotation definitely refers to Foscolo and not to Pino, thus showing that it was Foscolo and not Pino who played the principal rôle in this episode. Fassò, Luigi, *Ugo Foscolo; prose politiche e letterarie dal 1811 al 1816* (Vol. VIII of the *Edizione nazionale delle opere di Ugo Foscolo*) (Firenze, 1933).

26 Lemmi, *La restaurazione austriaca, op cit*, 176-77; *Studi intorno, op. cit.*, 73; Armaroli, *op. cit.*, 23.

27 Gallone wrote Bianchini: "Mothers even counselled their own sons to take off their hats and kick him, although he was a corpse by now. His figure was no longer that of a man but of a brute." Letter of April 20, 1814, Pellini, "La sommossa di Milano," *loc. cit*, 7. Also see "La Prineide di Tommasso Grossi," printed in Fabi, *op. cit.*, 211-21, for a realistic description of the excesses committed against Prina.

28 Lemmi, *La restaurazione austriaca, op cit*, 177-78; Helfert, *La caduta, op cit*, 69-71.

29 These proclamations are published in Pellini, *Pino, op. cit*, 18-20. Original copies can be found in the *Kriegs-Archiv*, Vienna, *Feld Akten (Italien)*, 1814, Fasc. 13, Nos. 77 and 88.

General Pino, who accompanied the troops, went to one of the balconies of the Scala theater and read the proclamations to the crowd below. This gesture was effective. The mob rapidly dispersed, some in the crowd shouting, " Long live King Pino! " [30]

Prina's corpse was carried to the Broletto palace. Later that night, the body was taken to the cemetery beyond the Comasina gate and buried. To prevent malefactors from digging up the body and mutilating it further, no marker was left upon the grave.[31]

During the night of April 20/21, outwardly at least, there seemed to be perfect calm in the capital of the Kingdom of Italy.[32] Early the next morning, however, the streets of the city were teeming with rioters, some of whom had returned to complete the devastation of Prina's palace; others, to find new objects of plunder or to kill other officials. The mob which had been in the city on the previous day was increased by a large number of peasants from the surrounding districts, who had streamed into the city to get their share of free entertainment and booty.[33] There were ominous signs that the 21st might be another day of bloody rioting and destruction.

In an attempt to prevent further trouble, the vicar of the cathedral of Milan, Mayor Durini, and the Milanese communal council issued proclamations to notify the people that a " *Three Days' Prayer to the Holy Guardian Angel* " would be held in the Church of S. Maria Segreta in order to call upon God to

30 Lemmi, *La restaurazione austriaca, op. cit.,* 178.

31 *Ibid.,* 178-79; Helfert, *La caduta, op. cit.,* 71-2; Cusani, *op. cit.,* VII, 142-45.

32 " It is eleven o'clock in the evening, and it appears that through the activity of the civic guard and particularly of its officers, the crowd has been entirely dispersed." Report to Eugene, 11 00 P. M., April 20, 1814, Beauharnais Archives, Princeton University, Fasc. 62, No. 16.

33 Report to Eugene, Milano, April 21, 1814, *ibid.,* No. 14; *Oesterreichischer Beobachter,* 1814, No. 130 (May 10, 1814), 708. Also see the descriptions given by Lemmi, *La restaurazione austriaca, op cit.,* 201-2; and by Helfert, *La caduta, op. cit.,* 76-8.

"direct, enlighten, and protect" the Milanese and that the country was being placed under the protection of the Allied Powers. All persons able to do so were requested " immediately to go to the quarters which would be assigned to them " and other citizens were asked to remain peacefully in their homes.[34] The provisional regency, which had been created on the morning of the 21st to take charge of the affairs of the kingdom,[35] issued proclamations to reassure the people that it was occupying itself only with the public good, and to appeal to them to help the civic guard in restoring order. Then, assuming a more severe tone, the regency notified the populace that henceforth the armed forces in the city would arrest all vagabonds and suspected persons whom they met.[36] General Pino also proclaimed: " All Citizens are required to cooperate with the Civic Guard to compel the mobs to disband. The armed forces will act vigorously to repress the culprits, to dissolve the mob, to protect tranquillity, and to support the peaceful inhabitants of the Capital." [37]

After the issuance of these proclamations, great numbers of people immediately hurried to the headquarters of the civic guard to enlist and to aid in protecting the city.[38] Nobles, merchants, shopkeepers, innkeepers, and traders, many of whom had assisted in plotting the revolution, came rushing up to help quell the rioters, fearful that the mob might turn against them and their property. Greatly reinforced as they were, the

34 Copies of these proclamations are in Pellini, *Pino, op. cit.*, 22-3, and 27-32.

35 See *post*, 128.

36 See Pellini, *Pino, op. cit.*, 24-7.

37 Fabi, *op. cit.*, 120; Cusani, *op. cit*, VII, 155.

38 One observer said that so many of them came that " in an instant three or four thousand civic guards were armed." Anonymous letter given by lawyer Tarella to Pellini, Pellini, Silvio, " Il 20 aprile 1814," *Napoleone. Rivista storica*, Anno I (1914), 50. Another contemporary report said that " in a short time over six thousand citizens had come together." *Oesterreichischer Beobachter*, 1814, No. 130 (May 10, 1814), 708.

civic guards now moved out boldly against the malefactors, who were armed with such weapons as clubs and stilettos.[39]

The chief center of disturbance was the Piazza del Duomo, opposite the Milanese cathedral, where the mob threatened to attack and sack the royal palace. The civic guards marched up to arrest some of the leaders and to scatter the rest of the mob. As a few detachments arrived, some of the populace turned to attack them. The guards got their bayonets ready, and prepared to charge. This gesture was enough to disperse the attackers. The crisis was now over. The military had gained complete control of the city.[40] Henceforth, it was easy for small detachments of troops to circulate about the city to disperse the few agitators who were still bent on trouble. Many of them were arrested;[41] others were merely told to go home; still others disappeared as if by magic. Order was quickly restored. The Milanese revolution had ended.

At the same time that the rebellion was going on in Milan, there were lesser disturbances in other parts of Lombardy. At Bergamo many countrymen invaded the city and attacked the municipal palace.[42] At Brescia an insurrection broke out as the last column of French troops passed through the city. A crowd of people attacked the dwelling of the prefect, Som-

39 Anonymous letter given by lawyer Tarella to Pellini, Pellini, "Il 20 aprile 1814," *loc cit.*, 50-1.

40 Lemmi, *La restaurazione austriaca, op. cit.*, 203-6, Helfert, *La caduta, op cit.*, 79-81; Cusani, *op. cit*, VII, 157-58.

41 Giovanelli wrote his friend that "in two days 1200 culpable and suspected persons found themselves in different prisons in the castle." Letter of May 7, 1814, Pellini, *Pino, op cit.*, 50. The anonymous observer whose letter was given to Pellini by Tarella said that on the night of April 21/22 "more than 200 or 300 arrests" were made Pellini, "Il 20 aprile 1814," *loc cit*, 51. Mantovani noted in his diary, on April 22, that during the night of April 20/21 more than 150 persons were arrested, and that more than 80 other persons were arrested on the morning of April 21. *Mantovani Diario*, Ambrosiana Library, *op cit*, V, 253

42 Mayor of Bergamo to Mayor of Milan, April 22, 1814, Gallavresi, Giuseppe, "Testimonianze tratte dalle carte Giovio per la storia dei fatti del 1814," *Bollettino ufficiale* del primo congresso storico del Risorgimento Italiano (1906), 135-36.

menzari, who managed, however, to escape.[43] At Verona a mob threatened to attack the prefect, Smancini, but they were kept in check by the Austrian garrison which was within the city.[44] At Monza an assembly of people moved to force an entry into the royal palace, but it was deterred when the intrepid and shrewd custodian of the palace passed out wine to the crowd and dismissed it.[45] Besides these sporadic flare-ups, it was also reported that disturbances took place in various parts of the department of Agogna,[46] and in Varese,[47] Como, and Novara.[48]

While the revolution in Milan and these disorders in other places were occurring, the viceroy was with his army in Mantua. There, on April 20, he received official notice of Napoleon's abdication at Fontainebleau. At once he sent General Pino a decree providing for the establishment of a provisional government, with Melzi as president, to act in the name of the viceroy, and ordering the convocation of the electoral colleges for an extraordinary sitting on May 10.[49]

43 *Oesterreichischer Beobachter*, 1814, No. 129 (May 9, 1814), 701; *Wiener Zeitung*, May 9, 1814, 518.

44 See the poem entitled· *L'anima del Prina che si presenta al principe Reuss e gli fa un ritratto di tutti gl'impiegati che furono in Verona sotto il prefetto Smancini*, by Stenterello. Printed in Castro, *Principio di secolo, op. cit.*, 154-55. Also see Lemmi, *La restaurazione austriaca, op. cit*, 179-80 Lemmi refers to the three disturbances which we have described above, but not to any of the others

45 April 24, 1814, *Mantovani Diario*, Ambrosiana Library, *op. cit.*, V, 256.

46 Borda to Battista, April 20, 1814, Gallavresi, *Carteggio di Borda, op. cit.*, 39; Borda to Gallotta, Milano, April 20, 1814, Fiorani, *loc. cit.*, 431.

47 Report to Eugene, Milano, April, 1814, Beauharnais Archives, Princeton University, Fasc. 62, No 36.

48 April 21, 1814, *Mantovani Diario*, Ambrosiana Library, *op. cit.*, V, 253, Pellini, *Pino, op. cit.*, 8.

49 Cusani, *op. cit.*, VII, 164-65; Fabi, *op. cit.*, Appendix XXXV, 146-48. This document was also printed as Inclusion No. 1 in the *Osservazioni del Generale Pino*, Ambrosiana Library, *op. cit.* As we have noted before, the *Osservazioni* has been printed verbatim by Pellini in his *Pino, op. cit.*, 96-112. Pellini, however, erroneously dates the above letter to General Pino as April 15, 1814. In the original copy in the Ambrosiana Library the letter is plainly dated April 20, 1814

On the 21st, Colonel Cavazza arrived in Mantua with the news of the uprising in Milan.[50] Astonished, bitter, and disappointed at the new turn of events, the viceroy wrote Melzi: " Truly I did not expect from the Milanese such reward for my long services." [51] Then he sent a dispatch to General Pino, asking him to take supreme command at Milan, and beseeching him to plead with the people to make no further depredations and " to await with calm the determinations of the High Allied Powers." [52]

On April 26, Eugene, realizing that the Milanese revolution had completely ruined his plans to make himself sovereign of an independent Kingdom of Italy, issued a proclamation in which he said farewell to the people of the Kingdom of Italy.[53] " I have been in your midst for nine years," he declared, " and my conscience assures me that during those nine years I have fulfilled all my obligations. It is a pleasure for me to say to you that you also have fulfilled all of yours. Wherever I shall be, your glory and your felicity will always be the first desire and the first wish of my heart." [54]

Later, probably on April 26 or early on the morning of April 27,[55] Prince Eugene left Mantua for Verona, arriving

50 Lemmi, *La restaurazione austriaca, op. cit.*, 213; Cusani, *op. cit.*, VII, 166.

51 Letter of April 21, 1814, Cantù, *Il principe Eugenio, op cit.*, VIII, 306-7 Also quoted in Lemmi, *La restaurazione austriaca, op. cit.*, 213-14.

52 Letter of April 21, 1814, *Osservazioni del Generale Pino*, Ambrosiana Library, *op cit*, Inclusion No. 3. Also see Pellini, *Pino, op. cit.*, 111-12; and Lemmi, *La restaurazione austriaca, op. cit.*, 213.

53 *Wiener Zeitung*, May 9, 1814, 518.

54 Prince Eugene, Proclamation to the people of the Kingdom of Italy, no date or place given, Beauharnais Archives, Princeton University, Fasc. 23, No. 125. According to what the *Wiener Zeitung*, May 9, 1814, 518, relates, there is no doubt that Eugene gave this proclamation at Mantua on April 26. This proclamation was also published in the *Giornale di Venezia*, No. 37 (April 29, 1814), 4, under the date of Mantua, April 26, 1814.

55 The *Wiener Zeitung*, May 9, 1814, 518, relates that he left Mantua at 2.00 A. M. on the morning of April 27. Zanoli, *op. cit.*, II, 311, says that he left at 3 00 A. M. on the same morning. Bellegarde, however, wrote Emperor Francis that Eugene left Mantua on April 26 and arrived in Verona in the

there in the evening of the 27th. As soon as he arrived, he hastened to send a letter to General Fontanelli, one of the two army deputies to the Allied Powers in Paris, informing him about what had happened in Milan, and ordering him and General Bertoletti to discontinue their mission to the Allies.[56] On the same evening, Count Bellegarde paid Prince Eugene a visit at Verona,[57] which the latter returned the next day.[58] On the 30th, Eugene left Verona with his wife and family, and proceeded across the Alps to the home of his father-in-law in Munich.[59]

When Eugene Beauharnais left Mantua, the Kingdom of Italy beyond the shadow of a doubt was at an end. It had been ingloriously overthrown in a short and bloody revolution, but the fact that it came to an end through an insurrection is easily explained. Many Italians had suffered for months from the vicissitudes of the Napoleonic regime, and they held the viceroy and his chief officials personally responsible for their grievances. Moreover, the Allied Powers, by flooding the peninsula with their liberal war proclamations, had led many an Italian to believe that when the Napoleonic regime was overthrown, the inhabitants of the kingdom might enjoy all the blessings of liberty and independence. Many a person must have felt that the time had come for him to express his own opinions about the future fate of his country. When, at this juncture, the Beauharnais faction attempted, in a manner which seemed underhanded to many persons, to create a Kingdom of Italy with the viceroy on the throne, many Milanese were, quite

evening of the same day. Letter of April 28, 1814, written at Verona, *Kriegs-Archiv*, Vienna, *Feld Akten (Italien)*, 1814, Fasc. 4, ad No 229½.

56 Written at Verona, April 27, 1814, Beauharnais Archives, Princeton University, Fasc. 23, No. 58. Also printed in Cusani, *op. cit.*, VII, 175-76.

57 Huegel Diary, *op. cit.*, April 27, 1814, 93.

58 *Ibid*, April 28, 1814, 93.

59 *Ibid.*, April 30, 1814, 93; Report from Verona, April 30, 1814, *Giornale di Venezia*, 1814, No. 40 (May 3, 1814), 3. Prince Eugene spent the remainder of his life in Bavaria. His father-in-law, King Maximilian of Bavaria, made him Duke of Leuchtenberg and Prince of Eichstadt. He died in Munich in 1824.

naturally, exceedingly angered. Hating and despising by then all vestiges of the Napoleonic regime and influenced as they were by the liberal propagandists in their midst, they felt that they could not stand by quietly and permit such an intrigue to succeed. They allowed themselves to be persuaded to begin an uprising against the senate, without foreseeing the bloody excesses which would proceed from it. The result was a disorderly revolution, which not only produced lamentable excesses but which, in addition, brought about the speedy entry of Austrian officials into Milan on the necessity of keeping order.

CHAPTER VIII

THE PROVISIONAL GOVERNMENT

THE evening of April 20, 1814, was a very grave one in the city of Milan. The government of the Kingdom of Italy had been wiped out in a single afternoon; the city itself was in the hands of an unruly mob, and no power remained to check the excesses of the revolutionists. The senate of the kingdom, after decreeing the abdication of the viceroy, had been forced to declare its sitting adjourned; the electoral colleges had not yet been convoked; and military dictatorship was impossible because of the lack of soldiers. Only one constitutional body, the municipal council of Milan, remained intact, but it possessed no legitimate power to act for the nation as a whole, since it represented only the commune of Milan.

The emergency, however, was too great to allow time for a discussion of questions of legality. To make some sort of provision for a government, Count Durini, the mayor of Milan, on the evening of April 20, called a meeting of the communal council for ten o'clock the next morning.[1] At this meeting, held in the Broletto palace, the council decided to have proclamations published to advise the people that the sales, tobacco, and salt

1 Lemmi, *La restaurazione austriaca, op. cit*, 199, and Helfert, *La caduta, op. cit.*, 74, relate that the communal council was convoked and assembled on the night of April 20/21. This is an error, which Marchesi, G. B., "Il podestà di Milano conte Antonio Durini," *Archivio Storico Lombardo*, XIX (1903), 161, has taken pains to point out. The communal council was convoked on the evening of April 20 to meet in the morning of the 21st. The relation of the provisional regency on the events of April 17-21 indicates that the council first met in the morning of April 21. Lemmi, *La restaurazione austriaca, op. cit.*, Appendix III, 399-400. The protocol of the communal council on April 21, 1814, also states that the council met at ten o'clock on the morning of April 21. *Museo del Risorgimento*, Milan, *Carte Beccaria*, Busta I, Carte 8, Fasc. I, Pezza 6, B. In his account, Carlo Verri said that on the evening of April 20, he received a letter inviting him to come to the meeting of the council in the city palace the next morning. Verri, *op. cit.*, 147. Furthermore, all the official notices of the decrees passed by the council which the writer has seen were dated no earlier than April 21.

taxes were to be lowered to one-half their former amount,[2] to order that the white and red cockade of Milan was to replace the tricolored revolutionary emblem,[3] and to assure the populace that the electoral colleges would be immediately convoked.[4] In addition, a provisional regency, with Carlo Verri as president, Giuseppe Pallavicini as secretary, and Giorgio Giulini, Alberto Litta, Giberto Borromeo, Giacomo Mellerio, Domenico Pino, and Giovanni Bazetta as their associates, was appointed to regulate all the affairs of the kingdom until more permanent governmental organs could be instituted.[5] Then, after having provided for a provisional government, the communal council wisely withdrew from its extra-legal activities and attempted nothing further in the way of passing decrees.[6]

Soon after its creation, the provisional regency began its sessions in the royal palace. At once it confirmed the reduction of taxes decreed by the communal council,[7] reduced the tax on sugar by two-thirds,[8] abolished the hated registration tax,[9] abolished the tax on arts and business,[10] and reduced the

2 Notification, Barbò, Milano, April 21, 1814, *Kriegs-Archiv*, Vienna, *Feld Akten (Italien)*, 1814, Fasc. 13, No. 83.

3 Printed in the *Giornale italiano*, of Milan, No. 112 (April 22, 1814). The *Giornale italiano* was the most important newspaper in Milan. Several of the official proclamations and decrees were printed in it, but nearly all of them can be found in more available sources. Besides the official decrees and proclamations, I have been able to find little of value for a study of the fall of the Kingdom of Italy in this paper. It devoted very little attention to the affairs of the Kingdom of Italy, and what little there was was so carefully censored that it was relatively unimportant.

4 Proclamation, Mayor and communal council of Milan, Milano, April 21, 1814, Fabi, *op. cit.*, Appendix XIX, 121-22.

5 Protocol of the communal council, Milano, April 21, 1814, *Museo del Risorgimento*, Milan, *Carte Beccaria*, Busta I, Carte 8, Fasc. I, Pezza 6, B.

6 Marchesi, *loc. cit.*, 164.

7 Decree, Barbò, Milano, April 23, 1814, *Raccolta degli atti del governo e delle disposizioni generali emanate dalle diverse autorità in oggetti sì amministrativi che giudiziarj* (Milano, 1816-19), 1814, 10. In future references this source will be cited as "*Atti del governo lombardo.*"

8 Decree, Barbò, Milano, April 23, 1814, *ibid.*, 11.

9 Decree, Provisional regency, Milano, April 21, 1814, *ibid.*, 5.

10 Decree, Provisional government, Milano, April 26, 1814, Fabi, *op. cit.*, Appendix XXXIV, b, 141.

postal rates on letters by one-half.[11] In addition, the regency decreed that all persons who had been imprisoned for evasion of the conscription laws, for failure to comply with the financial regulations, if their actions had not been accompanied by violence or any other crime, or because of their opinions, were to be immediately freed.[12] Only sons and supporters of families were exempted from military service,[13] and the punishment of the pillory was abolished for women who had committed only minor offenses.[14] The deduction of a fifth of the pay of all Italian troops which had been stipulated by a decree of January 7, 1814, was no longer to be continued.[15] With the exception that the portfolio of minister of interior was given to De Capitani,[16] all judicial and administrative authorities in the kingdom were provisionally retained in their posts, but the regency reserved for itself the right to make such changes in personnel as it might deem necessary.[17] With these measures, the provisional regency attempted to put out the flames of revolt kindled by the Milanese revolution.

On April 22, another governmental body held its first sitting in Milan. On that day the electoral colleges met.[18] As soon as

11 Decree, Provisional government, Milano, April 26, 1814, *ibid.*, Appendix XXXIV, d, 144-45.

12 Decree, Provisional regency, Milano, April 23, 1814, *Atti del governo lombardo, op. cit.*, 1814, 12-13.

13 Decree, Provisional regency, Milano, April 25, 1814, *ibid.*, 16.

14 Decree, Provisional regency, Milano, April 26, 1814, *ibid.*, 19-20.

15 Decree, Provisional regency, Milano, April 25, 1814, *ibid.*, 15.

16 Decree, Provisional regency, Milano, April 24, 1814, *ibid.*, 14.

17 Proclamation, Provisional regency, Milano, April 23, 1814, *ibid*, 8-9.

18 Only those delegates who represented the eight departments of Olona, Mincio, Alto Po, Agogna, Lario, Mella, Adda, and Serio, which had not yet been occupied by the Austrian troops, were admitted to the meeting. Verri, *op. cit.*, 154. The fact that the other members were disbarred from the sitting gave ground for charges of illegality. Senator Armaroli asserted that the electoral colleges had been "illegally convoked" and "illegally constituted," since there were present in the sitting only "Milanese electors" and "a few others from the non-invaded departments who were in Milan for government functions." Armaroli, *op. cit.*, 29. Even Ludovico

the meeting was opened, Ludovico Giovio was elected president. In assuming his office, Giovio gave an address in which he suggested to his colleagues that if the Italians were to have a glorious future, the electoral colleges must " demand liberal institutions, and an independent head, who, new and unknown to us, will become Italian and will welcome our votes and our benedictions." [19] Then, after their president had thus expressed their desire for independence, the colleges declared their sitting permanent and confirmed the measures which the communal council and the provisional regency had already taken.[20] The membership of the provisional regency was enlarged by the appointment of Giacomo Muggiasca, Giovanni Batista Vertova, Matteo Sommariva, Lucrezio Longo, Luigi Tonni, Giovanni Batista Tarsis, and Francesco Peregalli.[21] The Roman Catholic religion was declared to be the religion of the state, the continental system was abolished, all hunting rights, with a few exceptions, were abrogated, and the senate and the council of state were done away with.[22]

Giovio, who was chosen president of the electoral colleges, later wrote that the colleges were " illegitimats " because they had been " illegally " constituted. *Memoria di Giovio*, in Pellini, *Pino, op. cit.*, 91. Many senators complained that too few electors were present at the meetings to consider the electoral colleges a truly national and representative body, and protested that their deliberations were unconstitutional. Provisional regency, sitting of May 9, 1814, *Protocolli originali della reggenza provvisoria del Regno d'Italia nel 1814*, Brera Library, Milan A group of senators, including Veneri, Guicciardi, Paradisi, Moscati, Armaroli, Lamberti, Felici, Thiene, Serbelloni, and Massari, sent a letter of protest to Sommariva, the Austrian commissioner in Milan, on April 29, 1814, charging that the convocation of the electoral colleges was wholly without any constitutional justification. Armaroli, *op. cit.*, Appendix VIII, 71-5.

19 Fabi, *op cit ,* Appendix XXVIII, 130-31.

20 Proclamation, Electoral colleges to the Italian people, Milano, April 22, 1814, *Giornale italiano*, No. 113 (April 23, 1814) ; *Oesterreichischer Beobachter*, No. 130 (May 10, 1814), 709.

21 Decree, Electoral colleges, Milano, April 24, 1814, *Atti del governo lombardo, op. cit.*, 1814, 14.

22 Report from Milan, April 25, 1814, *Wiener Zeitung*, May 14, 1814, 537; *Giornale italiano*, No. 117 (April 27, 1814), 474.

On April 23, the electoral colleges sent to the Allies at Paris a deputation, composed of Marc'Antonio Fè, Federico Confalonieri, Giacomo Ciani, Alberto Litta, Giovanni Giacomo Trivulzio, Pietro Ballabio, Serafino Sommi, and Giovanni Luca Somaglia, with Giacomo Beccaria as secretary.[23] They were to request from the Allied Powers:

1. The absolute independence of the new Italian State, which will represent the Kingdom of Italy, with the same denomination or any other which it may please the high Allied Powers to give it.

2. The greatest possible extension of the boundaries of this new state, in combination with the interests of the Allies, and the new political balance of Europe.

3. A liberal constitution, having for its basis the division of the executive, legislative, and judicial powers, with the complete independence of the latter; admitting also a national representation designed to make laws, regulate the taxes, secure personal liberty, the liberty of the press, and of commerce.

4. Power to the Electoral Colleges to frame this Constitution.

5. A government monarchical, hereditary, in the order of primogeniture, and a Prince, who, by his origin and qualities, may cause to be effaced the calamities which have been suffered under the government abolished.[24]

23 Decree, Electoral colleges, April 23, 1814, *Giornale italiano*, No. 114 (April 24, 1814), 458.

24 Decree, Electoral colleges, April 23, 1814, *The London Times*, May 9, 1814. Also see *Giornale italiano*, No. 114 (April 24, 1814), 458; and Cusani, *op. cit.*, VII, 189-90. The form of government which the deputies were charged with demanding from the Allies is similar to the one projected in the permanent constitution, dated April 24, 1814, which was framed by the Royal Josephine Masonic lodge of Milan, and which was taken from Soveri Latuada by the Austrian police when he was arrested, along with several other conspirators of the Brescian-Milanese military conspiracy, in the latter part of November, 1814. Spadoni, Domenico, " Il processo per la congiura bresciano-milanese del 1814," *Atti* del XIII Congresso Nazionale della Società Nazionale per la Storia del Risorgimento italiano, tenutosi in Genova nei giorni 26-28 ottobre 1925, 86-8; Spadoni, *La congiura militare, op. cit*, Appendix 3, B, 284-86. Latuada had very close relations with various members of the Milanese communal council, the provisional government, and the electoral colleges, and was an intimate friend of General Pino, who, however, according to Latuada's relation to the Austrian police on December

In addition to sending deputies to the general Allied head-quarters at Paris, the various organs of the provisional government sent emissaries to the commanders of the Allied forces in Italy. On the morning of April 21, the communal council decided to send deputies to Marshal Bellegarde, Lord William Bentinck, and Joachim Murat.[25] Count Luigi Porro Lambertenghi was chosen to go to Bellegarde and Murat, and Baron Sigismondo Trecchi [26] was selected to go to Bentinck.[27] They

5, 1814, told him that the project was useless because the independence of the state was already assured and because a deputation had already been sent to the Allied Powers to demand it. Spadoni, "Il processo per la congiura," *loc. cit.*, 87; Spadoni, "Le società segrete nella rivoluzione milanese dell'aprile 1814," *loc. cit.*, 207. The Guelf constitution of October, 1813, also expressed a desire for a government in some ways similar to that demanded of the Allied Powers. See Spadoni, "Gli Statuti della Guelfia," *loc. cit.*, 704-38. Undoubtedly, many members of the provisional government were members of one or more of the secret political societies, and their views were similar to those of the societies.

25 Protocol of the communal council, Milano, April 21, 1814, *Museo del Risorgimento*, Milan, *Carte Beccaria*, Busta I, Carte 8, Fasc. I, Pezza 6, B.

26 Baron Trecchi was a member of the "pure Italian" party, and had many English friends, particularly among the liberal Whigs. Trecchi, Dario Biandrà, "Milano e gli Inglesi nel 1814. La missione del barone Trecchi," *Rassegna storica del Risorgimento*, Anno XV (aprile 1937), 526-27.

27 Salvisenti, Bernardo, "La missione Porro presso le Alte Potenze nel 1814," *La Lombardia nel Risorgimento*, Anno I-II (giugno 1914), 40; Spadoni, *Il moto del 20 aprile, op. cit.*, 61. Weil, *Eugène et Murat, op. cit.*, IV, 564, says that "the provisional regency and the municipal council had not only made an appeal for the intervention of the Austrian army, but sent Counts Porro and Serbelloni to Murat and Baron Trecchi to Bentinck to beseech them to come without delay to Milan." Lemmi, *La restaurazione austriaca, op. cit.*, 208, 210, states that "Counts Porro-Lambertenghi and Giovanni Serbelloni were sent to the general headquarters of Bellegarde and of the King of Naples," and Baron Sigismondo Trecchi to Bentinck. Cusani, *op. cit.*, VII, 181, says that Counts Porro Lambertenghi and Serbelloni were sent to Bellegarde's headquarters. Gallavresi, Giuseppe, "La rivoluzione lombarda del 1814 e la politica inglese secondo nuovi documenti," *Archivio Storico Lombardo*, Ser. IV, XI (1909), 106-7, maintains that Count Luigi Porro Lambertenghi was sent to Murat; Count Giovanni Serbelloni, to Bellegarde; and Baron Sigismondo Trecchi, to Bentinck. The writer does not know what Weil's, Lemmi's, Cusani's, and Gallavresi's sources of information were, but believes that they may have erred in relating that Count Serbelloni was also sent on a mission to the Allied commanders, and

were given letters addressed to the " High Allied Powers," entreating Bellegarde, Bentinck, and Murat " to hasten those political and military measures which will also assure to us that tranquillity which the High Powers are preparing for all Europe." [28]

Baron Trecchi was given, in addition to the above communication, a letter written by Mayor Durini on April 20, 1814, and addressed to Bentinck. This letter differed significantly from the one written by the communal council and sent to all three of the Allied commanders, Bentinck, Bellegarde, and

feels that the accounts of Spadoni and Salvisenti are more accurate. In his letter of April 27, 1814, to the communal council, Count Porro gave a detailed account of his mission. Although he mentioned Baron Trecchi several times, he made no mention of any person named Serbelloni. Salvisenti, *loc. cit*, 35-40. Likewise, Baron Trecchi, in his letter to the mayor of Milan, although mentioning Porro's progress on his mission, said nothing whatsoever about Serbelloni. Lemmi, *La restaurazione austriaca, op. cit.*, Appendix IV, 400-1. Furthermore, the writer has not seen the name of Serbelloni mentioned in any of the letters or documents relating to this particular mission which he has read.

28 Address of the communal council of Milan to the High Allied Powers, Milano, April 21, 1814, Lemmi, *La restaurazione austriaca, op. cit*, Appendix II, 395-97. With a slight but significant exception, the address, as quoted above, conforms to Article II of the protocol of the sitting of the communal council of April 21, 1814, as found in the *Museo del Risorgimento*, Milan, *Carte Beccaria*, Busta I, Carte 8, Fasc. I, No. 6, B. In the protocol, the representatives of the three Allied Powers in Italy were requested " to hasten all those political and military measures which will also assure to us that tranquillity *and independence* which the High Powers are preparing for all Europe." [The italics are mine.] The words " and independence " are written above the line in a manner which leads one to believe that they were probably added as an afterthought at a later date. Salvisenti, *loc cit.*, 34, has published another address to the Allied Powers, which he found in the *Archivio Porro*. It is dated 11.00 A. M., April 21, 1814, and signed by Somaglia, the president of the communal council, Mayor Durini, and several members of the council. It reads as follows: " Seeing the ever increasing tumult of the Population, and not being able to check the disorders in the Capital with the Municipal forces, the military Authorities of the High Allied Powers are entreated with the greatest solicitude to send the Heads of the Army to Milan to put an end to the disorders, and to prevent the sacking and every other terrible accident with which the Municipality is menaced." It is not known whether or not Porro and Trecchi made use of this document. Also see Spadoni, *Il moto del 20 aprile, op. cit*, 60-1 ftn.

Murat. It made a direct appeal for national independence. It began with the assertion that Bentinck's Leghorn proclamation[29] had made a deep impression upon the minds of the Italian people. Then it continued:

If your nation, always inalterable in its liberal principles, vigorously supports with one hand the peace of the world, and, with the other, protects the independence of the people and magnanimously offers its support for this worthy purpose, we raise our voices to you to permit us to participate in such benevolence.

It is true that a deputation of our Senate has gone to the High Allied Powers to promote the interests of our wretched country, but as it can not constitutionally represent the Italian nation, we can hope that the Allied sovereigns will not recognize in it the expression of the vote of the nation, and moreover, we do not know how to verify the object of its mission.

. . . To you, however, generous representative of a magnanimous nation, we address this spontaneous communication . . . to supplicate you to offer your strong hand to a loyal people, who long for that felicity which we see is already shining upon so many other nations. Yes, a liberal constitution, such as yours, the independence of a rather vast territory, which will make us strong in the eyes of other governments, and the freedom of our commerce are the unanimous and sincere demands of this unfortunate part of Italy, which, despoiled by a long war, has remained wretched in the midst of inexhaustible territorial riches, and ardently desires to return to its ancient prosperity and to bind with your nation those necessary commercial relations which nature has ordained for Italy.[30]

Thus it was from Lord Bentinck that the liberal leaders of the Milanese provisional government expected to receive the most efficacious assistance in obtaining independence and a constitutional government. Many of the members of the provisional government had a great admiration and respect for

29 See *ante*, 56-7.

30 Printed in Gallavresi, "La rivoluzione e la politica inglese," *loc. cit.*, 108-9; and in Trecchi, *loc. cit.*, 530-31.

England, and some of them had close connections with persons in London.[31] Many of them were influenced by Bentinck's liberal proclamations and felt that since he was such an avowed and open champion of the cause of Italian liberty and of constitutionalism, and since he was the representative of a powerful country, he would be much more likely to give them effective help in their plans to create a liberal and independent government than would either Murat or Bellegarde.

Porro and Trecchi left Milan immediately and arrived at Castel S. Giovanni on April 22. Here Colonel Gavenda gave them passports to continue their mission. Trecchi was given one to go to the headquarters of Lord Bentinck, and Porro one to go to General Nugent and to Count Bellegarde.[32] Apparently, Trecchi was joined on the way by a certain Lamberti.[33] Together they arrived in Genoa at two o'clock on the morning of April 24.[34]

Meanwhile, Count Porro left Castel S. Giovanni and arrived at Marshal Bellegarde's headquarters in Verona at nine o'clock on the morning of the 25th. He immediately presented himself to the Austrian commander, gave him the letter from the communal council, and assured him that at the present moment his mission had no other purpose than to ask for the protection of the Allied Powers. In spite of this statement, Porro, however, hastened to add that the largest portion of the population was

31 Borda to Gallotta, Milano, April 26, 1814, Fiorani, *loc. cit*, 433.

32 Porro to provisional government, Milano, April 27, 1814, Salvisenti, *loc. cit.*, 36.

33 Spadoni, *Il moto del 20 aprile*, *op. cit.*, 67, says that Lamberti was a deputy of the Milanese commercial classes. Gallavresi, " La rivoluzione e la politica inglese," *loc. cit.*, 116, relates that Lamberti was a mysterious emissary of General Nugent. That Spadoni's version is the correct one is indicated by the fact that, upon his arrival in Genoa, Lamberti presented to Bentinck an address signed by eighty persons from the banking and commercial circles of Milan. See *post*, 160.

34 " Sunday around two o'clock in the morning two deputies arrived from Milan with dispatches from His Excellency Lord Bentinck." Correspondence from Genoa, April 27, 1814, *Giornale italiano*, No. 121 (May 1, 1814). The last Sunday before April 27 was April 24.

filled with a desire for independence and wanted an Austrian prince as sovereign of an independent Kingdom of Italy. Bellegarde replied in a very friendly and encouraging manner and told him that he had already sent Lieutenant-General Sommariva and Count Strassoldo to Milan to cooperate with the provisional government. When Porro told the Austrian commander-in-chief that he was also charged with a mission to the King of Naples and that Baron Trecchi had been sent to Lord Bentinck, Bellegarde showed great displeasure,[35] and it appears that Porro's mission to Murat was never carried out.

Bellegarde expressed himself so favorably on the subject of independence that Count Porro was extremely hopeful.[36] It is not surprising that the Austrian field marshal encouraged Porro's expectations of obtaining an independent kingdom, for at this time many of the Habsburg officials in Italy seemed to be favorable to the creation of an independent kingdom under the scepter of an Austrian prince. On April 23, General Nugent told Count Porro that Austria and England were both " animated by very liberal sentiments," and that it would not be very difficult for the Lombards to obtain Francis of Austria-Este or some other Austrian prince as their sovereign.[37] The next day Nugent wrote Lord Bentinck: " They [the Milanese] intend to make the A. D. [Archduke] Francis their King, and I am sure you will promote this object. Your declaration will be of great use." [38] At Verona, Captain Sardagna told Porro that the plan of electing Francis of Austria-Este sovereign of the Kingdom of Italy was the best possible one for the interests of the inhabitants of the kingdom, and other prominent persons told the count that " Austria is content with seeing one of her Princes Sovereign " of the Kingdom of Italy.[39] Later Baron

35 Porro to provisional government, Milano, April 27, 1814, Salvisenti, *loc cit.*, 37-8.

36 *Ibid*, 37.

37 *Ibid*, 36-7.

38 Gallavresi, "La rivoluzione e la politica inglese," *loc. cit.*, 118.

39 Porro to provisional government, Milano, April 27, 1814, Salvisenti, *loc cit.*, 39-40.

Huegel, who was very close to the councils of Marshal Belle-garde, noted in his diary: " In giving them [the Milanese] a prince of our house, all the difficulties would be solved, and by adding to it [the Kingdom of Italy] Savoy and Piedmont, who do not want their actual king, an intermediary state, which would be very useful to us, would be formed."[40]

As many Austrian officials in Italy appeared to be favorable to the project of establishing a more or less independent King-dom of Italy with one of the Austrian archdukes as its king, it seemed likely that the plans of the liberal Milanese nobles and middle classes in control of the provisional government would succeed. But the fate of Lombardy was to be decided by the Allied Powers in Paris, and not by the Austrian officials in Italy. And the wishes of the Austrian Emperor and the other Allied sovereigns in Paris by the last of April and the first of May were quite different from those of the Habsburg agents in the Kingdom of Italy.

As we have seen, the territory of the former Kingdom of Italy west of the Mincio and north of the Po was, during the last days of April, 1814, under the administration of a hastily improvised Milanese provisional government. The parts of the kingdom which originally constituted the Duchy of Modena and part of the papal states were still under the administration of Austrian and Neapolitan military officials. The South Tyrol was under the supervision of the Austrian Baron von Rosch-mann. With the exception of the city of Venice, the Venetian departments east of the Mincio had been for several months under the governorship of the Austrian Prince Reuss-Plauen.

The city of Venice itself was, in accordance with the pro-visions of the Convention of Schiarino-Rizzino, handed over to the Austrians on April 20, 1814. The city had been block-aded by the British navy and the Austrian army [41] ever since

40 Entry of May 9, 1814, Huegel Diary, *op. cit.*, 98.

41 Peverelli, P., *Storia di Venezia dal 1798 sino ai nostri tempi* (Torino, 1852), I, 218.

the early part of October, 1813,[42] and early in November it was ordered that all communications between the city and the mainland were to be completely cut off.[43]

With the approach of the Austrian army on the mainland opposite the city, many refugees fled into the city, and a serious food shortage soon followed. As early as October 22, 1813, it was necessary to levy a tax upon such articles as bread and meat in order to discourage their consumption.[44] On December 4, a committee of six was formed to take charge of the provisioning of the inhabitants of the city.[45] In spite of these regulations, the food supply continued to decline, and late in February, 1814, a premium of five francs was promised for every bushel of wheat or rye of good quality, and one of three francs for every bushel of maize brought into the city.[46] Early in March, when conditions were so bad that many of the poorer people were suffering from famine,[47] these premiums were changed to five lire for a metric quintal (100 kilograms) of good wheat and rye and three lire for a quintal of maize, and premiums of ten lire for every quintal of rice and five lire for every quintal of vegetables were added.[48] By that time even bread was scarce,[49] and, to prevent actual starvation among the proletariat, the Venetian government ordered that a special

42 Cicogna Diary, October 7, 1813, Pilot, A., " Venezia nel blocco del 1813-14. Da noterelle inedite del Cicogna," *Nuovo Archivio Veneto*, Anno XIV (1914), 193. In future references this source will be given as " Cicogna Diary."

43 Proclamation, Radivojevics, Mira, November 7, 1814, *Archivio di Stato*, Venice, *Polizia*, 1813-14, Fasc. 6, A, No. 1138/5.

44 Cicogna Diary, *loc. cit.*, October 26, 1813, 194.

45 Peverelli, *op. cit.*, I, 229.

46 Notice, Gradenigo (the mayor of Venice), February 27, 1814, *Giornale dipartimentale dell'Adriatico*, No. 19 (March 2, 1814), 3.

47 On March 4, 1814, Cicogna noted in his diary that many of the poorer classes had not eaten meat for at least four months. Cicogna Diary, *loc. cit*, 199-200.

48 Notice, Gradenigo, March 9, 1814, *Giornale dipartimentale dell'Adriatico*, No. 22 (March 12, 1814), 3.

49 Cicogna Diary, *loc. cit.*, March 10, 1814, 200.

cheap bread be made to be sold only to the poor at a fixed price of four centesimi per pound.[50] Furthermore, in order to conserve to the fullest extent every particle of food left in the city, on March 21, it was ordered that all dogs in the city be shot.[51]

With many of the inhabitants on the point of starvation, and with many people ill on account of the deprivations which they had undergone,[52] the city could not hold out much longer. When news of the entry of the Allied army into Paris and of the signing of the Convention of Schiarino-Rizzino between Prince Eugene and the Austrians arrived in the city, Governor Seras and the generals in charge of the military defenses of the city invited the English and Austrian commanders in charge of the attack on Venice to meet with them to agree upon definite terms for the surrender of the city.[53] On April 20, the city was handed over to the Austrians,[54] and Prince Reuss-Plauen was put in charge of the direction of all its civil and military affairs.[55] On May 1, the French governor of the city, Seras, left Venice with his family.[56]

Governor Reuss immediately proclaimed that all existing laws and regulations of the city of Venice and the department of the Adriatic would, for the time being, be conserved and

50 Notice, Galvagna, March 19, 1814, *Giornale dipartimentale dell'Adriatico*, No. 25 (March 22, 1814), 1-2.

51 Notice, Mulazzani, March 21, 1814, *ibid.*, No. 26 (March 26, 1814), 1; Cicogna Diary, *loc. cit.*, March 24, 1814, 201.

52 Peverelli, *op. cit.*, I, 231-32.

53 Cicogna Diary, *loc. cit.*, April 19, 1814, 206.

54 Notice, April 20, 1814, *Collezione di leggi venete, op. cit.*, 1813-14, 140-41.

55 Proclamation, Seras and Marchal, Venezia, April 20, 1814, *Giornale di Venezia*, 1814, No. 35 (April 27, 1814), 1. Cicogna says that this proclamation was first published in Venice on April 25. Cicogna Diary, *loc. cit.*, April 26, 1814, 212. The *Giornale dipartimentale dell'Adriatico*, which was a biweekly paper, changed its name to *Giornale di Venezia* with the issue of April 27, 1814. At the same time it became a daily paper. The paper contains copies of many official decrees, but, like the *Giornale italiano*, of Milan, was so carefully censored that it contains very little news of the affairs of the Kingdom of Italy.

56 Cicogna Diary, *loc. cit.*, May 2, 1814, 214.

that all employees and functionaries who had remained at their posts would be provisionally kept in their positions.[57] At the same time the special taxes which the French had levied on foodstuffs and other commodities were reduced, and prices immediately fell to the level where they had been before the blockade was established.[58]

The population of the city joyfully greeted their Austrian and English conquerors, and took the opportunity offered by the change in government to vent their spleen against all things French. Even on the day before Venice actually surrendered, a large crowd of people took it upon themselves to create disturbances. The occasion for this outbreak was the appearance of two Austrian civil commissioners on the Riva degli Schiavoni. Crowds of idle pedestrians surged around to greet them. Under the intoxication of the moment some unknown person was stimulated into urging the crowd to follow him to a neighboring statue of Emperor Napoleon. There the hastily collected rabble began whistling and hissing, and threatened to dash the statue into bits. A body of soldiers was sent against them. When the captain entreated the mob to be calm, they turned against him and forced him to flee for refuge. More soldiers, however, soon arrived, and arrested several of the leading agitators. When nightfall came, the crowd finally went home, and the guards, taking advantage of the quiet, dismantled the statue and removed it to the safety of S. Giorgio Maggiore.[59]

57 Proclamation given at Padova, April 20, 1814, *Giornale di Venezia*, 1814, No. 35 (April 27, 1814), 1. Cicogna says that this proclamation was first published in the city on April 25. Cicogna Diary, *loc. cit.*, April 26, 1814, 212.

58 Cicogna Diary, *loc. cit.*, April 21, 1814, 210. In the *Giornale di Venezia*, 1814, No. 39 (May 2, 1814), 3-4, there was published a decree of Governor Reuss-Plauen, dated Padua, March 24, 1814, announcing the abolition of the Napoleonic continental system and the substitution for the French tariff rates of the rates in effect in the Venetian territory in 1805, when it was still under Austrian domination.

59 Cicogna Diary, *loc. cit.*, April 20, 1814, 207.

The Venetians continued to insult the French after the Austrians were in control of their city. People who had previously expressed their sympathy for the French in too ardent terms were insulted and beaten,[60] and the city was deluged with satires and diatribes against the French in general and Napoleon in particular.[61] The Austrians and English were accepted as liberators, and were joyously acclaimed at every turn.[62] The Venetians were disgusted with every vestige of the French rule, and looked toward a happier future from the Allied Powers.

60 *Ibid.*, April 20, and May 7, 1814, 207-8, 215.

61 *Ibid.*, April 30, May 23, and May 28, 1814, 214, 220, 221.

62 *Ibid.*, April 21, 1814, 209; Cervellini, G. B., "Il periodo veneziano di P. A. Paravia (dal carteggio inedito con G. Monico)," *Archivio Veneto*, Anno LXI (1931), 157.

CHAPTER IX

THE MILANESE PROVISIONAL GOVERNMENT AND THE AUSTRIANS

ON April 26, 1814, Marquis Annibale Sommariva, of Lodi, whom Marshal Bellegarde had dispatched to ·Milan, and his intendant and general assistant, Count Julius Strassoldo,[1] arrived at their destination.[2] They had been instructed that immediately upon their entry in the capital, they were to take control of the unoccupied portions of the Kingdom of Italy in the name of the Allied Powers, and were to issue a proclamation exhorting the people to remain tranquil and assuring them that the existing government would be provisionally conserved.

Sommariva and Strassoldo were to consider the Austrian occupation of the country as merely a temporary, military one, and they were not to make any changes in the government without Bellegarde's personal consent. All the governmental authorities who remained at their posts were for the present to be confirmed in their positions, but they were to be subordinated to the control of the commander of the Habsburg army. The two representatives were to pay close attention to public opinion and were to prevent at all costs the spread of a spirit of partisanship and intrigue. For this purpose, they were to maintain a strict censorship of the press, and were to take direct control of the police administration of the country. Care was to be taken to insure that no moves were made which might in any manner damage the interests of the Allied Powers.[3]

1 Bellegarde to Kaiser Franz, Verona, May 4, 1814, *Staats-Archiv*, Vienna, *Kaiser Franz Akten*, Fasc. 27, Sect. 1, Fo. 32.

2 " Today about eight o'clock in the morning I arrived here with Lieutenant Field Marshal Marquis Sommariva. The jubilation of the people on the street as they saw the uniform of the Lieutenant Field Marshal is indescribable." Strassoldo to Bellegarde, Mailand, April 26, 1814, *ibid.*, Fo. 35.

3 Bellegarde to Kaiser Franz, Verona, May 4, 1814, *ibid.*, Fo. 32-7; Bellegarde to Strassoldo, no date given but enclosed in the above letter, *ibid.*,

Upon his arrival in Milan, Sommariva handed the communal council a letter from Bellegarde, informing its members that Marquis Sommariva had been sent " to contribute with all possible means to the re-establishment of public order and tranquillity." [4] Then, according to instructions from his superior, he issued a proclamation to the Italian people to inform them that he was assuming control of the government in the name of the Allies and to beseech them to await faithfully and peacefully the decisions of the Allied Powers as to their fate.[5] To add emphasis to Sommariva's words, the provisional regency, on its own part, made this appeal : " Italians, you have developed your noble character, and the general sentiment of love for your country has excluded the possibility of opposition parties. Private interest is entirely forgotten by each of you ; repose, tranquillity, and the longing for a prudent and independent government are fixed in the hearts of all. There is no Italian who does not feel the need for a new order." [6]

After having informed the inhabitants of the city about the nature of his mission, Sommariva turned to the president of the provisional regency to suggest that he should arrange for an official in the ministry of war to be delegated to correspond directly with him on any inquiries which the Austrian commissioner might wish to make of him, and that another official should be appointed to answer any questions which either Sommariva or Strassoldo might ask about the state of public administration or public economy.[7] Then he had the regency announce that the Austrian one, three, fifteen, twenty, and thirty *kreutzer* copper pieces were to be freely interchangeable

Fo. 33; Bellegarde to Sommariva, Verona, April 29, 1814, *ibid.*, Fo. 38-9; Bellegarde to Sommariva, Verona, May 2, 1814, *ibid.*, Fo. 56-7.

4 Dated Verona, April 26, 1814, Lemmi, *La restaurazione austriaca, op cit.*, Appendix XI, 408-9.

5 Proclamation, Sommariva, Milano, April 26, 1814, *Atti del governo lombardo, op. cit.*, 1814, 18.

6 Dated Milano, April 27, 1814, *ibid*, 22-3.

7 Sommariva to Verri, Milano, April 26, 1814, *Museo del Risorgimento*, Milan, *Carte Beccaria*, Busta I, Carte 8, Fasc. I, Pezza 1.

with the local currency in the kingdom,[8] and that, although in the future taxes would be appreciably reduced, the financial exigencies of the moment were so great that the tax rate for the month of May was to be the same as that of the preceding month.[9]

On April 28, the military occupation of the Kingdom of Italy by Austrian troops, which had been stipulated in the Convention of Mantua, was completed. On that day Lieutenant Field Marshal Franz Fenner von Fennenberg occupied Brescia,[10] Lieutenant Field Marshal Anton Mayer von Heldenfeld entered Mantua,[11] and Lieutenant Field Marshal Adam Neipperg, at the head of fourteen thousand troops,[12] entered Milan. In all three places, the inhabitants greeted the arrival of the Austrian military forces with joyous enthusiasm and wild acclamation. In Milan, where the provisional regency had invited the people to receive the troops " with the loving and grateful hospitality which is due our liberators," [13] the reception was particularly enthusiastic and demonstrative. As early as eight o'clock in the morning, large throngs of persons jammed the streets along the line of march. Civic guards were stationed along the streets from nine o'clock in the morning until late in the afternoon, when Neipperg's forces finally arrived. As the Austrian troops began their entry into the city, pandemonium broke loose. Wild shouts of joy and enthusiasm resounded through the streets and public squares. Flowers were thrown down upon the marching soldiers from the windows and balconies of houses near-

8 Decree, Provisional regency, Milano, April 28, 1814, *Giornale italiano*, No. 119 (April 29, 1814), 482.

9 Decree, Provisional regency, Milano, April 29, 1814, *Atti del governo lombardo, op. cit.*, 1814, 26.

10 *Wiener Zeitung*, May 15, 1814, 542; *Oesterreichischer Beobachter*, No. 135 (May 15, 1814), 734.

11 Bellegarde to Kaiser Franz, Verona, April 28, 1814, *Kriegs-Archiv*, Vienna, *Feld Akten (Italien)*, 1814, Fasc. 4, ad No. 229½.

12 *Mantovani Diario, op cit*, April 27, 1814, V, 258

13 Provisional regency, sitting of April 27, 1814, *Protocolli originali della reggenza provvisoria*, Brera Library.

by. Everywhere large multitudes took this opportunity to express their gratification over their deliverance from the yoke of the once seemingly invincible French Emperor.[14]

With Sommariva, Strassoldo, and Neipperg in Milan, and Marshal Bellegarde not far away at Verona, the factions in the provisional government which aspired to create an independent Kingdom of Italy took several steps to impress the Austrians with the strength of their party. Just before adjourning their sitting on May 2, 1814, the electoral colleges issued a proclamation manifesting the unanimous vote of that body for independence.[15] Colonel Visconti and Benigno Bossi presented themselves to Marquis Sommariva to hand him an address of the civic guard demanding liberty for their country.[16] And on April 28, a delegation, composed of Fagnani, Rougier, Serbelloni, and Ottolini, and sent by the provisional regency,[17] arrived in Verona to render homage to Marshal Bellegarde, to inform him that the universal wish of the Lombards was to be ruled by a prince of the Habsburg house, and to request him to convey this sentiment to the Austrian Emperor.[18]

14 *Mantovani Diario, op. cit.*, April 28, 1814, V, 258; *Giornale italiano*, No. 119 (April 29, 1814), 482; Teresa Confalonieri Casati to Confalonieri, Milano, April 29, 1814, Gallavresi, Giuseppe, *Carteggio del Conte Federico Confalonieri, ed altri documenti spettanti alla sua biografia; con annotazione storiche* (Milano, 1910-13), I, 83-4.

15 Printed in the *Giornale italiano*, No. 123 (May 3, 1814), 500. Ludovico Giovio, the president of the electoral colleges, related in his memoirs that he himself had repeatedly pronounced the vote of that body for independence to Sommariva and Bellegarde. *Memoria di Giovio*, in Pellini, *Pino, op. cit.*, 92.

16 Teresa Confalonieri Casati to Confalonieri, Milano, May 2, 1814, Gallavresi, *Confalonieri, op. cit.*, I, 92-3; Castro, Giovanni de, " La restaurazione austriaca in Milano (1814-1817). Notizie desunte da diarj e testimonianze contemporanee," *Archivio Storico Lombardo*, Anno XV (1888), 608.

17 Provisional regency to Bellegarde, April 26, 1814, Lemmi, *La restaurazione austriaca, op. cit.*, Appendix XII, 409; Teresa Confalonieri Casati to Confalonieri, Milano, April 31, 1814, Gallavresi, *Confalonieri, op. cit.*, I, 90-1.

18 Bellegarde to Kaiser Franz, Verona, April 28, 1814, *Kriegs-Archiv*, Vienna, *Feld Akten (Italien)*, 1814, Fasc. 4, ad No. 229½; Bellegarde to Metternich, Verona, April 28, 1814, *Staats-Archiv*, Vienna, *Staatskanzlei, Provinzen, Lombardei-Venedig*, Fasc. 3, Sect. 3, Fo. 188-90.

A week later Bellegarde left Verona to proceed to Milan,[19] where he arrived on May 8 at the head of 12,000 troops.[20] His entrance into the city was greeted with a spirited ovation.[21] Large crowds of people were lined along the streets of the city to welcome him, and later other groups went to the house where he was lodged to manifest their exultation. A deputation of the provisional regency, consisting of Mellerio, Borromeo, Muggiasca, and Tarsis, went to the Austrian commander to greet him, and returned expressing satisfaction " with the extremely courteous and affable manner " with which Bellegarde had received them.[22] In the evening, when the Austrian Field Marshal appeared at the Scala theater, which was brilliantly lighted for the occasion, there was animated applause.[23]

With Bellegarde close at hand, several other deputations went to him to express their wishes in regard to the future fate of their country. A deputation headed by Count Giovio and purporting to represent the electoral colleges did not hesitate to declare that the inhabitants of the country wished to have an independent kingdom, "protected by wise laws and by a Prince who will receive our blessing." [24] In reply, Bellegarde assured the deputies that he had already brought their desires to the attention of the Allied Powers, and declared that he " did not doubt that the High Allied Powers, who have already done so much for the welfare of so many people, will also insure the felicity of the Italians." Then he added: " Await, therefore,

19 Bellegarde left Verona on May 6. Huegel Diary, *op. cit.*, May 6, 1814, 97.

20 Helfert, *La caduta, op. cit.*, 123; Lemmi, *La restaurazione austriaca, op. cit.*, 270.

21 Bellegarde to Metternich, Milano, May 9, 1814, Lemmi, *La restaurazione austriaca, op. cit.*, Appendix XIX, 423.

22 Provisional regency to deputation at Paris, Milano, May 9, 1814, *Museo del Risorgimento*, Milan, *Carte Beccaria*, Busta I, Carte 8, Fasc. I, No. 27.

23 Huegel Diary, *op. cit.*, May 8, 1814, 97; Teresa Confalonieri Casati to Confalonieri, Milano, May 8, 1814, Gallavresi, *Confalonieri, op. cit.*, I, 109.

24 *Wiener Zeitung*, May 26, 1814, 586; *Giornale italiano*, No. 130 (May 10, 1814), 530.

in peace the arrangements which the High Allied Powers will in a short time make for you." [25]

About the same time, Carlo Verri, the president of the provisional regency, called upon the Austrian commander to recommend not only the independence of the country but also the addition of considerable territory to the Kingdom of Italy which he hoped would be created. He suggested that at least the three papal legations and Genoa should be added to the kingdom, and asked whether or not Modena and Guastalla, Parma and Piacenza, and Piedmont had definitely passed into the hands of the house of Este, the Archduchess Maria Louisa, and the King of Sardinia, respectively. Bellegarde replied so positively in the affirmative to all these questions that Verri felt that there was " nothing to hope from the Germans." [26]

Bellegarde also received a deputation of the former senate of the Kingdom of Italy, composed of Guicciardi, Paradisi, and Veneri,[27] who came to protest that the position assumed by the electoral colleges of being the legitimate representation of the people of the kingdom was illegal, and asserted that all the enactments of that body were unconstitutional.[28] Bellegarde, however, was little moved by their denunciations. In spite of the arguments of the three senators, he hastened to write Count Verri that he would continue to recognize the provisional regency, approved as it had been by the electoral colleges, as the legitimate source of all governmental powers of the Kingdom of Italy, and invited him to devise, with the advice and

25 *Ibid.*

26 Sitting of May 9, 1814, *Protocolli della reggenza provvisoria*, Brera Library; Provisional regency to deputation at Paris, Milano, May 9, 1814, *Museo del Risorgimento*, Milan, *Carte Beccaria*, Busta I, Carte 8, Fasc. I, No. 26.

27 Teresa Confalonieri Casati to Confalonieri, Milano, May 11, 1814, Gallavresi, *Confalonieri*, *op. cit.*, I, 115.

28 Sitting of May 9, 1814, *Protocolli della reggenza provvisoria*, Brera Library.

consent of Marquis Sommariva, effective means of curbing the attempts of the senators to stir up trouble.[29]

Bellegarde's announcement to Verri that he recognized only the regency as the proper government of the kingdom was in accord with his policy of maintaining the *status quo* until the fate of the country was decided at Paris. Bellegarde, Sommariva, and Strassoldo lived up to this resolution, but some of the Habsburg officials in other parts of Lombardy occasionally took steps which caused complaints that they were trying to "Austrianize" the country. Even Bellegarde and his two commissioners in Milan frequently made moves which vexed the "pure Italians" in the Milanese government and made them suspicious of the intentions of Austria.

One of the first sources of irritation to the officials of the Kingdom of Italy came over the objections which the Austrian commissioners in Milan raised in regard to the irregular promotions which General Pino, apparently with the consent of the rest of the members of the regency, had made in the Italian army. Among others, Pino had promoted his close friends and associates, General Lechi, Ugo Foscolo, and General Dembowsky, to positions of a higher rank.[30] This move gave ground for much unfavorable criticism,[31] and Bellegarde hastened to express to Count Verri his disapproval of these appointments.[32] This disapprobation was highly obnoxious to General Pino, particularly since he had already been censured by the Austrian commander-in-chief for making several dispositions in regard to the quartering of Italian troops without first consulting

29 Letter of May 11, 1814, *Museo del Risorgimento*, Milan, *Carte Beccaria*, Busta I, Carte 8, Fasc. I, No. 40.

30 Rasini to Confalonieri, Milan, May 11, 1814, Casati, *op. cit.*, II, 298; Teresa Confalonieri Casati to Confalonieri, Milano, May 6, 1814, Gallavresi, *Confalonieri, op. cit.*, I, 105.

31 Pallavicini to Confalonieri, Milano, May 7, 1814, Gallavresi, *Confalonieri, op. cit.*, I, 107.

32 Provisional regency to deputation at Paris, Milano, May 9, 1814, *Museo del Risorgimento*, Milan, *Carte Beccaria*, Busta I, Carte 8, Fasc. I, No. 26.

him.[33] Pino complained in the sitting of the provisional regency on May 5, that the command of the Italian army in all but name had passed under the control of Marshal Bellegarde and Marquis Sommariva.[34] Pino was so much aroused that he even thought of sending in his resignation.[35]

Not only General Pino, but other Italian officials became ruffled over some of the manoeuvres of the Austrian plenipotentiaries. In particular, Count Strassoldo's passing over the heads of the Milanese government to obtain information on the status of the administration of the kingdom served to arouse their ire. When, at the outset, Sommariva, in conformity with his instructions, contented himself merely with asking the members of the provisional government to provide him with a report on the general state of all the branches of the administration, they responded favorably and made arrangements to comply with his request. On May 5, Count Strassoldo, however, sent a note directly to various ministers and other officers of the government, calling for financial statements and other public documents without any reference to the provisional regency or consultation with it. This procedure infuriated the members of the regency, who delegated General Pino to go to Marquis Sommariva to make a strong protest against Strassoldo's action. As a result, the Austrian commissioner agreed that in the future he would abstain from corresponding directly with the ministers.[36] The issue was settled in a satisfactory manner, but Strassoldo's tactlessness had served to increase the tension which was beginning to exist between the Austrian

33 Mc. Farlane to Castlereagh, Milano, May 4, 1814, Lemmi, *La restaurazione austriaca, op. cit.*, Appendix XVII, 420.

34 Sitting of May 5, 1814, *Protocolli della reggenza provvisoria*, Brera Library. Also see Spadoni, *Il moto del 20 aprile, op. cit.*, 113-14.

35 Mc. Farlane to Castlereagh, Milano, May 4, 1814, Lemmi, *La restaurazione austriaca, op. cit*, Appendix XVII, 420.

36 Provisional regency to deputation at Paris, Milano, May 6, 1814, *Museo del Risorgimento*, Milan, *Carte Beccaria*, Busta I, Carte 8, Fasc. I, No 23; MacFarlane to Bentinck, Milan, May 6, 1814, Gallavresi, "La rivoluzione e la politica inglese," *loc. cit*, 160.

commissioners and the members of the Milanese government. A clear-cut conflict of authority between the two was beginning to develop.

The ill-timed proclamation which Mayer von Heldenfeld, the Habsburg commissioner at Mantua, ordered published on April 28, increased the agitation and irritation of those in control of the administration of the kingdom. It read:

Mantuans! Finally after a long period of time during which destiny has separated us, there is good news in store for us, and we record with true expression of joy the attachment which you have on all occasions demonstrated and the fidelity which you have always manifested for the August House of Austria

We hope that these sentiments are not extinct, but that they have only been suppressed by political changes, and we rejoice to be able to return to live with You in true fraternal harmony and to enter into our ancient relations at the present time.[37]

In the opinion of the provisional government, this proclamation had an extremely unfortunate effect upon public opinion, and, furthermore, prejudiced the position of those parties which wanted to see an independent Kingdom of Italy established.[38] In their meeting of May 2, the members of the regency decided to send a copy of the proclamation, along with their objections to it, directly to Sommariva.[39]

The issuing of the proclamation at Mantua was followed by other actions which were graver. On May 2, Mayer von Heldenfeld formally ordered the prefect of the department of the

37 A copy of this proclamation is enclosed in the letter which the provisional regency sent to the Milanese deputation at Paris on May 3, 1814. This letter is in the *Museo del Risorgimento*, Milan, *Carte Beccaria*, Busta I, Carte 8, Fasc I, No. 359

38 Provisional regency to deputation at Paris, Milano, May 3, 1814, *ibid.*; Strassoldo to Bellegarde, Mailand, April 30, 1814, *Staats-Archiv*, Vienna, *Kaiser Franz Akten*, Fasc 27, Sect. 1, Fo. 54

39 Sitting of May 2, 1814, *Protocolli della reggenza provvisoria*, Brera Library; Provisional regency to deputation at Paris, Milano, May 3, 1814, *Museo del Risorgimento*, Milan, *Carte Beccaria*, Busta I, Carte 8, Fasc. 1, No. 359.

Mincio in the future not to send out any advice or proclamation of the Milanese government without first obtaining his consent.[40] It was reported that Mayer suggested to the police commissioner that police officials should wear the Austrian cockade,[41] and that the Austrians in Mantua were working hard to build up a pro-Austrian party.[42] The members of the Milanese regency were dismayed and immediately called upon Marquis Sommariva to ask him for an explanation of this new turn of events.[43] As a consequence of their spirited expostulations, Marshal Bellegarde notified Mayer that the civil affairs of Mantua were to remain solely under the direction of the provisional regency.[44]

The reports of the open propaganda of the Austrian party also annoyed the Italian officials. The prefect of the department of Mella wrote that Austrian emblems were being posted in many places in his department and that the Austrian military commander, who was obviously cognizant of what was happening, did nothing to interfere with the dissemination of pro-Austrian propaganda.[45] The prefect of Chiari referred to the fact that Austrian emblems were being posted in that place, and Count Verri, the president of the provisional regency, maintained that in Milan the Austrian troops were trying to substitute the Austrian cockade for the Italian.[46]

40 Letters of the provisional regency to deputation at Paris on May 5 and May 6, 1814, *Museo del Risorgimento*, Milan, *Carte Beccaria*, Busta I, Carte 8, Fasc. I, Nos. 21 and 23.

41 Provisional regency to deputation at Paris, Milano, May 10, 1814, *ibid.*, No. 28.

42 Electoral colleges to deputation at Paris, Milano, May 11, 1814, *ibid.*, No. 39.

43 Provisional regency to deputation at Paris, Milano, May 5, 1814, *ibid.*, No. 21.

44 Provisional regency to deputation at Paris, Milano, May 7, 1814, *ibid.*, No. 24.

45 Provisional regency to deputation at Paris, Milano, May 5, 1814, *ibid.*, No. 21.

46 Spadoni, *Il moto del 20 aprile, op cit*, 105. It should be noted that although Spadoni makes no attempt to separate the stories of the work of

To make matters worse, although some of the Austrian military officials apparently made no move to check the spread of pro-Austrian propaganda, they made determined efforts to check all attempts to proselyte the cause of independence among the Italian populace. As early as April 30, Count Strassoldo expressed deep concern over an article which had appeared on the previous day in the *Giornale italiano,*[47] asserting that the Austrians would conserve " that noble appearance which characterizes a nation, the first vote of which is for independence." [48] A few days later, the regency ordered printed and circulated in the kingdom a proclamation asserting that the " National Representation has manifested " to the Allied Powers " its vote for the independence of the Kingdom of Italy and for a Constitution, the liberal bases of which wisely counterbalance the respective powers " of government. " Spain, France, and Holland, on account of their recognition, bear witness that the magnanimity of the High Allied Powers has substituted, in a new kind of triumph, for the sanguinary glory of conquest, that more real and durable glory of re-establishing the felicity of Peoples through wise and liberal institutions." Since the example of these three countries showed that the Italian people could expect to obtain independence and a constitutional government from the Allies, they should remain " in that dignified position of calm which is befitting a People who await their destinies from the Nations of Europe, all of which come as and are loved as liberators." [49]

the Milanese provisional government, the manipulations of English and Austrian agents, and the activities of the Lombard deputation in Paris, he has made a good study of the period following the Milanese revolution. I have found his book quite helpful.

47 Letter to Bellegarde, *Staats-Archiv*, Vienna, *Kaiser Franz Akten*, Fasc. 27, Sect. 1, Fo. 53.

48 *Giornale italiano*, No. 119 (April 29, 1814), 482.

49 Proclamation, Milan, May 4, 1814, enclosed in Strassoldo to Bellegarde, Mailand, May 6, 1814, *Staats-Archiv*, Vienna, *Kaiser Franz Akten*, Fasc. 27, Sect. 1, Fo. 75.

When Count Strassoldo learned of the publication of this extremely liberal proclamation, before copies of it could be sent to the provinces, he hastened to call upon the provisional regency and vent his spleen upon those members who were present.[50] Sommariva, on his part, sent the Milanese government a note requesting its members " not to have anything published without first submitting it to him for his approval." [51] Mellerio went to Strassoldo to protest that the sole intention of the regency in having the proclamation printed was to moderate and calm public opinion, but Strassoldo turned a deaf ear to his arguments and absolutely refused to permit it to be posted.[52]

Ludovico Giovio, the president of the electoral colleges, also ran into difficulties with the Austrian officials when he tried to have some proclamations published. In spite of the protests of the Milanese government, he was given permission to have them printed only after such objectionable expressions as " constitutional " and " to the magnanimity of the British Nation " had been deleted from the text.[53]

It is no wonder that the members of the provisional regency complained that the Austrians were trying to extend their influence over the government in every conceivable manner. Habsburg agents had interfered with some of the appointments which the officials of the kingdom had made, had written directly to the ministers for information without prior consultation with the regency members, had given open encouragement to the intrigues of the pro-Austrian party, and had refused to

50 Provisional regency to deputation at Paris, Milano, May 6, 1814, *Museo del Risorgimento*, Milan, *Carte Beccaria*, Busta I, Carte 8, Fasc. I, No. 23.

51 Sommariva to provisional regency, Milano, May 6, 1814, enclosed in Strassoldo to Bellegarde, May 6, 1814, *Staats-Archiv*, Vienna, *Kaiser Franz Akten*, Fasc. 27, Sect. 1, Fo. 76.

52 Sitting of May 6, 1814, *Protocolli della reggenza provvisoria*, Brera Library. Also see Strassoldo to Bellegarde, Mailand, May 6, 1814, *Staats-Archiv*, Vienna, *Kaiser Franz Akten*, Fasc. 27, Sect. 1, Fo. 74.

53 Sitting of May 3, 1814, *Protocolli della reggenza provvisoria*, Brera Library; Electoral colleges to deputation at Paris, Milano, May 11, 1814, *Museo del Risorgimento*, Milan, *Carte Beccaria*, Busta I, Carte 8, Fasc. I, No. 39.

permit the provisional government to publish liberal proclamations. Sommariva even went so far as to order the members of the regency to make a clear distinction between the legislative and administrative authorities and not to execute anything which might fall under the first heading without consulting him in advance.[54] And Strassoldo brought pressure upon the members of the Milanese government to abolish the office of police directory and to concentrate its functions in the ministry of interior.[55] The members of the provisional regency were indignant at this seeming infringement on their affairs and wrote their deputation at Paris: " The Austrians are trying every day to extend their own influence in questions of public affairs and to despoil the provisional Government of that authority which has been conferred upon it by the National Representation and which was, moreover, confirmed by the High Allied Powers." [56]

Considerable dissatisfaction also arose over the lodging and maintenance of the Austrian officers and troops in the city of Milan. Although immediately after the arrival of Sommariva and Strassoldo in the capital on April 26, it was decreed that only the officers were to be quartered in private houses,[57] and although the conduct of these officers was, on the whole, courteous and above reproach,[58] there were so many of them in

54 Sommariva to Verri, Milano, May 3, 1814, *Staats-Archiv*, Vienna, *Kaiser Franz Akten*, Fasc. 27, Sect. 1, Fo. 67-8.

55 Strassoldo to Bellegarde, Mailand, May 3, 1814, *ibid.*, Fo. 63; Decree, Provisional regency, May 5, 1814, *Atti del governo lombardo, op. cit.*, 1814, 33. Strassoldo thought that Paolo de Capitani, who had been made minister of interior on April 24 (Decree, Provisional regency, Milano, April 24, 1814, *ibid*, 14.), could be counted upon to keep a much stricter supervision over the police than the former unreliable and inefficient police directory. Strassoldo to Bellegarde, Mailand, May 3, 1814, *Staats-Archiv*, Vienna, *Kaiser Franz Akten*, Fasc. 27, Sect 1, Fo. 63; Bellegarde to Kaiser Franz, May 9, 1814, *ibid.*, Fo 61.

56 Letter of May 6, 1814, *Museo del Risorgimento*, Milan, *Carte Beccaria*, Busta I, Carte 8, Fasc. I, No 23.

57 *Wiener Zeitung*, May 14, 1814, 538.

58 Pallavicini to Confalonieri, Milano, May 7, 1814, Gallavresi, *Confalonieri, op. cit*, I, 107.

Milan that giving them lodging caused considerable hardship.[59] Moreover, there were so few barracks for the soldiers that a large number of them were also quartered in private houses.[60]

The expenses of maintaining this large retinue of officers and troops were enormous. Mantovani estimated that it cost the government over ninety thousand lire per day.[61] The provisional regency complained that the cost was so great that it was " a war Contribution." [62] Count Verri lamented to Bellegarde that the maintenance of the Austrian troops was such a drain upon the finances of the state that it was wholly impossible for the government to continue to support them,[63] and begged the Austrian intendant, Baron Rossetti, to have the number of troops reduced. Rossetti, however, peremptorily dismissed the subject with the statement that " the army could not be put on a peace footing in a country which was considered as conquered." [64] There was no hope of alleviation. The expenses still continued.

As we have seen, within two weeks after their arrival in Milan, the Austrians had succeeded in irritating many of the members of the provisional government. In many cases, this unfortunate state of affairs was a result of lack of prudence and tact; in others, it was due to a conflict of authority. Strassoldo, Sommariva, and Bellegarde had been ordered to go to Milan to oversee the government and to keep peace and tranquillity until the supreme Allied councils would definitely pronounce

59 Teresa Confalonieri Casati wrote her husband on May 8 that there were over eight hundred officers, with a large retinue of horses and servants, in the city. *Ibid*, 109. In addition, there were about 15,000 troops. Provisional regency to deputation at Paris, Milano, May 9, 1814, *Museo del Risorgimento*, Milan, *Carte Beccaria*, Busta I, Carte 8, Fasc. I, No 27.

60 Mantovani estimated that six thousand soldiers were taken care of in this manner. *Mantovani Diario, op. cit.*, May 11, 1814, V, 262.

61 *Ibid.*

62 Letter to deputation at Paris, Milano, May 9, 1814, *Museo del Risorgimento*, Milan, *Carte Beccaria*, Busta I, Carte 8, Fasc. I, No. 27.

63 Provisional regency to deputation at Paris, May 9, 1814, *ibid.*, No. 26.

64 Verri to deputation at Paris, Milano, May 13, 1814, *ibid*, No 36.

themselves on the fate of the kingdom. They were the representatives of a nation whose arms had conquered the Kingdom
of Italy, and, as such, felt that their own authority was superior
to that of the hastily devised provisional regency. Moreover,
schooled as they were in the philosophy of Austrian conservatism, the three Austrian officials looked askance upon the
liberal proclamations which the members of the government
wished to issue to the Italian people. They felt that they would
serve only to stimulate mischief-makers to cause trouble.

Most of the members of the Milanese provisional government, on the other hand, belonged to the liberal factions. They
believed in the doctrines, considered so dangerous by the con-
servatives of the era, of liberalism and constitutionalism. They
ardently desired independence and constitutional government,
and had little respect for the conservative opinions of the Habsburg commissioners. Furthermore, they believed that the
supreme authority over the Kingdom of Italy was vested in
their hands. They had been assigned their duties by the Milanese
authorities during the course of the revolution of April 20, and
their position had been confirmed by the electoral colleges, the
members of which claimed that they represented the will of the
people of the kingdom. Since they had sent deputies to Marshal
Bellegarde asking him to send representatives to Milan to aid
them in keeping order, the members of the provisional government undoubtedly felt that the position of those commissioners
was secondary to their own.

Moreover, it appears that there was a considerable amount
of confusion, intrigue, and disorder within the provisional government itself. Teresa Confalonieri Casati, the wife of Federico
Confalonieri and herself an ardent supporter of the independence party, complained to her husband: " There is general discontent on account of all the half measures which are taken and
on account of the little uniformity of the orders which are sent
from the diverse authorities who are in command at this
moment." [65] Count Durini, the mayor of Milan, on May 10,

[65] Letter of May 11, 1814, Gallavresi, *Confalonieri, op. cit.*, I, 115.

handed in his resignation to the provisional regency, on the ground that "there are so many disorders which are following each other in the actual state of affairs that I now consider myself unable to carry out the functions which have been assigned to me or to oppose the disorders which are predicted to occur." [66]

The divided command and disorders to which Teresa Confalonieri and Durini referred appear to have been concentrated in the regency itself. The regency seems to have been permeated with intrigues and cabals.[67] Verri, the president, and Pino, the commander of all the military forces of the kingdom, both of whom were ardent liberals, were said to have become the masters of the government. The other members of the regency were merely their tools. Each was accused of engaging in various intrigues to get more power than the other and of exalting the idea of a powerful, independent kingdom with a constitutional head and a national legislature in order to win popular support.[68]

In the light of evidence such as the foregoing, it appears that some of the members of the Milanese provisional government may at times have been looking toward their own personal advancement in complaining about the interference of the Austrian commissioners in governmental affairs. Nevertheless, it seems that the regency, as a whole, was motivated chiefly by a sense of patriotism and by a desire to provide for the well-being of their country. The Austrian representatives, too, acted only

66 Quoted in Marchesi, *loc. cit.*, 166.

67 On May 11, 1814, Rasini wrote Confalonieri: "Our affairs are not going well. Cabals and intrigues are still the order of the day. The Regency does not live up to our expectations." Casati, *op. cit.*, II, 297. Two days later, Porro Lambertenghi wrote Confalonieri: "I do not speak of our internal cabals of the senators who were foiled, nor of the ambitions of some among us." Gallavresi, *Confalonieri, op. cit.*, I, 123. In referring to this remark, Gallavresi says that in all probability Porro was referring to Pino. See *ibid.*, 123 ftn.

68 Rasini to Confalonieri, Milano, May 11, 1814, Casati, *op. cit.*, II, 297-98; Alberico Felber to Confalonieri, Milano, May 2, 1814, *ibid.*, 295.

in accord with their instructions. The real reason for the quarrel between the members of the provisional government and the Austrian commissioners must be ascribed to a conflict of authority, and not to personal intrigues. No matter how conciliatory the members of the Milanese government, on the one hand, and the representatives of the Habsburgs, on the other, might have been, it is very probable that a certain amount of friction would have arisen between them.

CHAPTER X

ENGLISH INTRIGUES AND PUBLIC OPINION

On Sunday morning, April 24, Baron Sigismondo Trecchi arrived in Genoa at the headquarters of Lord William Bentinck, the commander-in-chief of the British forces in the Mediterranean. He brought with him dispatches from the Milanese communal council and from Mayor Durini, requesting Lord William to take measures to insure the tranquillity of the Kingdom of Italy and beseeching him to use his influence for the establishment of an independent kingdom with a liberal and constitutional government.[1]

The Milanese emissary was cordially received by Bentinck, who promised to send Lieutenant-General MacFarlane to Milan "to re-establish public order and tranquillity and to contribute to the happiness of the City of Milan."[2] MacFarlane was instructed to try to check both popular excesses against the

1 See *ante*, 132-34.

2 Bentinck to president of the Milanese communal council, Gênes, April 26, 1814, Lemmi, *La restaurazione austriaca, op cit.*, Appendix X, 407-8, Trecchi, *loc. cit.*, 538. According to Trecchi's own account to Durini, Bentinck promised to send MacFarlane to Milan "to examine the political state" of the country, and, on his own part, to endeavor to obtain his government's support for the claims of the Italians. Letter of April 25, 1814, Lemmi, *La restaurazione austriaca, op. cit.*, Appendix IX, 406-7, Trecchi, *loc. cit.*, 536-37. Either Bentinck was more enthusiastic in words than in writing or Trecchi allowed his eagerness to exaggerate the real nature of the reception which Bentinck had accorded him, for in his reply to the letter from the communal council, Bentinck confined himself to saying that which we quoted above. Furthermore, Bentinck wrote Castlereagh that he had sent MacFarlane to Milan "to act as mediator between the different parties and to recommend to all to await patiently the decision of the Allied Sovereigns." Letter of April 27, 1814, Gallavresi, "La rivoluzione e la politica inglese," *loc. cit.*, 126. And to Bellegarde he related that he had told MacFarlane "to employ whatever means of conciliation and persuasion seemed convenient to calm the effervescence of spirits and to engage all parties to await with calm and tranquillity the decision of the Allied Powers on the future fate of the Country." Letter sent from Genoa on May 1, 1814, *ibid.*, 138.

viceroy's partisans and vengeance on their part in case they should be successful in regaining their control of the kingdom, and " to advise all parties to await the decision of the Allied Powers."[3] Trecchi and MacFarlane left Genoa on the 26th and arrived in Milan on the following day.[4] On May 5, Mac-Farlane was joined by Sir Robert Wilson, the English attaché to the Austrian army, who had come down from the imperial headquarters at Verona.[5]

Besides Trecchi, there were several other Milanese who went to Bentinck to represent certain classes of persons or organizations other than the provisional government. A certain Bartolo Lamberti, carrying with him an address containing about eighty signatures, representing all the banking and the most important commercial houses of Milan,[6] came across Trecchi on the way and accompanied him to the city of Genoa. Lamberti had four audiences with Bentinck. In them Lord William assured him " that England would spontaneously protect the freedom of commerce," but he regretted that all the steps taken to bring about an independent Kingdom of Italy " have been made too late."[7]

On April 28, Soveri Latuada, a prominent Freemason and the intimate friend of General Pino, arrived in Genoa to procure Lord William's support for an independent kingdom. He handed Bentinck " letters from the communal council and from Pino" as well as a "representation signed by over three hundred persons from distinguished Milanese families." Bentinck, however, dismissed him in a peremptory manner, replying to his

3 The instructions are dated Genoa, April 26, 1814, Gallavresi, "La rivoluzione e la politica inglese," *loc. cit.*, 124.

4 Trecchi, *loc. cit.*, 539; Lemmi, *La restaurazione austriaca, op. cit.*, 211.

5 " Sir Robert Wilson came here yesterday." MacFarlane to Bentinck, Milan, May 6, 1814, Gallavresi, "La rivoluzione e la politica inglese," *loc. cit.*, 153.

6 Spadoni, "Le società segrete nella rivoluzione milanese dell'aprile 1814," *loc. cit.*, 203.

7 Note received by Ballabio on May 9, 1814, *Museo del Risorgimento*, Milan, *Carte Beccaria*, Busta I, Carte 8, Fasc. III, No. 15.

protestations "that it was too late and that, moreover, the Milanese have made the revolution not for independence, but to have the Austrians." [8] The plans of Lamberti, Latuada, and their friends failed to bear fruit. It was only Baron Trecchi's official mission from the provisional government which prompted Lord William to intervene in Milan by sending General MacFarlane thither to act as mediator among the various parties.

Upon his arrival in Milan on April 27, General MacFarlane was officially welcomed by a deputation composed of Mellerio and Borromeo. MacFarlane treated the two Milanese in a courteous manner. When Mellerio and Borromeo told him that the universal vote of the populace was for independence, he " did not hesitate to reply that this vote was inspired by their love for their country." Then he suggested that " among all the Princes, the most desirable one and the one who can be most easily obtained is Archduke Francis of Este." [9]

This demonstration of MacFarlane's liberalism, in addition to the fact that he was the representative of Lord William Bentinck, an avowed champion of liberalism, was enough to make many Milenese liberals regard him as a real "Messiah of Liberty." Soon " generals, statesmen, merchants, and persons from every social class " came to him to express their desires for independence and for " a constitutional head, independent of all foreign influence." [10]

A deputation from the electoral colleges was sent to the English general to express the desire of the colleges for " a free constitution, a good Prince, and boundaries extensive enough to facilitate the exportation of our territorial pro-

8 Quoted in Spadoni, "Le società segrete nella rivoluzione milanese dell' aprile 1814," *loc. cit.*, 201-2. Also see Spadoni, " Il processo per la congiura," *loc. cit.*, 86-7.

9 Sitting of April 29, 1814, *Protocolli originali della reggenza provvisoria*, Brera Library.

10 Mc. Farlane to Bentinck, Milano, April 29, 1814, Lemmi, *La restaurazione austriaca, op. cit.*, Appendix XVI, 418.

ducts." [11] In reply, MacFarlane assured the deputies that both Lord Bentinck and he had "a keen interest in the welfare of Italy" and "know that independence is the first good of a country." [12]

On April 30, the English representative in Milan received an address from the Milanese civic guard, which had been written by the Italian litterateur, Ugo Foscolo.[18] In it, the guard called for the establishment of a "powerful Country, a just Constitution," and an Italian "Prince who will promise to consecrate all his thoughts, strength, and blood to remedy Italy's misfortunes." [14] At the same time, General Pino handed MacFarlane a note addressed to Lord Bentinck, in which he made this appeal:

Your proclamation given at Leghorn has electrified the spirit of the Italians.

The Milanese have given the example, and breathe only Independence.

It is reserved for you, my Lord, and for England, to regenerate Italy, or at least a part of our countries.

The Italians offer their blood and their grateful hearts to you.

My Lord, do not abandon Italy.[15]

Representatives of private groups, as well as deputations from the government and the military forces, gravitated around Bentinck's representative in Milan to express their wishes in regard to the future of the Kingdom of Italy. On April 30, a

11 *Museo del Risorgimento*, Milan, *Carte Beccaria*, Busta I, Carte 8, Fasc. III, No. 29 This note was received by the deputation in Paris on May 17. A copy of this address, written in French and differing slightly from the copy in the *Carte Beccaria*, can also be found in Gallavresi, "La rivoluzione e la politica inglese," *loc. cit.*, 146.

12 *Museo del Risorgimento*, Milan, *Carte Beccaria*, Busta I, Carte 8, Fasc. III, No 29

13 Foscolo, "Lettera Apologetica," in *Opere complete di Ugo Foscolo*, *op. cit.*, I, 702.

14 Dated April 30, 1814, Foscolo, "Prose Politiche," in *ibid.*, II, 558-59.

15 Dated April 29, 1814, Gallavresi, "La rivoluzione e la politica inglese," *loc. cit.*, 137-38.

certain Cadolino, who professed to represent the college of merchants of Cremona, handed him a memorandum in which, along with the usual demands for independence and a constitution, the annexation of vast territories, including, among other places, Genoa, and ports on both the Adriatic and the Mediterranean, were demanded. Such an addition, it was asserted, " would render the Kingdom of Italy strong enough to balance Italian politics " and to enable " a flourishing commerce " to exist.[16] The merchants of Bergamo handed MacFarlane a more modest petition, asking merely for English protection, " freedom of commerce, and for a liberal constitution." [17] In Milan, a number of " pure Italians " hastened to obtain the signatures of three thousand persons to a memorial demanding an English king for Italy.[18] The petition was handed to General MacFarlane, who sent it to London.[19]

When General Wilson arrived in Milan, he, too, received a number of Milanese patriots and listened to their arguments in favor of Italian independence. A record of a few of these conferences is extant. Soon after his arrival, Tarsis and Peregalli, who were members of the provisional regency, went to him to compliment him in the name of that body. In their interview, these two men, among other things, asserted that " Europe owed to the generosity of England the re-establishment of that equilibrium which is going to be introduced in its political system." Thereupon, Wilson suggested that " the Kingdom of Italy would also figure in forming part of this equilibrium," and added that as late as the month of January the Austrian Emperor had promised the independence of Italy.[20] On the morning of May 7, while visiting Count Verri, Wilson again

16 *Ibid.*, 147-48.

17 *Ibid.*, 149-50.

18 Domenico Giovanelli to a friend, Milano, May 7, 1814, Pellini, *Pino, op. cit* , 51.

19 Borda to Battista, Milano, May 3, 1814, Gallavresi, *Carteggio di Borda, op cit.*, 48.

20 Quoted in Spadoni, *Il moto del 20 aprile, op. cit* , 120-21.

repeated in a positive manner the same statement in regard to the Austrian Emperor's promises which he had made to Tarsis and Peregalli.[21] In making this rash assertion, the English general was encouraging the Milanese liberals to believe that his government was promoting the creation of a new balance of power in Europe, in which independent, national states, with liberal governments, would be established to prevent Austria and France from becoming too strong. Wilson, as well as Bentinck and MacFarlane, was still working to bring into existence an independent, liberal state in northern Italy in order to strengthen Britain's political and economic influence in that region. This was certainly not what the British Foreign Office at this late date wanted its Italian representatives to do.

As we have seen, MacFarlane and Wilson lent a willing ear to all the pleas for independence which were made to them by various groups of Italians. Wilson had always been very sympathetic to the cause of liberalism and national independence. As an ardent champion of liberalism, he espoused the cause of Italian freedom in a spirited and determined manner long before he arrived in Milan. While still at Verona with the Austrian army, he had, on April 27, noted in his diary: " The state of this country . . . requires the most prompt attention and the wisest counsels. If the political establishment is not in harmony with public feeling, there will certainly be a general revolt. The Austrian Government is perhaps the most unpopular of all; for it is too poor to be liberal, and the manners of the Germans are at direct variance with Italian habits and character." [22] Holding such beliefs, the English general encouraged the " pure Italian " factions in Lombardy as much as he possibly could.

MacFarlane, on the other hand, asserted that prior to his arrival in Milan, he held opinions which were at least in part

21 Provisional regency to deputation at Paris, Milano, May 7, 1814, *Museo del Risorgimento*, Milan, *Carte Beccaria*, Busta I; Carte 8, Fasc. I, No. 24.

22 Wilson Diary, *op. cit.*, II, 360.

opposed to the cause of liberalism and independence.[23] If his statement was made in good faith, obviously the multifarious petitions which were presented to him caused him to change his sentiments within a few days after his arrival in the Lombard capital. At any rate, exactly one week after his arrival in Milan, he advised Castlereagh that if the decision of the Allies at Paris had " for its object the dismemberment of the Kingdom of Italy and the restitution of the diverse provinces to the sovereignty of their ancient masters, there is every reason to fear that seeds of discord will be sown and that this country will become the theater of new revolutions." [24] Regardless of what his original position may have been, by early May MacFarlane had become an avowed and ardent champion of Italian liberalism and independence.

Since Wilson and MacFarlane held such a liberal point of view, they would be expected to take sides with the provisional government in its opposition to some of the policies pursued by Strassoldo and Sommariva. MacFarlane, in fact, began interfering in the Austro-Italian quarrels immediately after his arrival in Milan. A day or two after he had come to the capital of the kingdom, when some persons came to MacFarlane to demand " that a British functionary should be associated with that of Austria to assist the Provisional Government till the fate of Italy is decided," the British agent immediately supported their contention, and advised his superior in Genoa that " not only for the Kingdom of Italy, but for the Piedmont, British as well as Austrian Commissaries should be nominated." [25]

23 On April 29, 1814, MacFarlane wrote Bentinck· " You know me to possess sentiments which are more favourable to absolute power than to perfect Independence." Gallavresi, " La rıvoluzione e la politica inglese," *loc. cit.*, 135.

24 Letter of May 4, 1814, Lemmi, *La restaurazione austriaca, op. cit*, Appendix XVII, 421-22.

25 MacFarlane to Bentinck, Milan, April 29, 1814, Gallavresi, " La rivoluzione e la politica inglese," *loc. cit.*, 135. An Italian translation of this letter can also be found in Lemmi, *La restaurazıone austriaca, op. cit*, Appendix XVI, 418-19.

Later MacFarlane and Wilson took a more active part in supporting the provisional regency in its opposition to the actions of the Austrian generals. When Pino informed them of the suppression of the proclamation referring to the liberal constitutions that had been granted to other European countries,[26] Wilson hastened to assure him that he could find nothing in the proclamation that should displease any of the Allied Powers, and MacFarlane, on his part, went to Strassoldo to try to influence him to permit its publication.[27] When the two generals were advised of the fact that Sommariva had written directly to the ministers for information,[28] they "declared openly that the conduct of the Austrians evidently tended to usurp exclusive power over this Country," and asked General Pino to launch a determined protest against this usurpation of the powers of the provisional government.[29]

After General Pino's departure, MacFarlane and Wilson went directly to Sommariva to advise him "to pursue a delicate and conciliatory system of administration in his relations with the Regency." Sommariva plainly showed his displeasure at this interference, replying that "he had his instructions from Marshal Bellgarde" [sic] and asking whether Bentinck, under whose instructions they were acting, was not under the orders of the Austrian commander-in-chief. MacFarlane showed him his instructions and added that he had been told "to promote conciliation & harmony amongst all parties." He told the Austrian commissioners that if "that end could be obtained by no others [sic] means," he "should be forced to the necessity

26 See ante, 152-53.

27 Provisional regency to deputation at Paris, Milano, May 6, 1814, Museo del Risorgimento, Milan, Carte Beccaria, Busta I, Carte 8, Fasc. I, No. 23; MacFarlane to Bentinck, Milan, May 6, 1814, Gallavresi, "La rivoluzione e la politica inglese," loc. cit., 160; Strassoldo to Bellegarde, Mailand, May 6, 1814, Staats-Archiv, Vienna, Kaiser Franz Akten, Fasc. 27, Sect. 1, Fo. 74-8.

28 See ante, 149.

29 Provisional regency to deputation at Paris, Milano, May 6, 1814, Museo del Risorgimento, Milan, Carte Beccaria, Busta I, Carte 8, Fasc. I, No. 23.

of protesting officially against any measures in [*sic*] the part of the Austrian Authorities which should have for their object the annihilation of the Provisional Regency." According to MacFarlane's relation, "this declaration had its effect, & M. Sommariva said he would be happy to avail himself of" his "counsel & assistance in whatever might relate to the interests of the common cause." [30]

MacFarlane and Wilson apparently did not confine their efforts merely to making protests over alleged Austrian interference in Italian affairs, but actually seem to have encouraged the Italians to resist the Austrian commissioners. In his fragmentary memoirs, Count Giovio, the president of the electoral colleges, insinuated that, in a remarkable conference which he had with General MacFarlane, the latter mysteriously attempted to incite him to offer a spirited resistance to the Austrians. MacFarlane intimated that the Italians should appeal directly to Lord Castlereagh. Although Castlereagh "was far from being a liberal man" and had "principles quite contrary to the spirit of the century," Bentinck's emissary in Milan asserted that if he refused to act upon the votes of the people, another parliament would shortly be called together and an appeal could be sent directly to it.[31] These were strange words from a man who was supposedly representing the British Foreign Office.

Wilson and MacFarlane suggested that the provisional regency could counteract any influence which the Austrians might have by means of a national plebiscite. Such a vote, they assured the regency, would demonstrate to the Allied Powers that the majority of the people actually wanted independence.[32]

30 MacFarlane to Bentinck, Milan, May 6, 1814, Gallavresi, "La rivoluzione e la politica inglese," *loc. cit.*, 160.

31 Gallavresi, "Giovio," *loc. cit.*, 242-43. Also see Gallavresi, "La rivoluzione e la politica inglese," *loc. cit.*, 148.

32 Provisional regency to deputation at Paris, Milano, May 9, 1814, *Museo del Risorgimento*, Milan, *Carte Beccaria*, Busta I, Carte 8, Fasc. I, No. 26; MacFarlane to Bentinck, Milan, May 9, 1814, Gallavresi, "La rivoluzione e la politica inglese," *loc. cit.*, 162.

" If the vote of the Italian Nation for its independence were
officially made known to England," Wilson declared a few days
later, " this country would by all means interpose its mediation
between the Other Powers to sustain it, since this vote was
conformable with the liberal views and also with the interests
of Great Britain." [33]

The encouragement which the two British representatives
gave to the liberal factions made them very popular among wide
circles of Milanese society. Baron Huegel, in describing the
eagerness with which many of the inhabitants of the capital
were expecting Bentinck's arrival in the city, noted in his
diary: " It is the Messiah who must be re-establishing the
Kingdom of God in Italy who is expected." [34] Alberico Felber
advised Confalonieri that MacFarlane " was exciting " such a
" large party in his favor " that " every time he is presented
at the theater there is repeated and remarkably loud applause,
whereas there is none for Sommariva." [35] And General Pino
remarked to the other members of the provisional regency on
May 1 that the applause which was given " to the English
General on the previous evening and this morning was such as
to demonstrate a decided partiality for them [the English],
which must be badly received on the part of the Austrians." [36]

General Pino surmised correctly when he guessed that Mac-
Farlane's cordial reception by many Milanese was ill received
by the Habsburg officials in Milan. Strassoldo seized upon the
fact that MacFarlane had received more applause at the Scala
theater than the Austrians as proof that he was not in Milan as
" a disinterested spectator," [37] and complained bitterly that

33 Verri to deputation at Paris, Milano, May 13, 1814, *Museo del
Risorgimento*, Milan, *Carte Beccaria*, Busta I, Carte 8, Fasc. I, No. 36.

34 Huegel Diary, *op cit*, May 12, 1814, 99.

35 Letter of May 2, 1814, Casati, *op. cit.*, II, 296.

36 Sitting of May 1, 1814, *Protocolli della reggenza provvisoria*, Brera
Library.

37 Strassoldo to Bellegarde, Mailand, April 30, 1814, *Staats-Archiv*, Vienna,
Kaiser Franz Akten, Fasc. 27, Sect. 1, Fo. 55.

MacFarlane's presence in Milan had a very pernicious effect upon public opinion.[38] Bellegarde expressed himself as fearing that MacFarlane's actions served only to give new hope to the independence party which existed in the kingdom,[39] and Baron Huegel noted in his diary: " In concert with Vilson [*sic*], he [MacFarlane] is working upon the public spirit and is making the members of the provisional government believe that they are a kind of sovereign." [40]

The Austrians, however, did not long have to suffer the presence of the British emissaries in Milan. As soon as Castlereagh received word that Bentinck had sent MacFarlane to Milan, he hastened to advise him: "With respect to the measures to be adopted in regard to the Milanese, I do not wish your lordship to continue General M'Farlane [*sic*] there, now the Austrians have advanced. It may complicate injuriously the concerns of Italy, any interference on the part of your lordship, placed at such a distance as you are from the seat of the Allied Councils; and I am desirous that your lordship should not take any steps to encourage the fermentation which at present seems to prevail in Italy, on questions of Government." [41] The next day he continued: " In Italy, it is now the more necessary to abstain, if we wish to act in concert with Austria and Sardinia. Whilst we had to drive the French out of Italy, we were justified in running all risks; but the present state of Europe requires no such expedient; and, with a view to general peace and tranquillity, I should prefer seeing the Italians await the insensible influence of what is going on elsewhere, than hazard their own internal quiet by an effort at this moment." [42]

This last letter gives a clue to the British government's Italian policy. During the years preceding Napoleon's overthrow, the

38 Letter to Bellegarde, May 3, 1814, *ibid.*, Fo. 62-3.

39 Letter to Emperor Francis, Mailand, May 9, 1814, *ibid.*, Fo. 60.

40 Huegel Diary, *op. cit.*, May 9, 1814, 98.

41 Letter sent from Paris on May 6, 1814, Castlereagh Correspondence, *op. cit.*, X, 15.

42 Letter of May 7, 1814, *ibid.*, 18.

Foreign Office had found it expedient to encourage liberal and national movements, in Italy as well as in other places under French domination, as excellent weapons against the French Emperor. Now that the war was over Lord Castlereagh turned his back upon liberalism and nationalism. True to his principles of conservatism, he aimed to discourage any experimentation which might provoke further revolution or warfare. As he warned Lord Bentinck, although " a great moral change " was " coming on in Europe " and although " the principles of freedom " were " in full operation," the " danger is that the transition may be too sudden to ripen into anything likely to make the world better or happier. We have new constitutions launched in France, Spain, Holland, and Sicily. Let us see the result before we encourage further attempts." [43]

When Bentinck received Castlereagh's orders, he left Genoa for Milan and reached there on the 14th of May. Upon his arrival, accompanied by MacFarlane and Wilson, he paid a visit to the president of the provisional regency. There he showed Verri his instructions, but advised him not to be too much discouraged. He told him that he would immediately send General MacFarlane to Paris and London, and intimated that MacFarlane would personally inform the members of the British government of the desires of the Milanese.[44] On May 15, MacFarlane left Milan to proceed to Paris and London.[45] His departure was followed by that of Bentinck on the 16th,[46] and that of Wilson on the 20th.[47]

English agents were no longer in Milan to stir up the hopes of the independence parties, but they had left too late to prevent irreparable mischief and no little embarrassment for the British

---

[43] Quoted in Webster, *Castlereagh, op. cit.*, 286.

[44] Verri to deputation at Paris, Milano, May 14, 1814, *Museo del Risorgimento*, Milan, *Carte Beccaria*, Busta I, Carte 8, Fasc. I, No. 48.

[45] Huegel Diary, *op. cit.*, May 15, 1814, 100-1. Also see Lemmi, *La restaurazione austriaca, op. cit.*, 258.

[46] Huegel Diary, *op. cit.*, May 16, 1814, 101.

[47] *Ibid.*, May 20, 1814, 102.

Foreign Office.   It is true that MacFarlane, Wilson, and Bentinck had acted wholly contrary to the intentions of both the Allied Powers and the British cabinet, but many persons thought that they were following the instructions of their government.   At Paris, Castlereagh was repeatedly called upon to explain the doings of the three gentlemen to Metternich and Emperor Francis, as well as to the Italian deputation. To the latter he frankly admitted:

> I think that the first duty of an honest and enlightened cabinet is to deceive neither individuals nor nations. I would deceive you if I should promise to support your cause. I must frankly confess that our military officials many times hold a direction and language not analogous to that of the cabinet.[48]

The British representatives justified their actions in Milan on the ground that an overwhelming majority of the people longed for an independent and constitutional government. All three of them expressed themselves emphatically upon this subject. MacFarlane wrote Bentinck two days after his arrival in the city that the Milanese " consider England as their Guardian Angel," and " look to Austria with dread and dismay." [49] A few days later he wrote that " among the ancient nobility there are several who would voluntarily wish to have the old Austrian provincial government restored, because it had a mild, economical, and paternal system of administration, but even they prefer, together with all the other social classes, a constitution, a prince, and a government perfectly independent of any other country, if it is possible." [50] And still later he asserted: " The

48 Report of the deputies at Paris to Verri, Paris, May 15, 1814, Bianchi, *op. cit.*, I, 340.

49 Letter of April 29, 1814, Gallavresi, " La rivoluzione e la politica inglese," *loc. cit.*, 135, Lemmi, *La restaurazione austriaca, op. cit.*, Appendix XVI, 418-19.

50 To Bentinck, Milano, May 4, 1814, Lemmi, *La restaurazione austriaca, op. cit.*, Appendix XVII, 420.

Italians, your Lordship may rest assured, would receive a British Prince unanimously." [51]

Wilson was just as emphatic as MacFarlane in insisting that nearly all the people in Milan wanted independence. On May 7, he noted in his diary: " The Austrian party is limited to some few chamberlains of the court and two or three Toisons d'Or." [52] And on May 6, he wrote to Castlereagh: " Independence is the unequivocal demand of the men of letters, the army and the People." [53] Lord Bentinck expressed himself in a similar vein. On May 1, he wrote: " These Italians have fallen into most unlucky hands, for they hate the Austrians & I am fearful if the same odious conduct is pursued in Milan & Piedmont as in Verona, the present popular Govt. may possibly break out into positive violence against them. In proportion as they are hated, so is the British name invariably treated with enthusiastick [sic] respect." [54]

MacFarlane, Wilson, and Bentinck were obviously prejudiced opponents of the Austrians and very strong supporters of the advanced Italian liberal factions. Strassoldo, Sommariva, and Bellegarde, the three Austrian officials in Milan, expressed opinions on the nature of Milanese public opinion which differed from those of the English agents, but Sommariva and Bellegarde admitted the existence of an appreciable amount of sentiment in favor of an independent kingdom. Strassoldo asserted that " a rather considerable group of persons, mindful of the prosperity which they had in the former Austrian Lombardy, wish once more to become subjected to the mild Austrian scepter." Another party desired an independent kingdom, " with an Austrian archduke as its independent prince." Excepting the French party, which was almost completely negligible, the

51 Letter to Bentinck, Milan, May 6, 1814, Gallavresi, "La rivoluzione e la politica inglese," *loc. cit*, 153.

52 Wilson Diary, *op. cit.*, II, 364-65.

53 Gallavresi, "La rivoluzione e la politica inglese," *loc. cit.*, 152.

54 Letter to Castlereagh, *ibid.*, 140.

smallest party in Milan, Strassoldo maintained, was the English party, " the members of which were mainly tradespeople." [55]

Strassoldo judged that " in general the people and the nobility are, with the exception of a few exalted heads, well disposed towards Austria," [56] but Sommariva admitted that a large number of people wanted " an independent constitutional government " with " an Austrian prince as sovereign." [57] Bellegarde, too, maintained that there was a general desire on the part of the Lombards to be ruled by a prince of the Habsburg house.[58] " Hatred of the French," he observed, " has decidedly manifested itself. Everywhere there is satisfaction over the good fortune of being freed from their yoke; but at the same time, as the idea is supported and nourished by foreign influence, the wish to remain independent is becoming more prominent." [59] The Austrian general was greatly perturbed by the growth of a spirit of partisanship in Milan. " The people desire and like us," he wrote Metternich, " but there are several factions in which we inspire anxiety and fear." [60] These factions, Bellegarde charged, acted already as if they thought that " the fate of the kingdom rested in their hands." [61]

The observations of both the English and the Austrian representatives, although differing much in minor details, bear witness to the fact that a large number of Milanese in late April and May, 1814, desired the creation of an independent Kingdom of Italy with some form of constitutional govern-

---

55 Strassoldo to Bellegarde, Mailand, April 30, 1814, *Staats-Archiv*, Vienna, *Kaiser Franz Akten*, Fasc. 27, Sect. 1, Fo. 49-50.

56 Strassoldo to Bellegarde, Mailand, May 3, 1814, *ibid.*, Fo. 62.

57 Sommariva to Bellegarde, Mailand, April 28, 1814, *Kriegs-Archiv*, Vienna, *Feld Akten (Italien)*, 1814, Fasc. 4, No. 226.

58 Bellegarde to Kaiser Franz, Verona, April 28, 1814, *ibid.*, ad No. 229½.

59 Bellegarde to Kaiser Franz, Mailand, May 9, 1814, *ibid.*, Fasc. 5, No. 35½.

60 Letter of May 9, 1814, Lemmi, *La restaurazione austriaca, op. cit.*, Appendix XIX, 423.

61 Bellegarde to Kaiser Franz, Mailand, May 9, 1814, *Staats-Archiv*, Vienna, *Kaiser Franz Akten*, Fasc. 27, Sect. 1, Fo. 60.

ment. The various proclamations which the electoral colleges and the provisional regency made, the instructions which they gave to their deputies in Paris, and the manner in which they expressed themselves before both the Austrian and the English officials demonstrate that the majority of the members of the provisional government were heartily in favor of creating an independent and constitutional government. The friendly reception which so many Milanese accorded to MacFarlane and Wilson shows that many of them welcomed their liberal ideas. The fact that addresses demanding an independent government were sent to the central government from the municipal bodies of many cities, towns, and hamlets [62] reveals that the independence movement was not confined wholly to the capital of the kingdom. The " pure Italian " party had a large following in Milan, as well as in other parts of Lombardy, particularly among the middle class and intellectual circles. Just how numerous its adherents were can perhaps never be accurately estimated. It can only be said that among the " politically active " classes of the population, they appeared to be much stronger than the factions which were content with a mere restoration of the old Austrian regime like that which had existed before the French Revolution.

It should be noted that the ranks of the " pure Italian " party were not entirely filled with persons working for the cause of Italian unification. Many people were influenced by a narrow " Lombard " program. When they used the terms " national liberty " and " national customs " in their various addresses to the Austrian and English agents in Milan and to the Milanese people, they had in mind the liberty and independence of Lombardy, rather than that of the Italian people as a whole. The concept of an Italian national group appears to have meant little to them in 1814. A large number of Milanese liberals were satisfied with obtaining " Lombard independence," and did not

62 Verri to Giovio, May 4, 1814, Gallavresi, " Testimonianze tratte dalle carte Giovio per la storia dei fatti del 1814," loc cit., 134.

concern themselves with the unification of the entire Italian nationality into a single, large state.

Some Lombards, though, acted and thought in terms of an "Italian" rather than just a "Lombard" nationalism. They were filled with an ardent longing to accomplish the unification and independence of the whole Apennine peninsula and not merely that of their own particular locality. Those who seconded Joachim Murat's intrigues definitely desired to bring about the creation of a powerful kingdom extending from the Alps to Sicily, which was to be under the control of the King of Naples. Most of the members of the secret societies, too, seem to have thought in terms of the whole Italian nation. And those persons who had been influenced by the writings of such propagandists as Alfieri, Gioia, Cuoco, Monti, and Barzoni, were stirred by a genuine Italian patriotism. It appears, however, that in the spring of 1814, this group was not so large in Lombardy as the liberal faction which was primarily interested in securing merely Lombard independence.

Although in the late spring of 1814, the various liberal and national groups were not so large in the Venetian departments as in Lombardy, there was a considerable amount of dissatisfaction with the existing provisional Austrian regime and a noticeable sentiment in favor of independence in the Venetian territory. In various parts of the Venetian *terra firma,* and especially in the mountain districts, the bad crops of the preceding year and the high taxes and heavy military requisitions exacted from them first by the French and then by the Austrians left many people almost completely destitute.[63] Since as early as May, 1814, the wine and fruit crops for the year were considered a complete loss and the prospects for a good grain crop appeared poor,[64] the Venetians saw little chance of their condition being improved in the near future.

63 Hager Reports, as summarized in the *Staats-Conferenz* Protocol of June 26, 1814, *Staats-Archiv*, Vienna, *Conferenz Akten*, Ser. b, 1814, No. 1143; Hager to *Staats-Conferenz*, June 7, 1814, *ibid.*, No. 1163; Hager Report, July 13, 1814, *ibid.*, No. 1388; Wiedemann-Warnhelm, *op. cit.*, 47, 67.

64 Hager to *Staats-Conferenz*, June 17, 1814, *Staats-Archiv*, Vienna, *Conferenz Akten*, Ser. b, 1814, No. 1174.

Most of the inhabitants of the Venetian *terra firma* were still as impoverished in May, 1814, as they had been when the Austrians first occupied the country in October of the preceding year. Many of them blamed the Austrians for their plight and made increasingly loud demands for the alleviation of those oppressions and grievances which they held responsible for their poverty. The most bitter complaints of the population were about the heavy taxes, forced military contributions, and compulsory loans which the Habsburg authorities continued to levy upon the population even after the military campaign against the French had ended in April, 1814. It was maintained that all the old French exactions were still continued and that the Austrians had added new ones. Landowners complained that they paid more in taxes and contributions to the Austrian government than the total revenue from their land during the preceding year. Other people complained that the exactions levied upon them were still so heavy and that the tax collectors were still so harsh and relentless in fulfilling their duties after the end of the war that they were left almost penniless after paying what was demanded of them by the officials.[65]

The continued arrogance and cruelty of Austrian officers and soldiers in Italy, already obnoxious to many Venetians in the winter of 1813/14, also irritated many people. It was charged by many Venetians that the Austrians considered Italy an enemy country, and that they frequently offended and mistreated the inhabitants.[66] The continued existence of the old provisional government and the apparent failure of the Austrians to make seriously needed administrative changes in any reason-

65 Hager Reports of May 17, June 7, and June 17, 1814, *ibid*, Nos. 1102, 1163, and 1174; Hager Report, May 23, 1814, *Staats-Archiv*, Vienna, *Kabinets-Akten*, 1814, No. 1583.

66 Hager Report, May 17, 1814, *Staats-Archiv*, Vienna, *Conferenz Akten*, Ser. b, 1814, No. 1102; Hager Report, May 23, 1814, *Staats-Archiv*, Vienna, *Kabinets-Akten*, 1814, No. 1583.

able period of time annoyed many people.[67] Since no definite
pronouncement had yet been made on the fate of the country,
many Venetians felt that their future status would not be
definitely determined until the Congress of Vienna was held.[68]
The fact that in over six months of Austrian rule many of the
hated officials of the former French regime, accused as they
were of officiousness, harshness, and dishonesty, had not yet
been dismissed vexed many Venetians,[69] and the actions of
Governor Reuss-Plauen's chief assistant, Count Thurn, described as a man " hated by the whole world," and charged
with being haughty and proud and with having the governor
completely under his control, angered them.[70]

Since many of the inhabitants of the Venetian provinces
were very much dissatisfied with the Austrian regime and held
it responsible for their poverty and misery, it is not surprising
to find that there was a fairly large group of people among
them who wanted a government that would be independent of
all Austrian influence. The Venetian " citizen," Cicogna, on
May 9, 1814, noted in his diary that since it appeared that the
Austrians would not restore the Venetian Republic, the common
wish of the Venetian people was to have " a prince of the House

67 Report to Raab, Venice, July 16, 1814, *Carte segrete ed atti ufficiali
della polizia austriaca in Italia dal 4 giugno 1814 al 22 marzo 1848* (Torino,
1851-52), I, 22; *Staats-Kabinet* Protocol, sitting of June 29, 1814, *Staats-
Archiv*, Vienna, *Kabinets-Akten*, 1814, No. 1583. The *Staats-Kabinet* maintained that one of the chief reasons for the slowness in making necessary
changes in Venetia was that every little detail had to be reported to the
Emperor. Since the Emperor was usually away from Vienna, the *Staats-
Kabinet* explained, this could not be done without a considerable loss of
time. *Ibid.*

68 Hager Report, June 30, 1814, *Staats-Archiv*, Vienna, *Conferenz Akten*,
Ser. b, 1814, No. 1281.

69 Hager Reports of May 17, June 17, and July 16, 1814, *ibid.*, Nos. 1102,
1174, and 1407.

70 Hager Report, May 17, 1814, *ibid.*, 1102; Hager Reports of May 11,
and May 23, 1814, *Staats-Archiv*, Vienna, *Kabinets-Akten*, 1814, Nos. 1551
and 1583.

of Austria reign in a Venetian State " that would be " independent from the Austrian Emperor." [71]

The Austrian government did not fail to recognize a desire for independence among many inhabitants of the Venetian departments. In his reports of May 5 and May 7, 1814, to the Austrian central police directory, Baron von Raab, the Austrian police director in the Italian provinces, wrote that there was a large party in the Venetian territory which wished a restoration of the old republic, although he added that their " wishes are not of such a nature as to cause alarm." [72] He was disturbed by the activities of the Freemasons in various parts of Venetia, and particularly in Verona, and maintained that they were gaining proselytes for the so-called " English party " every day.[73]

On May 12, Governor Reuss-Plauen reported to Baron Hager, the president of the aulic police directory, that "the hope of a rebirth of the Venetian Republic has not yet been suppressed among the members of the aristocracy." This hope, Reuss said, " has been strengthened by the assertions of English seamen that Venice will not remain with Austria." [74]

Baron Hager also expressed alarm over the liberal spirit prevailing in certain parts of Venetia. He asserted that the English, especially after Lord Bentinck's proclamation about the restoration of the old Genoese Republic in late April, 1814, had stirred up a strong party in favor of independence in the Venetian departments, as well as in Lombardy. The Freemasons and other persons strongly influenced by English propaganda were openly working for the independence of the country, which

71 Cicogna Diary, *loc. cit.*, 217.

72 As summarized in the Hager Report of May 17, 1814, *Staats-Archiv*, Vienna, *Conferenz Akten*, Ser. b, 1814, No. 1102.

73 Raab to Hager, Padua, June 25, 1814, *Archivio di Stato*, Milan, *Atti segreti*, 1814, Busta I, No. 65.

74 As summarized in Hager to *Staats-Conferenz*, June 2, 1814, *Staats-Archiv*, Vienna, *Conferenz Akten*, Ser. b, 1814, No. 1152.

was to be under the protection of the English.[75] The English consul in Venice, Hager declared, was using his influence to encourage the idea of Venetian independence. Since the Venetians were not yet certain what the fate of their country would be, and since those in favor of independence were thus encouraged by the British, a rather considerable number of Venetians, particularly among the nobility, hoped " for the restoration of the Republic." [76] From the reports of the Austrian officials it seems that not only in Lombardy but also in Venice there was considerable sentiment in favor of independence in the late spring of 1814.

75 Hager Report, June 7, 1814, *Staats-Archiv*, Vienna, *Kabinets-Akten*, 1814, No 1603.

76 Hager Report, July 8, 1814, *Staats-Archiv*, Vienna, *Conferenz Akten*, Ser. b, 1814, No. 1346.

CHAPTER XI

THE MILANESE DEPUTATION AT PARIS

" THE undersigned," in regard to " the partitions agreed upon " in " the secret treaty signed at Prague on the 27th of July, 1813," and " in consequence of the fact that the plan established by articles No. 4, 9, 10, 14, 23, 25, 30, and 32 of the said treaty ought to have taken place in Italy as well as in Germany, is authorized in the name of his Court to communicate to Your Excellency, in the form of a secret protest, that His Imperial and Royal Majesty is firm in his intentions of not relinquishing that which was stipulated in the said articles of the same treaty relative to Italian affairs." In this manner begins a letter which Prince Metternich is alleged to have sent to Lord Castlereagh on May 26, 1814, and which was published in Nicomede Bianchi's *Storia documentata della diplomazia europea in Italia dall'anno 1814 all'anno 1861* (1865-72).[1] In almost identically the same way, with only a few inconsequential changes in wording, reads the beginning of another letter which is supposed to have been sent to Castlereagh on March 26, 1814, and which was published in Cesare Cantù's *Il principe Eugenio, memorie del Regno d'Italia* (1880).[2]

Both letters, tallying almost perfectly in wording,[3] then proceed to stipulate the secret terms in regard to Italy which were supposedly agreed upon at Prague. In the 4th, 9th, and 10th articles of the Treaty of Prague, read the words, " the supreme direction and definite organization " of Italian affairs were, " with the exception of the ancient States belonging to the king

---

1 Vol. I, 333-34.

2 Vol. IX, 158-60. The name of the supposed writer of this letter is not given, but the context of the letter indicates that the supposed writer of the alleged letter was Metternich.

3 Some of the few minor differences which exist in the wording of the two letters are probably due to the fact that while the letter in Bianchi is in French, the one in Cantù is written in Italian. Where there is disagreement, the writer's translation follows the letter included in Bianchi.

of Sardinia, reserved to H. I. and R. M. [His Imperial and Royal Majesty], in concert with the Cabinet of St. James." In Article 12 it was stipulated that " the House of Austria has an incontestable right " to the papal states " as King of Rome as well as in its position of hereditary emperor and head of the German Empire." [4]

Articles 23 and 24 " partially assigned to H. I. and R. M. [His Imperial and Royal Majesty] the territory known under the name of the kingdom of Italy, including the States of Genoa and Parma, which were to be disposed of in favor of a prince of his family. The duchy of Modena, Reggio, and Massa-Carrara, which belongs to the house of Este, and the territories of the ancient principality of Lucca and Piombino, which were to be given to the Grand-Duke of Tuscany, were, however, to be exempted from the provisions of these articles." The Illyrian provinces were to be incorporated directly into the Austrian Empire, according to Article 25. In Article 30, it was alleged in the letters, " England confirmed in advance everything that Austria would wish to do in Italy, and promised to engage the Allied Powers, at the general peace, likewise to recognize the partitions which have been made in the definitive plan on this subject." And in Article 32 it was " recognized that the Italian States, with the exception of Piedmont, . . . will be given to Austria as conquered countries." [5]

It is from these two letters that the myth arose, which has been accepted by nearly all the Italian and many other writers,[6] that at Prague England gave Austria a free hand in Italy. Evidence, however, indicates that the documents were nothing but an out-and-out forgery. In the first place, the fact that in spite of almost identical wording the two documents bear

[4] Both letters use the expression, "its position of hereditary emperor and head of the German Empire."

[5] Bianchi, *op. cit*, I, 333-34.

[6] Even Francesco Lemmi, in his *La restaurazione austriaca, op. cit.*, 219, and Freiherr von Helfert, in his *Kaiser Franz, op. cit.*, 1, have accepted this myth. Many other writers have accepted without question the statement that England gave Austria a free hand in Italy in the secret treaty of Prague.

different dates would tend to make one distrustful. Further-more, a few sections of the letters are suspiciously inaccurate. Contrary to the implications in Articles 23 and 24, Lucca and Piombino never formed a part of the Kingdom of Italy, and there is no evidence besides these two letters to support the thesis that the Habsburgs ever wished or were ever promised the incorporation of Genoa in their extensive domains. Then, too, so far as the writer knows, no other documents referring to these secret articles supposedly composed at Prague have ever been found.[7] On the other hand, he has found several sources which seem to demonstrate conclusively that the fate of some of the countries allegedly promised to Austria in the secret articles of this treaty, and notably that of the territory now under consideration, Lombardy, was not decided until long after July, 1813.

At the conference at Prague, in July, 1813, an effort was made to get Napoleon's consent to a peace project which had been formulated by the Allied Powers. The concessions which the Allies, this time with the full approval of the British govern-ment, agreed to demand from the French Emperor in case he would not consent to an immediate peace were the same as those which Prussia and Russia had proposed to the Austrian

7 Charles K. Webster, the British historian, in referring to the document in Bianchi, says: "The document itself shows by internal evidence its falsity, and the British and Austrian archives and all the rest of the cor-respondence of these years prove conclusively that no such treaty was made." In his *Castlereagh, op cit.*, 286. The Italian historian, Giuseppe Gallavresi, asserts that the complete silence of the archives in Vienna, Berlin, and London "seems to take away all faith in a supposed treaty, the existence of which, moreover, appears to be incompatible with the attitude of the representatives of the allied powers in Italy for a considerable time after-wards." In his "La rivoluzione e la politica inglese," *loc. cit.*, 99 ftn. Albert Sorel, the profound and careful French scholar on the diplomacy of the Revolutionary and Napoleonic eras, declares that he found no traces of any such treaty in either the British Record Office or in the Berlin and Vienna archives. In his *L'Europe et la révolution française* (5th ed., Paris, 1885-1904), VIII, 162 ftn. The present writer has been unable to discover any documentary evidence of the existence of this secret treaty in the Viennese or the Milanese archives or in any published sources.

government on May 16, and which had been agreed upon by
Russia, Prussia, and Austria in the Treaty of Reichenbach, of
June 27, 1813.[8] In these negotiations, it was agreed that the
Confederation of the Rhine was to be dissolved, Holland was
to be separated from France, the Bourbons were to be restored
in Spain, and the French were to be forced to give up all the
territory which they held on the right bank of the Rhine. Of
more importance to our own story, the Austrians were promised
the restoration of all the territories which they had possessed
in 1805 in Italy and in Germany. In addition, it was stipulated
that the whole of Italy was to be freed from French control and
influence.[9] The promise of the return to Austria of all the
territories which she had held in both Italy and Germany in
1805 was confirmed by the secret articles appended to the
Treaty of Toeplitz, of September 9, 1813.[10] In 1805, Austria's
territorial possessions in Italy *were limited to the Venetian
provinces.* The Venetian territory, first occupied by Austrian
troops in October, 1813, was definitely promised to the Habsburgs by the Allied Powers in the summer of 1813, but the fate
of Austria's former Lombard provinces was still left undecided.

The Habsburgs seem to have been fully satisfied with the
stipulations in regard to Italy which had been made at Prague
and Toeplitz. On September 24, 1813, Aberdeen wrote Castlereagh that Metternich had told him " that in the event of the
success of the Allied armies, the line of the Mincio was the

8 See Humboldt to Metternich, Prague, 1813, Gebhardt, Bruno, *Wilhelm
von Humboldt's politische Denkschriften* (Berlin, 1903), II, 86; and Sorel,
op. cit., VIII, 162.

9 Sorel, *op. cit.*, VIII, 162; Fournier, August, *Napoleon the First, a
Biography* (New York, 1903), 616; Humboldt to Metternich, Prague,
1813, Gebhardt, *op. cit.*, II, 86. An excellent discussion of the negotiations which were held in the summer of 1813 between Austria and the members of the coalition against Napoleon can be found in Sorel, *op. cit.*, VIII,
84-180. A brief but good discussion of Metternich's part in these negotiations
can be found in Srbik, Heinrich Ritter von, *Metternich, der Staatsmann und
der Mensch* (Muenchen, 1925), I, 156-63

10 *The British and Foreign State Papers*, I, Pt. 1, 96.

frontier to which Austria looked."[11] The Mincio river was the dividing line between Lombardy and Venetia. In early November, 1813, when the Allied Powers sent the French diplomat, Saint Aignan, to the French headquarters with proffers of peace on condition that Napoleon accept the natural boundaries of France, the Rhine, the Alps, and the Pyrenees, as a basis for it, Metternich told Saint Aignan that " in Italy Austria would receive a frontier which would be the object of further negotiation" and that it was imperative that "the Italian states, like Germany, should be governed in a manner independent from France or any other preponderant Power."[12] And on May 7, 1814, the Milanese provisional regency was told by Sir Robert Wilson that "as late as last January Emperor Francis gave his assent to the independence of this Country."[13] This hardly sounds as if a nefarious conspiracy were concocted at Prague in July, 1813, to hand over Italy to the tender mercies of the Habsburgs.

When, then, did the Allied Powers decide to give Lombardy to Austria? During the last days of 1813, Genoa was given to the King of Sardinia,[14] in order to strengthen this buffer state on France's border so that any future French attempt to invade the Apennine peninsula could more easily be checked.[15] The

11 Balfour, Lady Frances, *The Life of George Fourth Earl of Aberdeen* (London, 1922), 102.

12 Note, St. Aignan, Francfort, November 9, 1814, *Staats-Archiv*, Vienna, *Frankreich Varia*, Fasc. 78, Sect. 2, Fo. 244.

13 Provisional regency to deputation at Paris, Milano, May 7, 1814, *Museo del Risorgimento*, Milan, *Carte Beccaria*, Busta I, Carte 8, Fasc. I, No. 24.

14 "Provided it be clearly with the entire concurrence of the inhabitants you may take possession of Genoa in the name and on the behalf of his Sardinian Majesty." Bathurst to Bentinck, December 28, 1813, Hansard, *op. cit.*, XXX (March 6 to May 1, 1815), 387-88. "I have to acknowledge the receipt of your 'private and secret' letter of the 18th December. Sir John Dalrymple has not yet sent me the conditions under which the Genoese have been transferred to the King of Sardinia, but I expect them immediately." Bentinck to Castlereagh, January 7, 1814, Castlereagh Correspondence, *op. cit.*, IX, 147.

15 It should be noted that it was part of the general policy of the Allied Powers to establish barriers on the frontiers of France that would help to

fate of Lombardy, however, was still an open question. A memorandum of the British cabinet, dated December 26, 1813, reveals that " the Milanese, Modena, Parma and Placentia [*sic*] are to be subject to discussion." [16] On January 31, 1814, Bellegarde wrote Count Mier: " Prince Metternich, in one of his anterior dispatches told me that it was useful that the question of the fate of the Milanese remains in a complete suspense." [17] At the conferences held at Langres, Troyes, and Châtillon, in late January and in February, 1814, no mention was made of the fate of Lombardy, and the only agreement reached in regard to the Apennine peninsula was to leave Italy divided into independent buffer states between Austria and France.[18] Although this does not necessarily mean that the Allied Powers intended that Lombardy was to be one of these independent states, it does

check any future French attempts to expand. It was also partly for this reason that the Allies decided to give Belgium to Holland.

16 Webster, C. K., *British Diplomacy, 1813-1815 (Select Documents Dealing with the Reconstruction of Europe)* (London, 1921), 125.

17 Huegel Diary, *op. cit.*, 32 ftn.

18 Gallavresi maintains that the Allies decided to give Lombardy to the Austrians at Troyes in February, 1814. "La rivoluzione e la politica inglese," *loc. cit.*, 128. Documentary evidence, however, does not support the contention that such a deal was made either at the conference at Troyes or at the conferences at Langres and Châtillon. The instructions in regard to Italy which were given at Langres to the plenipotentiaries of Austria, Russia, England, and Prussia for their use at the conferences of peace with Napoleon at Châtillon read: " Italy divided into independent states, between Austria's Italian possessions and France." Dated Langres, January 29, 1814, Demelitsch, Fedor von, "Actenstuecke zur Geschichte der Coalition vom Jahre 1814," *Fontes Rerum Austriacarum*, XLIX (1899), 291. The documents on the Conference of Châtillon which are in the Viennese *Staats-Archiv, Frankreich Varia*, Fasc. 78, make no mention of the agreement to which Gallavresi refers, but, on the other hand, contain several letters which indicate that there was an accord on Italy's being divided into independent buffer states between Austria and France. The protocol of the fifth conference at Châtillon limits its references to Italy to the following statement: " The ancient republic of Venice will become a province of the Austrian monarchy." Nothing at all was said about Lombardy. *Ibid.*, Sect. 2, Fo. 241. Sorel, *op. cit.*, VIII, 242-308, and Srbik, *op. cit*, I, 172-75, indicate that in all the negotiations at the conferences of Langres, Troyes, and Châtillon, the only agreement that was reached in regard to Italy was that it was to be divided into independent states.

indicate that no specific agreement in regard to Lombardy was reached at that particular time.

Other indications, however, seem to show that the future of Lombardy was probably not determined until sometime after these conferences. On March 30, 1814, Castlereagh wrote Bentinck: " Your lordship is fully apprized of the earnest interest the Prince Regent takes in the restoration of the King of Sardinia and the Grand Duke of Tuscany to their ancient dominions; you will give every aid to both, but you will studiously abstain from encouraging any measure which might commit your Court, or the Allies, with respect to the ultimate disposition of any of the other territories in the north of Italy, *the destination of which must remain to be discussed upon a peace.*" [19] On April 27, 1814, he wrote Liverpool that although the Allies were masters of Italy in a military sense, they " must weigh well the political complications, which are not merely personal to the Sovereign claimants, but mixed up with a good deal of internal and extensive jealousy amongst the mass of the Italian population." [20] Words such as these seem to indicate that the future disposition of the western part of the Kingdom of Italy was still an open question in March and April, 1814.

The actions of the Austrian plenipotentiaries in Milan during the latter part of April tend to confirm this opinion. Bellegarde, as we have seen, ordered Sommariva and Strassoldo to take possession of the government in Milan *in the name of the Allied Powers* and not in that of Austria.[21] If the status of the country had been decided, the territory would have undoubtedly been taken in the name of the Habsburgs. Bentinck had been ordered in December, 1813, to take possession of Genoa in the name of the King of Sardinia.[22] And when Nugent marched into Modena and Reggio, he took possession of the two principalities

19 Hansard, *op. cit.*, XXXI (May 2 to July 12, 1815), 71. The italics are mine.

20 Castlereagh Correspondence, *op cit.*, IX, 510.

21 See *ante*, 142.

22 Bathurst to Bentinck, December 28, 1813, Hansard, *op cit*, XXX, 387-88.

in the name of Archduke Francis of Este.[23] Furthermore, Marshal Bellegarde, General Nugent, and Baron Huegel openly expressed themselves in favor of an independent Kingdom of Italy with the Archduke Francis of Austria-Este as its monarch.[24] It hardly seems plausible that they would have done so if they had been told that the country was to be incorporated into the Austrian Empire.

On May 3, 1814, however, Federico Confalonieri, the president of the Italian deputation at Paris, wrote his wife that " Venice and Lombardy have, beyond all doubt, been assigned to Austria," and that Parma was to go to Maria Louisa, and Piedmont, Tuscany, Modena, and the greater portion of the papal states were to be returned to their respective former rulers.[25] On the next day he continued: " *A month ago we still had time to make some move in regard to our political existence,* but here nothing remains for us to do but to implore it. What will they grant us? Austria is the arbiter and absolute master of our destiny. The scope of our mission has changed. It is no longer a question of demanding a liberal constitution, independence, a kingdom, etc., etc., from the Allied Powers; it is only a question of imploring them as a father to grant these to us." [26]

Moreover, on May 4, 1814, Bellegarde wrote a letter to Emperor Francis, the general tenor of which clearly shows that at the time of the writing of the letter Bellegarde knew that Lombardy was definitely to be incorporated into the Austrian Empire.[27] On April 25, while conferring with Porro Lambertenghi, the emissary whom the Milanese communal council had sent to him, Count Bellegarde had expressed himself as being

23 Mier to Metternich, Reggio, March 11, 1814, Weil, *Eugène et Murat, op. cit.*, V, 58.

24 See especially *ante*, 136-37.

25 Casati, *op. cit.*, II, 7.

26 Letter to his wife, *ibid.*, 8. The italics are mine. Also quoted in Lemmi, *La restaurazione austriaca, op. cit.*, 263-64.

27 Note, for example, the following concluding section: "On my arrival in Milan, I will let the future happy fate of Lombardy be more definitely made known, will give all administrative branches a more definite organi-

in favor of an independent Kingdom of Italy with an Austrian archduke as king.[28] The actions and behaviour of the Austrian officials in Lombardy indicate that Bellegarde was not deliberately trying to deceive Porro, and that he had not yet received instructions or any indications that the fate of Lombardy had been decided by the Allied Powers. Thus it would seem that the Allied Powers probably decided to give Lombardy to Austria during the period intervening between the time a letter notifying Bellegarde of this fact could have reached him before April 25, and the time when a similar letter would have reached him before May 4.

On May 7, 1814, the Milanese deputation at Paris wrote the provisional regency that an accord between the Allied Powers to give both the Venetian and the Milanese territories to the Habsburgs as conquered territory *" was reached about twelve days before the arrival of the Deputation."* [29] Federico Confalonieri, accompanied by the secretary of the deputation, Marquis Beccaria, arrived in Paris on April 30.[30] Trivulzio and Sommi came to Paris on May 3.[31] Litta, Ciani, Ballabio, and Somaglia must have arrived there sometime late on the 4th.[32] Fè did not arrive until May 10.[33]

zation, and will put into effect all the regulations which Your Majesty may wish to put into effect to establish the future administration of this province according to Your paternal and sagacious views, so that their recuperation from eighteen years of heavy oppression and their lasting well-being can be brought into complete harmony with the interests of the Empire." *Staats-Archiv*, Vienna, *Kaiser Franz Akten*, Fasc. 27, Sect. 1, Fo. 47-8.

28 See *ante*, 135-36

29 *Museo del Risorgimento*, Milan, *Carte Beccaria*, Busta I, Carte 8, Fasc. II, No. 3. The italics are mine.

30 Confalonieri to his wife, Parigi, April 30, 1814, Casati, *op. cit.*, II, 3.

31 See Confalonieri to his wife, Parigi, May 3, 1814, *ibid.*, 8; and Helfert, *La caduta, op. cit*, 115.

32 On May 4, 1814, Confalonieri wrote his wife that Litta, Somaglia, and Fè had not yet arrived in Paris. Casati, *op. cit.*, II, 9. On May 7, 1814, the deputation, however, wrote the provisional regency that "since the 4th of May all of the deputation, with the exception of Signor Count Fè, found themselves reunited in Paris." *Museo del Risorgimento*, Milan, *Carte Beccaria*, Busta I, Carte 8, Fasc. II, No. 3.

33 Deputation to provisional regency, Parigi, May 12, 1814, *ibid.*, No. 9.

Since five of the seven deputies arrived in Paris on either May 3 or May 4, and since all but one were there on May 4, it appears probable that the deputation considered May 4 as the date of their arrival in the French capital. If this is true, the Allied Powers, according to the statement of the Milanese deputies, agreed to the unification of Lombardy with the Austrian Empire on about April 22. Of course, the Milanese deputies could have been mistaken in their assumption that an agreement had been reached about twelve days before their arrival in Paris, but, on the other hand, Marshal Bellegarde's actions tend to show that he received word that Lombardy was to be given to the Habsburgs sometime between April 25 and May 4. Moreover, in his letters to his wife, Confalonieri indicated that the Allied Powers reached an agreement in regard to the disposition of Lombardy sometime between the beginning of April and May 3. Apparently, at least all circumstantial evidence points in that direction, the fate of Lombardy was definitely decided sometime during the latter part of April, 1814.

On September 8, 1814, Cardinal Consalvi wrote Cardinal Pacca that on the previous day Prince Metternich had told him that at first the Austrian government wished to have the Mincio for the boundary of its Italian territory and did not want Lombardy.[34] The Habsburgs were forced to take that country, Metternich asserted, " for the sole reason . . . of *killing Italian Jacobinism in Milan.*" Since Milan was the center of radical agitation for the unification of the whole peninsula under a constitutional government, Metternich explained, Austria's own

34 In regard to this assertion of Prince Metternich, it should be mentioned that on October 25, 1814, the Archduke John noted in his diary: " I am not at all pleased with the division of territory. Austria has received a great deal in Italy, to its misfortune. I would never have placed the boundaries beyond the Po and the Chiese. I would have given Lombardy to the King of Sardinia as King of the Lombards, because it would be useful to have a powerful prince there, as it is in Holland in the North." Freksa, Frederick, *A Peace Congress of Intrigue (A Vivid, Intimate Account of the Congress of Vienna, composed of the Personal Memoirs of its Important Participants)* (New York, 1919), 239.

possessions in Venetia would be imperiled if she did not also have Lombardy under her control.[35]

Cardinal Consalvi's letter seems to give the clue as to why the Allied Powers finally decided to incorporate Lombardy, as well as Venetia, with the Austrian Empire. If they made their decision during the last days of April, the Allied statesmen undoubtedly knew of the Milanese revolution of April 20 at the time that they reached a final agreement. If they made up their minds around the 22nd, as the letter which the Milanese deputation wrote to the provisional regency appears to indicate, they probably based their determination, at least in part, on reports of the large amount of liberal agitation in Milan immediately before and after the senate meeting on April 17. Furthermore, if the weather were clear, the news of the events of April 20th might have reached Paris as early as the 22nd via the most rapid system of communication which existed. Even if the Allied Powers decided to give Lombardy to the Habsburgs as early as the middle of April, 1814, they could not have failed to know how strong the " pure Italian " party was at that time.

All the indications of the strength of the liberal factions in Lombardy in March and April, 1814, must have proved to the conservative Habsburg government that a dangerous " Jacobin spirit " existed in the capital of the Kingdom of Italy. They must also have made a profound impression upon Lord Castlereagh, the conservative Tory foreign minister of Great Britain, and upon the conservative government of Frederick William III of Prussia. To these three governments, as well as to the governments of the other Allied Powers, all these demonstrations of liberalism must have shown that Milan was a hotbed of revolutionary sentiment. After having suffered from over twenty years of almost perpetual warfare, many of the high

35 Rinieri, P. Ilario, *Corrispondenza inedita dei cardinali Consalvi e Pacca nel tempo del Congresso di Vienna (1814-1815) ; ricavata dall'archivio secreto vaticano, corredata di sommarii e note. Preceduta da uno studio storico sugli stati d'Europa nel tempo dell'impero napoleonico, e sul nuovo assestamento europeo e da un diario inedito del Mse. di San Marzano* (Roma, 1903), 5.

government officials of the various Allied Powers had a " Jacobin phobia," and were not prone to tolerate the existence of conditions which might easily lead to the outbreak of new revolutions and new warfare. An independent Kingdom of Italy could be very dangerous; therefore, the Allied Powers decided to give Lombardy, as well as Venetia, to the Habsburgs.[36]

According to the instructions which were given to the members of the Paris deputation by the electoral colleges on April 23, they were to ask the Allied Powers for a new liberal and independent monarchical state,[37] and were to tell Generals Fontanelli and Bertoletti, the two representatives of the army who had been sent to Paris by Prince Eugene just prior to the Milanese revolution, to leave Paris immediately.[38] Somewhat later the deputies were informed that the Milanese provisional government was favorable to the proposal of having the Archduke Francis of Este as king of their country,[39] and were asked to request the Allied Powers to have returned to Italy the statues, pictures, manuscripts, and other valuable objects of a similar nature which the French had plundered and taken away from Italy.[40] In addition, they were to implore the Allied Powers to permit the union of Genoa with the new Kingdom of Italy which the Milanese liberals hoped would be created.[41]

36 It should be noted that although Lemmi accepts Bianchi's contention that Austria was given a free hand in the Kingdom of Italy at the conferences at Prague, in July, 1813, he says that the Milanese revolution of April 20 played a large part in definitely influencing the Habsburgs, as well as the other Allied Powers, to annex Lombardy to the Austrian Empire. See his *La restaurazione austriaca, op. cit.*, 219-21.

37 See *ante*, 131.

38 Determination, Provisional regency, Milano, April 23, 1814, *Museo del Risorgimento*, Milan, *Carte Beccaria*, Busta I, Carte 8, Fasc. I, no number given.

39 Provisional regency to deputation at Paris, Milano, April 27, 1814, *ibid.*, No. 3.

40 Giovio to president of the provisional regency, Milano, April 29, 1814, *ibid.*, Pezza 3.

41 Provisional regency to deputation at Paris, Milano, May 3, 1814, *ibid.*, No. 359.

Soon after Confalonieri and Beccaria arrived in Paris on April 30, Fontanelli and Bertoletti, who during their sojourn in Paris had attempted to influence various prominent Allied officials to hand the Kingdom of Italy over to Prince Eugene, departed from the city.[42] At the same time, the Milanese deputies made use of every practical opportunity to learn the destiny that might have been prepared for the Kingdom of Italy and to gain audiences with officials of the Russian, Prussian, and Austrian governments. The ministers of the first two governments did not reply immediately, but Prince Metternich and Count Stadion manifested a desire to confer with the deputation. The deputies decided to commission Count Litta, who had held a distinguished position under the Austrian government, to go to them.[43]

On the morning of May 6, Count Litta was received by Metternich and Stadion. Prince Metternich, after a cordial reception, explained that, since the Kingdom of Italy was considered territory conquered by Austrian arms, there could never be any discussion of absolute independence. Litta thought that, in the circumstances, the best thing which could be done would be to have a new kingdom created, with Milan as its capital and an Austrian archduke as viceroy, to which would be united all the provinces of Italy which would be under Austrian control. Metternich encouraged this idea, and suggested that this state could well be named the Kingdom of Italy. Count Stadion also expressed similar sentiments.[44]

On May 7, the Italian deputies were received by the Austrian Emperor, who told them that their country had been given to him by the Allied Powers. He knew, of course, that they had

---

42 Confalonieri to his wife, Parigi, May 3, 1814, Casati, *op. cit.*, II, 5-6.

43 Deputation to provisional regency, Parigi, May 7, 1814, *Museo del Risorgimento*, Milan, *Carte Beccaria*, Busta I, Carte 8, Fasc. II, No. 3.

44 *Ibid*. Also see Verga, Ettore, " La deputazione dei collegi elettorali del regno d'Italia a Parigi nel 1814," *Archivio Storico Lombardo*, Anno XXXI (1904), 318. This article contains the only adequate study that has been made of the activities of the Lombard deputation at Paris. The writer has found it quite useful.

THE MILANESE AT PARIS 193

come to Paris to demand the independence of the kingdom.
Although he was unable to grant this, Francis asserted that he
could and would give the Milanese many things that would
make them proud of the fact that they were to be Austrian
subjects. In the first place, although he was still undecided as
to the name for the new province, at the moment he was con-
templating calling it the " Longobardian Kingdom." This name,
he believed, would recall to the Milanese all the ancient glories
of their country.

The country was to be governed, in the name of the Emperor,
by an Austrian archduke, and its capital was to be the city of
Milan. The Italian army was to form a separate and distinct
corps of the imperial army, and the Italian language, institutions, and customs were, as far as possible, to be preserved.
Furthermore, the Emperor assured the Italians that he would
attempt, at all costs, to revive the commerce and industry of
their country, and would begin negotiations with the French
government to have all the art treasures taken from Italy
during the Revolutionary and Napoleonic period restored.[45]

By this time the deputies were convinced that it was utterly
impossible for them to do anything in the way of obtaining the
independence of their country. The members of the Milanese
provisional government, however, for some time continued to
live in the ethereal blue of unrealistic optimism. When, on the
morning of May 13, the provisional regency received the dispatches of the deputation informing its members about the
conference which they had had with Emperor Francis, the
president of the regency, after having brought the matter to
Sir Robert Wilson's attention, advised the deputies immediately

45 Confalonieri to his wife, Parigi, May 8, 1814, Casati, *op. cit.*, II, 9-11;
Deputation to provisional regency, Parigi, dated May 7, but actually dis-
patched on May 8, 1814, *Museo del Risorgimento*, Milan, *Carte Beccaria*,
Busta I, Carte 8, Fasc. II, No. 6. Two days later, upon the Austrian
Emperor's request, Count Litta gave him a list of the names of " upright
and sagacious men " whom the Emperor could consult about the various
branches of the administration of the Kingdom of Italy. Litta to Kaiser
Franz, May 9, 1814, *ibid.*, Pezza 5, No. 14; Verga, *loc. cit.*, 320.

to call upon Lord Castlereagh to express to him the unanimous desire of the Italian people for independence and to invoke the protection of England. If the deputies felt that Castlereagh favored giving Lombardy to the Habsburgs, they should at once send one of their members directly to London to get the English government to overrule Castlereagh's manipulations. They were also to request the Austrian Emperor to grant the people absolute independence with an Austrian prince as king.[46]

The next day, after Lord Bentinck had arrived in Milan and had assured him that " such a beautiful vote " as that of the Italians for independence would still be granted, Verri insisted in a letter to the deputies that the " destinies of this Country do not yet seem to be absolutely fixed, in spite of all that has passed in Paris," and urged the deputies to confer with the British ministers " over the most noble cause of National independence." [47] At the same time, Verri requested the deputies to protest to the Allies against Count Bubna's having occupied the department of Agogna in the name of the King of Sardinia.[48]

It was not until May 24—just one day before Bellegarde officially took charge of the kingdom in the name of the Austrian Emperor—that the provisional regency at last demonstrated that it realized that the cause of Italian independence was doomed. On that day its president finally wrote the deputation that it was useless and imprudent to make any further attempts to obtain independence. The deputies were henceforth to direct their efforts toward obtaining the greatest possible number of advantages for their country. They were to insist that the country " should at least have the denomination of Kingdom, should be administered with Laws conforming to the customs and needs of the People, and should have a National Representation." In the new regime, the Italians were

46 Verri to deputation at Paris, Milano, May 13, 1814, *Museo del Risorgimento*, Milan, *Carte Beccaria*, Busta I, Carte 8, Fasc I, No. 36.

47 Letter of May 14, 1814, *ibid*, No. 48.

48 Verri to deputation at Paris, no date given, *ibid.*, No. 46.

to have exclusive right to all the state offices, and the Emperor should consult prominent Italians before deciding what type of government was to be instituted in Lombardy.[49]

The members of the Milanese deputation did not need the stimulus of the various dispatches from the provisional regency. Before the arrival of these letters, the deputies were hard at work consulting various representatives of the Allied Powers in an attempt to influence them to change their position in regard to the future of Lombardy. They held conferences with the Russian ministers, Nesselrode and Pozzo di Borgo, and with the Prussian minister, Wilhelm von Humboldt, without receiving any encouragement.[50] Tsar Alexander merely told them that he hoped that they would "be content with the arrangements which have been made." [51]

Federico Confalonieri went to Castlereagh and to Lord Aberdeen to see if he could interest them in the cause of the Milanese liberals. Castlereagh told him, in response to his protestations that it was to the best interests of his state to have independence and a constitutional government, that it was not necessary to give the Milanese a constitution in order to insure their happiness and prosperity. In the history of the house of Austria, he insisted, "there can be found no traces of abuse of power and force." Neither did Confalonieri receive any consolation from Lord Aberdeen, for he spoke in the same vein as Castlereagh.[52]

On the afternoon of May 27, the deputies had another conference with the Austrian Emperor. Emperor Francis expressed the hope that he would be able to calm the agitation which had been heedlessly stirred up in Milan "by several Englishmen."

49 *Ibid*, No. 71.

50 Report of deputies to Verri, Parigi, May 18, 1814, Casati, *op. cit.*, II, 17. The same letter is published in Bianchi, *op. cit.*, I, 339-43, under date of May 15, 1814.

51 Deputation to provisional regency, Parigi, May 22, 1814, *Museo del Risorgimento*, Milan, *Carte Beccaria*, Busta I, Carte 8, Fasc. II, No. 49

52 Report of deputies to Verri, Parigi, May 18 (or May 15?), 1814, Casati, *op. cit.*, II, 16-22, Bianchi, *op. cit.*, I, 339-43.

He promised that he would accept and wear the Lombard Crown of Iron, and reiterated his intentions to establish a court at Milan and to make that city the center of the administration of the kingdom.

Count Litta, who had been delegated by the other deputies to do most of the talking, asked that the new state be given the greatest possible territorial extension. He maintained that it was necessary to have at least Agogna, Alessandria, the Valtelline, Brescia, and Bergamo included in the new kingdom. This expansion, however, the Emperor declared that he could not approve. Agogna belonged to the King of Sardinia. As to the rest of these territories, he could not promise their incorporation into the kingdom, since he could scarcely decree their annexation to another country before first consulting the wishes of the people residing in these principalities.

Turning to the subject of the troops stationed in the country, the deputies insisted that a substantial reduction of their number was urgent. Francis recognized the fact that at that moment the situation in this respect was burdensome to the inhabitants, but promised that these conditions would soon cease to exist. Then he proceeded to relate how he hoped to improve the status of his Italian subjects in other ways. To insure greater freedom of commerce, he would see to it that all tolls on the Mincio were abolished, and that those on the Po ceased as soon as arrangements could be made with the Parmese and papal governments. Taxes would be no higher than those in any other part of his domain. All the obligations of the *Monte Napoleone* [53] would be paid in full, and all national goods which had been sold during the previous regime were to remain in the hands of their possessors. Moreover, as soon as a commission could be appointed to draw up a constitution for the country, several Italian citizens would be called to Vienna to assist it. [54]

[53] All the debts, as well as the whole pension system, of the former Kingdom of Italy had been consolidated in the *Monte Napoleone*.

[54] Deputation to provisional regency, Parigi, May 27, 1814, *Museo del*

Emperor Francis's words at the interview showed that the Habsburgs intended to be absolute masters of both Venetia and Lombardy. The deputies could turn to them only as docile subjects beseeching their paternal ruler to grant their wishes. In the last few days of the congress, the deputies, in compliance with their instructions, confined their activities chiefly to presenting various memorials and petitions to the Habsburg ministers in Paris. These concerned mainly the disposition of the art treasures which the French had removed from Italy, and the territorial arrangements which were to be made for the department of Agogna and for the Valtelline. On May 24, the deputies handed to Prince Metternich a list of the chief works of art and the manuscripts which the French had taken from Lombardy during the campaign of 1796.[55] On the same day they protested to Metternich against Count Bubna's occupation of the department of Agogna in the name of His Sardinian Majesty,[56] and in the course of the next few days three memorials outlining the losses which would ensue for Lombardy if the department were taken from it were given to the Austrian foreign minister.[57]

The Milanese deputies were just as active, and, in the long run, much more successful, in protesting against the occupation of Bormio, Chiavenna, and the Valtelline by the Grisons. On May 4, three thousand Grison troops had invaded these districts, carrying with them a proclamation of the Grison government advising the inhabitants that, with the consent of the Allied Powers, the soldiers were occupying their territory to facilitate its incorporation again into Grison territory.[58] As

Risorgimento, Milan, Carte Beccaria, Busta I, Carte 8, Fasc. II, No. 60; Confalonieri to his wife, Parigi, May 28, 1814, Casati, op. cit., II, 26-31.

55 A copy of this memoir is in the Staats-Archiv, Vienna, Frankreich Varia, Fasc. 79, Sect. 2, Fo. 50.

56 Deputation to Metternich, Parigi, May 24, 1814, ibid., Fo. 60.

57 Museo del Risorgimento, Milan, Carte Beccaria, Busta I, Carte 8, Fasc. II, Pezza 1, No. 68; Pezza 3, ad No. 59; and No. 84. Also see Verga, loc. cit., 323

58 Dated May 3, 1814, Staats-Archiv, Vienna, Staatskanzlei, Provinzen, Lombardei-Venedig, Fasc. 3, Sect. 3, Fo. 199.

soon as he heard of this invasion of Italian soil, Sommariva announced that he had already taken possession of this territory, along with the other unconquered parts of the Kingdom of Italy, in the name of the Allied Powers, and invited the Grisons to renounce their project.[59]

Having heard of these events, the Milanese deputation at Paris hastened to object to Metternich about the insolence of the Grisons' invading and demanding a country which was purely Italian.[60] On the 25th, the deputies handed Metternich a memorial from the inhabitants of the Valtelline, Chiavenna, and Bormio, in which they manifested their alarm over the possibility of their falling again under the yoke of the Grisons and expressed their ardent wish to remain united with the Kingdom of Italy.[61]

In spite of these protests, the fate of these principalities was not settled until the spring of 1815. The inhabitants were almost unanimously opposed to falling under the rule of the Grisons, and at the Congress of Vienna, they presented several petitions beseeching the Allied Powers to permit them to remain united with Lombardy and to pass under Austrian sovereignty. The Grisons were just as insistent that the territory be given to them. The Habsburgs were in favor of returning the Valtelline to the Swiss on the condition that its residents enjoy the same civil liberties and independence as the people living in the other Swiss cantons. The inhabitants of the Valtelline, Chiavenna, and Bormio, however, absolutely refused to countenance it. In the end, the Allied Powers finally decided to annex these territories to Lombardy.[62]

59 Bellegarde to Metternich, Milan, May 9, 1814, *ibid.*, Fo. 198-201.

60 Verga, *loc. cit.*, 325; Deputation to provisional regency, Parigi, May 23, 1814, *Museo del Risorgimento*, Milan, *Carte Beccaria*, Busta I, Carte 8, Fasc. II, No. 50.

61 A copy of this memoir is in the *Staats-Archiv*, Vienna, *Staatskanzlei, Provinzen, Lombardei-Venedig*, Fasc. 40, Sect. 1, Fo. 152-58.

62 For the protocols of the sittings of the committee on Swiss affairs in the Congress of Vienna, in which the fate of the Valtelline, Chiavenna, and Bormio was discussed, see Klueber, Johann Ludwig, *Acten des Wiener*

Besides presenting the various memorials which we have mentioned, the deputies were unable to accomplish much after their conference with the Habsburg Emperor on May 27. The days of the Congress of Paris were numbered, even though the Allied statesmen had done little to settle the multifarious problems connected with the making of the definitive peace treaty which confronted them. On May 30, the Treaty of Paris was signed. Besides confirming the decision of the Allied Powers to give Lombardy-Venetia to the Habsburgs, the treaty stipulated that Genoa was to go to Sardinia,[63] that Switzerland was to be independent, that Belgium was to go to Holland, and that the boundaries of France were to be the same as those which that country had had on January 1, 1792. Besides this, little had been agreed upon. The most important problems confronting the Allies were still left unsolved. Nothing had been decided concerning the rest of Italy, concerning the burning question of the fate of Poland and Saxony, or concerning the future organization of Germany. The treaty was, at the most, only a partial settlement. Nevertheless, on June 2, the Emperor of Austria, Tsar of Russia, and King of Prussia left Paris.[64]

On June 7, the deputies protested to Count Stadion because Bellegarde on May 25 had decreed the abolition of the electoral colleges,[65] and gave him a memorial in which they stated their reasons for insisting that it was necessary that Lombardy have some form of national representation.[66] On June 11, the deputies handed Stadion a written protest about Bellegarde's establishment of a new customs line on the Adige between Mantua

Congresses in den Jahren 1814 und 1815 (Erlangen, 1815-19), V, 117-328; and D'Angeberg, Comte, Le Congrès de Vienne et les traités de 1815 (Paris, 1864), 1933.

63 In the Treaty of Fontainebleau, of April 11, 1814, it had also been stipulated that Parma was to go to Maria Louisa.

64 Deputation to provisional regency, Parigi, June 3, 1814, Museo del Risorgimento, Milan, Carte Beccaria, Busta I, Carte 8, Fasc. II, No. 76.

65 Deputation to provisional regency, Parigi, June 7, 1814, ibid., No. 84.

66 A copy of this memorial is in ibid., No. 6.

and the Veronese.[67] This was the last official act of the Milanese deputation. On the next day, it officially declared itself dissolved. Fè had already left the city several days before. On June 12, Federico Confalonieri left for London, and was followed a little later by Litta, Somaglia, and Ballabio. Trivulzio departed for Holland, and Sommi, for Switzerland. Ciani and Beccaria were the only members of the deputation who returned directly to Milan.[68]

[67] Deputation to Stadion, Parigi, June 11, 1814, *ibid.*, No. 92.

[68] Confalonieri to his wife, Parigi, June 11, 1814, Casati, *op. cit*, II, 36-7. Also see Lemmi, *La restaurazione austriaca, op. cit.*, 266.

CHAPTER XII

THE END OF THE KINGDOM OF ITALY

In late April, 1814, Lombardy became a part of the Habsburg Empire. The Milanese revolution, the manipulations of the liberals in the Milanese provisional government, the intrigues of disobedient British Whigs, and the machinations of secret societies had been in vain. Lombardy, as well as Venetia, was the possession of the Austrian Emperor, who was given a free hand by his allies to do with it as he wished. It was his duty to establish in it, as well as in Venetia, a government which would heal the wounds left by over a dozen years of French domination and to set up in northern Italy a new order which would insure that enduring peace for which the Allied Powers had looked for more than twenty years.

Being in sole possession of Lombardy, Emperor Francis was charged with providing the country, first, with a provisional Austrian regime, and later, with a more durable and permanent government which would reconcile the customs, habits, and desires of the Lombards with the political philosophy and the organization of the Austrian Empire. The second could be delayed for a period of months, and, perhaps, years; the first had to be supplied immediately.

Francis did not tarry in making arrangements for the provisional government of the country. On May 14, from Paris, he wrote Marshal Bellegarde to give him an outline of the general policies which he was to follow in setting up a temporary government for the Milanese. In addition to retaining his position of commander-in-chief of the imperial army in Italy, Bellegarde was to assume the functions of Austrian commissioner, with the duty of conducting the civil administration in all of Lombardy and in those parts of the former Venetian Republic between the Mincio and Adige rivers which had not yet been placed under the jurisdiction of the Habsburg government.

Bellegarde was commanded to permit the Milanese provisional government temporarily to continue its work, but he himself was to assume the presidency. Since the country had been conquered, there could be " no talk of a constitution, a senate or other similar bodies, or of representation." Accordingly, the electoral colleges, if they still existed, were to be abolished. Insofar as he thought it advisable, the new Austrian commissioner was immediately to issue a proclamation notifying the population of the foregoing prescriptions. Furthermore, he was to announce that henceforth he would speak, not in the name of the Allied Powers, but only in that of the Emperor. Whenever any Italians questioned him about the future of their country, Bellegarde was to inform them that the Emperor would do what was best for them, as well as for his other subjects.

With the exception that he was to have the electoral colleges dissolved, the newly appointed commissioner was to make no changes in the government of the country unless he was convinced that they were indispensable and that they were fully in accord with the precepts which Emperor Francis had ordered him to follow. If Bellegarde required any help in conducting the administration, he was immediately to bring this need to the Emperor's attention. If he wanted information or advice from any of the inhabitants, he could, after carefully informing himself about them, consult the individuals whose names were on the list of dependable and capable persons given by the Lombard deputation at Paris to the Emperor and sent by him to Bellegarde.

The imperial commissioner was to make reports on the conditions of the country directly to the Emperor. In them he was to pay particular attention to the nature of public opinion and the conditions of the Italian army. He was, furthermore, to dismiss all the officers and soldiers of the Italian army who were not citizens of the former Lombard or Venetian states.[1]

1 Kaiser Franz to Bellegarde, Paris, May 14, 1814, *Staats-Archiv*, Vienna, *Conferenz Akten*, Ser. b, 1814, No. 996.

Emperor Francis sent Prince Reuss-Plauen, who was in charge of the government of the Venetian provinces, a copy of the foregoing instructions, and directed him to ascertain, in an inconspicuous way, whether the people in the Venetian provinces desired a separate Venetian province or whether they wished to remain in an administrative unit with Lombardy, as they had been during the time of the Kingdom of Italy.[2] At the same time, the Emperor asked Count Zichy, the president of the Austrian State Conference, to inform the heads of the various branches of the imperial administration about the Emperor's determination in regard to Lombardy and to request them immediately to make proposals on the best way of creating a permanent government for Lombardy which would be similar to that in Austria's hereditary German states. Zichy was to arrange for the immediate translation of the Austrian law books into Italian, and was to propose to the Emperor the name of a capable person to supervise the establishment of a judicial organization in the newly acquired provinces.[3]

Such were the Emperor's first official instructions in regard to the future of the Milanese. Perhaps the underlying motives which prompted the inclusion of some of the items are revealed in a letter which Prince Metternich sent to Marshal Bellegarde on May 15, in order to call his attention to several factors which he thought were " of such a nature that they should serve him as a point of departure in all the proceedings which are in the process of being undertaken or which will be made " in Lombardy. In the letter Metternich expressed great anxiety because of the existence in the Apennine peninsula of " the so-called *Italian* spirit," which " the Emperor Napoleon, the King of Naples, and General Lord W. Bentinck, and even some of our own agents, have in a powerful manner contributed to exciting and sustaining." Bellegarde was " in no manner " to favor this spirit.

2 Kaiser Franz to Reuss, Paris, May 14, 1814, *ibid.*
3 Kaiser Franz to Zichy, Paris, May 14, 1814, *ibid.*

"The best counterpoise against this Italian pretension," Metternich continued, "is without doubt to be found in parcelling out Italy," a policy which is "very much in agreement with the political views of the Powers. For several centuries many local animosities and jealousies have existed in Italy. These hatreds have never allowed the union of all the diverse elements" found in the peninsula, "and they have survived. The territory allotted to Austria is bounded by the *Ticino* and the *Po*; nothing, therefore, prevents us from attempting to revive the *Lombard* spirit. With this in mind, His Majesty has decided to add to his other titles that of *King of Lombardy,* and to include the Crown of Iron" in the imperial coat of arms. Metternich advised Bellegarde that he should, when taking possession of the government, announce this determination of the Emperor, and told him that he was to "administer the country between the *Po and the Ticino exclusively* in the name of Austria." [4] Bellegarde was thus to use the traditional Habsburg policy of *divide et impera* in coping with the new liberal and national spirit prevailing in certain quarters in Lombardy.

Before the instructions from the Emperor and the letter from Metternich arrived in Milan, Bellegarde, on May 12, following other directions from the Austrian cabinet, had issued a proclamation announcing that Lombardy was definitely to be an Austrian territory. On the same day, a *Te Deum* was celebrated in the Cathedral of Milan, and the Scala theater was illuminated, as was the entire city. According to the field marshal's report, the inhabitants everywhere expressed their great joy, and many cities and communities, when they heard of the news, sent deputies carrying addresses expressing their loyalty and appreciation to Bellegarde. [5]

4 *Staats-Archiv,* Vienna, *Staatskanzlei, Provinzen, Lombardei-Venedig,* Fasc. 3, Sect. 2, Fo. 50-3. A good summary of this letter is in Weil, *Murat, op. cit.,* I, 88-90.

5 Bellegarde Report of May 21, 1814, *Staats-Archiv,* Vienna, *Conferenz Akten,* Ser. b, 1814, No. 1248.

On May 22 Marshal Bellegarde received the Emperor's instructions.[6] Three days later, on May 25, he issued a proclamation in which he notified the people that he had been appointed Austrian commissioner plenipotentiary for the provinces belonging to ancient Lombardy, including Mantua and the departments on the left bank of the Po which did not depend upon the imperial government in Venice. The proclamation announced, in addition, that the senate, council of state, and electoral colleges were abolished, and that all unions and congresses which could not be justified were to be interdicted.[7]

On May 26, Bellegarde took over the presidency of the Milanese provisional government.[8] Two days later the provisional regency, upon Bellegarde's instigation, established a provisional customs line on all the borders of Lombardy.[9] About the same time, several officials from those sections of the former Kingdom of Italy which were no longer part of Lombardy were dismissed.[10] On June 1, 1814, Mayer von Heldenfeld, who was in command at Mantua, issued a proclamation prohibiting the existence of all secret societies and threatening all persons belonging to them with heavy penalties.[11]

To all intents and purposes, practically every one of the trappings of the former Kingdom of Italy had been abolished. On June 2, 1814, Metternich, in behalf of the Emperor, wrote Count Bellegarde to remove the very last of them. Bellegarde

6 *Mantovani Diario, op. cit.*, May 23, 1814, V, 269.

7 Proclamation, Bellegarde, Milano, May 25, 1814, *Atti del governo lombardo, op. cit.*, 1814, 52-3; *Mantovani Diario, op. cit.*, May 25, 1814, V, 270-71. Lemmi, *La restaurazione austriaca, op. cit.*, 277, and Helfert, *La caduta, op. cit.*, 132, erroneously relate that the senate, council of state, and electoral colleges were not declared abolished until May 26.

8 *Wiener Zeitung*, June 11, 1814, 642; *Giornale italiano*, No. 148 (May 28, 1814), 604.

9 Decree, Provisional regency, Milano, May 28, 1814, *Atti del governo lombardo, op. cit.*, 1814, 54-6.

10 *Mantovani Diario, op. cit.*, May 31, 1814, V, 272.

11 *Wiener Zeitung*, July 4, 1814, 735; *Giornale di Venezia*, No. 81 (June 21, 1814), 4.

was ordered to proclaim Austrian rule in all parts of the provinces, to require every state official to take a special oath of allegiance to the Habsburg Emperor, and to announce to the people that the Emperor would at once occupy himself with giving their country a definite organization.[12]

June 12 was the day chosen by Marshal Bellegarde to carry out the Emperor's instructions. A proclamation, signed by Bellegarde, was posted on the streets, reading: " People of Lombardy, Mantua, Brescia, Bergamo, and Crema, a happy destiny awaits you; your provinces are definitely added to the Austrian Empire. You will all be united and equally protected under the scepter of the august emperor and king, FRANCIS I, adored father of his subjects, and the desired sovereign of those states which have the happy lot of being subject to him." [13] A *Te Deum* was sung in the Milanese cathedral to celebrate the signing of the Treaty of Paris on May 30, and a religious procession, headed by most of the chief officials of the state, was held. In the evening the city was illuminated.[14]

On the next day, a decree was passed by the provisional regency, which declared that all the emblems and coats-of-arms of the preceding government had ceased to exist and would be removed by the public authorities. Moreover, the use of the Milanese cockade was forbidden. For the formula on official documents of " during the provisional regency," the expression, " during the reign of His Majesty, Francis I, Emperor and King," was to be substituted.[15] With this action, the last vestiges of the Milanese provisional government were removed   Lombardy, henceforth, was merely a part of the Habsburg Empire. It was destined to remain as such until 1859.

---

12 *Staats-Archiv*, Vienna, *Staatskanzlei, Provinzen, Lombardei-Venedig*, Fasc. 3, Sect. 2, Fo. 58.

13 Proclamation of June 12, 1814, *Atti del governo lombardo, op cit.*, 1814, 60-1.

14 *Giornale italiano*, No 164 (June 13, 1814), 670; *Mantovam Diario, op. cit*, June 12, 1814, V, 278-79.

15 *Atti del governo lombardo, op. cit.*, 1814, 62-4. Also see Cusani, *op cit*, VII, 200; and Lemmi, *La restaurazione austriaca, op cit.*, 278.

There was joy in the ranks of the Austrian party, which included most of " the nobility, the clergy, and the peasants " in the country.[16] In addition, a substantial number of persons from some of the other classes belonged to the pro-Austrian group. These people, worn out by the extravagances of eighteen years of French rule, longed for the mild and paternalistic Austrian government which had existed in Lombardy prior to the French invasion. Other persons who were not pro-Austrian or pro-liberal or pro-national were happy because they felt that the Habsburgs would give the country that peace, security, and economic stability which they desperately desired.

The Italian liberals, however, were discontented and disgusted with the new order of things which was being established in the country. " The military, the state employees, and the middle classes " were particularly anti-Austrian and were bitterly disillusioned because an independent constitutional state could not be established.[17] During the eighteen years of French rule, liberalism had become a creed to a substantial minority of the population, particularly the middle class, as well as to a small section of the liberal nobility, and they were bitter because their hopes of creating a model constitutional state had been dashed to the ground.

By far the most dissatisfied element in Lombardy was the Italian army. For a long time, this organization had been a " hotbed " for the incipient nationalism and liberalism which were developing in the Kingdom of Italy. Several of its officers were among the leading figures in the secret political societies, and some of them were strong supporters of Joachim Murat in his attempts in the spring of 1814 to make himself king of a united Italy. For months before the final collapse of the Kingdom of Italy, in April, 1814, the members of the army had been unpaid. When Prince Eugene was ready to leave Mantua on April 26, the officers and soldiers of the army were so

16 Bellegarde Report, May 31, 1814, *Staats-Archiv*, Vienna, *Conferenz Akten*, Ser. b, 1814, No. 1249.

17 *Ibid.*

vociferous in demanding their back pay from him that Eugene had great difficulty in calming them.[18]

As soon as Eugene was overthrown, the army sent a series of demands to the Milanese provisional government, insisting that it support these requests before the Allied Powers.[19] In them, the army requested the government to support invalids, veterans, and military orphans, provide pensions, and continue to educate the sons of soldiers, as the previous French government had done. Furthermore, all military ranks, decorations, and pensions should be preserved, all prisoners of war should be freed, and the necessary funds should be procured for maintaining the troops on their existing basis.[20]

That the Italian soldiers would not obtain the fulfillment of all these demands was obvious when the Austrian Emperor, as soon as he learned that the Habsburg army in Italy had been victorious, ordered Bellegarde to dissolve the Italian army.[21] This command would have been a fatal blow to the Italian army if Bellegarde had carried out the Emperor's instructions immediately. Before doing so, however, the Austrian commander in Italy took the initiative to protest against the measure as being perilous and cruel,[22] and to suggest that the Italian

18 *Wiener Zeitung*, May 9, 1814, 518; Bellegarde to Metternich, Verona, April 26, 1814, *Staats-Archiv*, Vienna, *Staatskanzlei, Provinzen, Lombardei-Venedig*, Fasc. 3, Sect. 3, Fo. 172. The latter document is also published in Lemmi, *La restaurazione austriaca, op. cit.*, Appendix XIV, 412-17.

19 Bellegarde to Metternich, Verona, April 26, 1814, *Staats-Archiv*, Vienna, *Staatskanzlei, Provinzen, Lombardei-Venedig*, Fasc. 3, Sect. 3, Fo. 173. Also in Lemmi, *La restaurazione austriaca, op. cit.*, Appendix XIV, 414.

20 *Staats-Archiv*, Vienna, *Staatskanzlei, Provinzen, Lombardei-Venedig*, Fasc. 3, Sect. 3, Fo. 181. Also in Lemmi, *La restaurazione austriaca, op. cit.*, Appendix V, 402-3.

21 Bellegarde to Metternich, Verona, April 26, 1814, *Staats-Archiv*, Vienna, *Staatskanzlei, Provinzen, Lombardei-Venedig*, Fasc. 3, Sect. 3, Fo. 173, Lemmi, *La restaurazione austriaca, op. cit.*, Appendix XIV, 414.

22 Bellegarde to Metternich, Verona, April 26, 1814, *Staats-Archiv*, Vienna, *Staatskanzlei, Provinzen, Lombardei-Venedig*, Fasc. 3, Sect. 3, Fo. 170-71, Lemmi, *La restaurazione austriaca, op. cit.*, Appendix XIII, 410-12. This is a different letter from the one cited above and which will be cited in the following footnote.

soldiers could be very useful to the Habsburgs and that the largest possible number of Italian regiments should be formed.[23]

The cabinet in Vienna finished by yielding, at least in part, to the spirited and insistent objections of the field marshal, and spoke no longer of the dissolution of the Italian army.[24] But it was necessary immediately to come to some kind of a decision, for the conduct of the Italian soldiers was such that it was highly imperative that something be done at once. There were numerous desertions, for not only did many of the soldiers hate the Germans, but they feared that if they were incorporated into the Austrian army, their pay would be much less than it had been under the previous French government.[25] Bitterly discontented and disillusioned, many Italian soldiers committed excesses. At Cremona, the troops under the orders of General Zucchi devised all sorts of revolutionary slogans, and demanded " death for all ex-nobles, priests, and aristocrats." At Milan some of the soldiers were almost as truculent in denouncing their enemies.[26] Fights between Italian and Austrian soldiers occurred repeatedly. On May 24, there was a bloody brawl in Milan when some Hungarian grenadiers were attacked by a few Italian troops.[27] Baron Huegel witnessed a fight between Italian and Austrian soldiers in which several of the participants on both sides were wounded.[28] Countess Confalonieri wrote her husband that she had seen such a fight in which swords were used and in which she beheld a German wound in a horrible

23 Bellegarde to Metternich, April 26, 1814, *Staats-Archiv*, Vienna, *Staatskanzlei, Provinzen, Lombardei-Venedig*, Fasc. 3, Sect. 3, Fo. 173-74, Lemmi, *La restaurazione austriaca, op. cit.*, 309-10, and Appendix XIV, 414-15.

24 Lemmi, *La restaurazione austriaca, op. cit.*, 311.

25 Pallavicini to Confalonieri, Milano, May 7, 1814, Gallavresi, *Confalonieri, op cit.*, I, 106-7; Huegel Diary, *op. cit.*, May 19, 1814, 101-2.

26 Teresa Confalonieri Casati to Confalonieri, Milano, May 6, 1814, Gallavresi, *Confalonieri, op. cit.*, I, 105.

27 Hager to *Staats-Conferenz*, June 8, 1814, *Staats-Archiv*, Vienna, *Conferenz Akten*, Ser. b, 1814, No. 1153.

28 Huegel Diary, *op. cit.*, May 22, 1814, 102.

manner a soldier of the Italian royal guard.[29] Disorders and even insubordination were rampant.[30] The light infantry troops of the royal guard revolted against their officers,[31] and many other soldiers were ready to follow their example.

The situation was so acute that Marshal Bellegarde found it necessary to appoint a military commission, on May 20, to make inquiries into the conduct of the soldiers and single out those who were guilty of infractions of the discipline of the army.[32] Later, on May 30, Bellegarde published a proclamation in which he announced that the Italian troops would become Austrian troops and that " the Austrian Emperor had decided to accept in the ranks of his army those officers " belonging to the above troops " who had not strayed from the path of duty or honor." [33] On June 1, the royal guard regiments were dismissed, since they did not fit into the Austrian form of military organization, and a commission, composed of two Austrian and two Italian generals, was appointed to put into effect the reorganization of those Italian army corps which were to become a part of the Habsburg military forces.[34] The problem of what disposition was to be made of the former Italian army was now solved, but not to the satisfaction of a large number of the members of that organization. Many Italian officers and soldiers remained discontented with their lot, and, during the summer and fall of 1814, became a center of radical opposition to the Habsburg regime.

By early June, 1814, the last vestiges of the French regime had been removed from every part of the former Kingdom of

29 Letter of May 24, 1814, Gallavresi, *Confalonieri, op. cit.*, I, 151.

30 *Mantovani Diario, op. cit.*, May 22, 1814, V, 267.

31 Huegel Diary, *op. cit*, May 21, 1814, 202.

32 *Mantovani Diario, op. cit.*, May 22, 1814, V, 267-68; Teresa Confalonieri Casati to Confalonieri, May 21, 1814, Gallavresi, *Confalonieri, op. cit.*, I, 143.

33 *Oesterreichischer Beobachter*, No. 164 (June 13, 1814), 877-78; Lemmi, *La restaurazione austriaca, op. cit.*, 312; Helfert, *La caduta, op. cit*, 140-41.

34 Helfert, *La caduta, op. cit.*, 141; Lemmi, *La restaurazione austriaca, op. cit.*, 312.

Italy. In Lombardy, as we have seen, the government had been placed under the direct control of Field Marshal Bellegarde. In Modena, the people were awaiting their legitimate ruler, the Archduke Francis IV of Este, who finally returned to the capital of the duchy on July 16. In the departments of Reno, Lower Po, and Rubicone, which comprised the territory of the three former papal Legations of Bologna, Ferrara, and Romagna, Count Strassoldo[35] was in charge of the civil and military administration, pending the final settlement of their fate.[36]

On May 15, Prince Reuss-Plauen, the governor of the Venetian territory, entered the city of Venice to take formal possession of the government of the city in the name of the Austrian Emperor. He and his entourage were met at Marghera by the mayor of the city and other prominent Venetians, who escorted them to the Piazza di San Marco. At the Piazza, the Austrians were received in a manner which, in the opinion of the Venetian citizen, Cicogna, " was even more magnificent, more beautiful, and richer than was usual in the good years of the city." [37] They were greeted with a military salute, and a military parade was held. Large throngs of people were lined along the Piazza and in the streets to greet the governor, and the Grand Canal was full of boats. In the evening the city was beautifully illuminated.[38]

By early June, 1814, the seat of the Venetian government, which, during the course of the military campaign, had been at the general headquarters of the army, had been moved to Padua. Here Prince Reuss-Plauen, and his two chief assistants, Count Thurn and Anton von Raab, the latter in charge of the Italian police, directed the administration of the country. The

35 In early May, 1814, Count Strassoldo had been ordered to leave Milan to assume the post of Austrian commissioner in charge of the provisional government of these three departments.

36 Helfert, *La caduta, op. cit*, 156.

37 Cicogna Diary, *loc. cit.*, May 16, 1814, 217.

38 *Ibid.*, 217-18; *Giornale di Venezia*, No. 51 (May 16, 1814), 4, and No. 53 (May 18, 1814), 3-4; *Wiener Zeitung*, June 1, 1814, 605.

jurisdiction of their government extended to the Adige on the west and the Po on the south. Although the Austrians had been in control of most of the Venetian territory for more than half a year, no formal proclamation that the country was definitely to be incorporated into Austria had yet been made, and some people still believed that their fate had not yet been decided.[39] Nearly all the oppressive burdens from which the populace had been suffering since the last part of 1813, when the Austrians had first occupied the country, still existed.[40] None of the taxes had yet been reduced, with the exception that Governor Reuss-Plauen, acting on his own initiative in the hope of obtaining the subsequent approval of the Austrian Emperor,[41] had, on May 25, issued a proclamation advising the people that the payment of the June quota of the land tax was to be deferred until the month of July,[42] after the harvest would be over. Many people were on the verge of starvation, and some of them, in sheer desperation, turned to robbery and violence.[43]

As we have seen, by early June, 1814, the Kingdom of Italy, which had been created by Napoleon in 1805, was definitely overthrown. The Venetian departments of the kingdom had been occupied by Austrian troops since October, 1813. The territory west of the Mincio and north of the Po, however, had remained under French control until April 16, 1814, when the French-Italian army under the command of Prince Eugene Beauharnais, Napoleon's viceroy in the kingdom, laid down its arms.

39 Hager Report, June 30, 1814, *Staats-Archiv*, Vienna, *Conferenz Akten*, Ser. b, 1814, No. 1281.

40 Note especially the two protocols of the *Staats-Conferenz* of June 21, 1814, *ibid.*, Nos. 1120 and 1146.

41 Reuss Report, Padua, May 27, 1814, as summarized in the *Staats-Conferenz* protocol of June 21, 1814, *ibid.*, No. 1143.

42 *Collezione di leggi venete, op. cit.*, 1813-14, I, 240-41. No significant tax reductions were announced in the Venetian departments until August 4, 1814, when the capitation, the sales, and the registration taxes were lowered. See *ibid.*, II, 19-24.

43 Hager Report, June 17, 1814, *Staats-Archiv*, Vienna, *Conferenz Akten*, Ser. b, 1814, No. 1174; Helfert, *Kaiser Franz, op. cit.*, 24.

By April, 1814, when the French had finally been defeated, in Italy as well as elsewhere, the overwhelming majority of the inhabitants of the parts of the kingdom still under French administration wanted the immediate overthrow of the French government. A large number of them, influenced as they had, been by the liberal and national propaganda of the patriotic writers, of the British agents, of the emissaries of Joachim Murat, of the members of the secret societies, and even of some of the Austrian generals in Italy, longed to have created in its place a new Kingdom of Italy, wholly independent of all foreign control and governed according to liberal principles.

When, at this moment, Prince Eugene and his friends made moves designed to influence the Allied Powers to establish a new kingdom with Eugene as its monarch, persons from the ranks of all the groups opposed to the French—pro-Austrians, " pure Italians," and members of the secret societies—cooperated to prevent the viceroy's plot from succeeding. They staged the bloody and destructive Milanese revolution of April 20, as a result of which the existing French government was overthrown and a new provisional government, dominated by the " pure Italian " factions, was temporarily established in its place.

The Milanese revolution sealed the fate of the western part of the Kingdom of Italy. Venetia had been promised to Austria by the Allied Powers in the Treaty of Prague, of July 27, 1813. The future destiny of Lombardy, however, was not definitely decided until the reports of the large amount of liberal and revolutionary sentiment in Milan in April, 1814, induced the conservative governments of the Allied Powers to give the country to the Habsburgs.

A large number of persons in both Venetia and Lombardy were very much dissatisfied with the prospects of becoming Austrian subjects. Many Venetians, governed as they had been by Austrian military officials for more than half a year, had been angered by the retention of many former French officials in the new Austrian government, by the officious and disrespectful conduct of Austrian soldiers, by the compulsory circulation of depreciated Austrian currency in the country, and, above all, by the high taxes and military requisitions which the Habsburg officials had levied upon them. Some of them were bitter because the Venetian Republic had not been restored.

The Lombards had not been subjected to these grievances, but by early June, 1814, many of them, particularly the Italian army and the middle classes, were hostile to the Austrians. They were irritated and disillusioned because, after the English agents, MacFarlane, Wilson, and Bentinck, and even some of the Habsburg officials themselves, had encouraged them to believe that their hopes for the establishment of an independent kingdom would be satisfied, they were placed under Austrian domination.

Some of the Italian " patriots," most of them officers of the Italian army, conceived a plot in the summer of 1814 to drive the Austrians out of Italy. Fortunately for the Habsburgs, the scheme—the so-called Brescian-Milanese military conspiracy— was nipped in the bud in the fall of 1814, and its ringleaders were arrested and imprisoned.[44] Thereafter, no active plot to overthrow the new Austrian regime was planned in Lombardy-Venetia for a number of years. When, during the period of the " Hundred Days " in 1815, Napoleon's brother-in-law, Joachim Murat, unfurled the banner of independence and unification in Italy and issued clarion calls to the Italians to follow him in his fight against the Austrians, the Lombards and the Venetians turned a deaf ear to his pleas. The liberal leaders of the Italian army had been discredited by their unsuccessful attempt to revolt during the previous year, the bourgeoisie was tired of struggling, and, furthermore, was hostile to Murat, and most

44 The best account of the Brescian-Milanese conspiracy is in the two volumes in the *Collezione storica del Risorgimento italiano* written by Domenico Spadoni and entitled: *Milano e la congiura militare nel 1814 per l'indipendenza italiana: La congiura militare e il suo processo* (Modena, 1937), and *Milano e la congiura militare nel 1814 per l'indipendenza italiana: I giudizi di Mantova e la sorte dei congiurati* (Modena, 1937).

of the members of the other classes " were indifferent to the cause of national independence." [45]

From 1814 to 1859, the Lombard and Venetian portions of the former Kingdom of Italy formed a small portion of the vast expanse of the Habsburg Empire—a portion in which some of the Italians submitted with pleasure to Austrian sovereignty, but others yielded with increasing dissatisfaction. [46] For a time, the Austrians were able to throttle the national and liberal spirit which had germinated in Italy during the course of the Revolutionary and Napoleonic period. In 1848, however, when a large number of Lombards and Venetians, as well as other Italians, had been converted to the liberal and national program, the Italian " patriots " made a spirited attempt to cast off the Austrian yoke. They failed to accomplish their goal. Later, however, by taking advantage of the Austro-French-Sardinian War of 1859, the Austro-Prussian War of 1866, and the Franco-Prussian War of 1870, they succeeded in creating a liberal and national state—a new Kingdom of Italy. The hopes and aspirations of the " pure Italians " of 1814 were at last fulfilled.

45 Lemmi, Francesco, " Gioacchino Murat et le aspirazıoni unitarie nel 1815," *Archivio storico per le Province Napoletane*, Anno XXVI (1901), 195-96.

46 For an excellent study of the nature of the liberal opposition to the Habsburgs during most of this period, see Greenfield, Kent Roberts, *Economics and Liberalism in the Risorgimento. A Study of Nationalism in Lombardy, 1814-1848* (Baltimore, Md , 1934).

BIBLIOGRAPHY

ARCHIVAL MATERIAL

Milan:

Ambrosiana Library:

> *Le Lamentazioni, ossiano le notti del Gle. Pino, con note interessanti la Rivoluzione di Milano del 20 Aple. 1814.* A handwritten copy. Filed under the signature of S. C. V. V. 26, No. 10. An attack on the plotters of the Milanese revolution of April 20, 1814

> Mantovani, Luigi, *Diario politico-ecclesiastico di Milano.* Under the signature of M. S IV. 5.

> *Memoria di Lodovico Giovio intorno all'opuscolo intitolato: 'Sulla rivoluzione di Milano seguita nel giorno 20 aprile, e nei successivi 1814. Li 7 febbrajo 1815.'* A handwritten copy of this document is filed under the signature of S. C V. V. 26, No 6. A brief but excellent source for the events of April 20, 1814. Giovio was the president of the electoral colleges of the Kingdom of Italy.

> *Opuscolo sopra la Rivoluzione di Milano e la Morte di Prina M. nel 20 aprile 1814.* S C.V.V 26. Contains valuable pamphlets, both handwritten and printed, on the Milanese revolution of April 20, 1814.

> *Osservazioni del Generale Pino sopra alcune asserzioni dell'autore dell'opuscolo che ha per titolo. 'Sulla rivoluzione di Milano, seguita il 20 aprile 1814, ec. Parigi in novembre. Italia, 1815.'* S C V.V. 26, No. 7. Interesting, but of no particular value.

> *Sulla rivoluzione di Milano seguita nel giorno 20 aprile 1814, sul primo suo governo provvisorio e sulle quivi tenute adunanze de'collegj elettorali. Memoria storica con documenti.* Parigi, Novembre 1814. Printed anonymously, but written by Senator Leopoldo Armaroli. Filed under the signature of S C.V.V. 26, No 5. A good source for the Milanese revolution of April 20, 1814

Archivio di Stato:

> *Atti segreti,* 1814.

Brera Library:

> *Protocolli originali della reggenza provvisoria del Regno d'Italia nel 1814.* Filed under the name of De Pagave Excellent for the period following the Milanese revolution.

Museo del Risorgimento italiano:

> *Carte del Giacomo Beccaria.* The best available source on the events following the Milanese revolution.

Princeton University:

Archives of Eugene Beauharnais Contains some new material on the Milanese revolution.

Venice·

Archivio di Stato (Contains much unused material)·
Atti Hiller, 1813.
Dazi Consumo, 1814.
Finanze, 1813
Imposte, 1814.
Organizzazione, 1813, 1814.
Polizia, 1813, 1814
Pubblico Politico, 1813.

Vienna

Haus- Hof- und Staats- Archiv (Cited as *Staats-Archiv* in all but the
first reference):
Conferenz Akten, Ser a and b, 1813, 1814. An excellent source
Frankreich Varia.
Kabinets-Akten, 1813, 1814. Contains summaries of many of the
police reports which were destroyed in July, 1927, when the
Ministry of Justice Palace was burned
Kaiser Franz Akten. A source thus far largely unused by Italian
historians writing on the fall of the Kingdom of Italy.
Staatskanzlei, Provinzen, Lombardei-Venedig.
Staats-Rath Akten, 1814

Hofkammer Archiv·
Central- Organisirungs- Hof- Commission Akten, 1814
Kredit Akten, 1813, 1814.

Archiv des Ministeriums des Innern:
Hofkanzlei. Most of this material was destroyed in the burning of
the Ministry of Justice building in 1927

Kriegs-Archiv:
Feld Akten (Italien), 1813, 1814 Contains several valuable, unused
documents.
Kriegs-Ministerium Akten, 1813, 1814.

PRINTED CONTEMPORARY RECORDS

" Agriculture and Statistics of Italy (A Review of Chateauvieux, Frédéric
Sullin de, *Lettres écrites d'Italia en 1812 et 1813, à M. Charles Pictet, . .*) "
The Edinburgh Review, XXVIII (1817), 31-58.

Allgemeine Zeitung Mit allerhoechsten Privilegien, 1813, 1814

*The Annual Register, or a View of the History, Politics, and Literature,
for the Year 1813.* Cradock and Joy, London, 1814

*The Annual Register, or a View of the History, Politics, and Literature,
for the Year 1814.* Baldwin, Cradock, and Joy, London, 1815

*Appello ad Alessandro, Imperatore e Autocrate di tutte le Russie, sul
destino dell'Italia* Scritto nelle tre lingue [English, Italian, and French]

dall'editore dell'*Italico* [Bozzi Granville]. Ricardo and Taylor, London, 1814. An original copy of this appeal is in the Milanese *Biblioteca del Risorgimento italiano*.

Bandini, Gino,
Giornali e scritti politici clandestini della Carboneria romagnola (1819-21). In the *Biblioteca storica del Risorgimento italiano*, Ser. V, No. 8. Albrighi, Segati e C., Roma, 1908.

Bollettino delle leggi della Repubblica Italiana e del regno d'Italia. 27 vols., no publisher given, Milano, 1802-14

The British and Foreign State Papers, 1813, 1814

Cantù, Cesare (edit.),
Corrispondenze di dipomatici della repubblica e del Regno d'Italia, 1796-1814. Agnelli, Milano, 1884.

Cantù, Cesare (edit.),
Il principe Eugenio, memorie del Regno d'Italia. 9 vols., Corona e Caimi, Milano, 1880 A valuable collection of Prince Eugene's correspondence

Carducci, Giosue,
Letture del risorgimento italiano. 2 vols., Zanichelli, Bologna, 1896-97. Contains excerpts from the writings of prominent Italian nationalists.

Carte segrete ed atti ufficiali della polizia austriaca in Italia dal 4 giugno 1814 al 22 marzo 1848. 3 vols., Capolago, Torino, 1851-52

Casati, Gabrio (edit.),
Federico Confalonieri, Memorie e lettere. 2 vols., Hoepli, Milano, 1889. Confalonieri was a liberal Milanese noble who played a large rôle in the events which led to the fall of the Kingdom of Italy

Casini, Tommaso,
La rivoluzione di Milano dell'aprile 1814. Relazioni storiche di Leopoldo Armaroli e Carlo Verri, Senatori del Regno italico. In the *Biblioteca storica del Risorgimento italiano*, I, No. 3. Società editrice Dante Alighieri, Roma, 1897. The best source for the Milanese revolution of April 20, 1814.

Cipolla, C.,
"Un Documento Austriaco sui Massoni e sui Carbonari" *Rassegna Nazionale*, XXIV (1885), 478-500.

Collezione di leggi e regolamenti pubblicati dall'imp. regio governo delle province venete, 1813, 1814 Andreola, Venezia, 1814-15. Although this collection has been practically unused, it is an invaluable source. It contains all the official decrees and regulations.

Coraccini, Frédéric,
Histoire de l'administration du royaume d'Italie pendant la domination française. Audin, Paris, 1823. This is a French translation of Coraccini, Federico, *Storia dell'amministrazione del regno d'Italia durante il dominio francese*. Veladini, Lugano, 1823 The book was also published under the

following title: *Mémoires sur la cour du Prince Eugène et sur le royaume d'Italie pendant la domination de Napoléon Bonaparte.* Par un Français attaché à la cour du vice-roi d'Italie. Audin, Paris, 1826. My citations are to the first of these three editions. This work has been much used by scholars.

D'Angeberg, Comte [Chodźko, Jacob Leonard],
  Le Congrès de Vienne et les traités de 1815. 2 vols, Lahure, Paris, 1864.

D'Angeberg, Comte [Chodźko, Jacob Leonard],
  Recueil des traités, conventions et actes diplomatiques concernant l'Autriche et l'Italie. Amyot, Paris, 1859.

Demelitsch, Fedor von,
  "Actenstuecke zur Geschichte der Coalition vom Jahre 1814" *Fontes Rerum Austriacarum,* XLIX, Pt 2 (1899), 227-447.

  Dernière campagne de l'armée franco-italienne, sous les ordres d'Eugène-Beauharnais, en 1813 et 1814, Suivie de Mémoires secrets sur la révolution de Milan, du 20 avril 1814, et les deux conjurations du 25 avril 1815; la campagne des Autrichiens contre Murat; sa mort tragique, et la situation politique actuelle des divers États d'Italie. Par le chevalier S J***, témoin oculaire. Dentu, Paris, 1817. Good for the Italian campaign of 1813-14

Du Casse, A,
  Mémoires et correspondance politique et militaire du Prince Eugène. 10 vols, Lévy, Paris, 1858-60 A much quoted source.

Fassò, Luigi (edit),
  Ugo Foscolo; prose politiche e letterarie dal 1811 al 1816 Vol VIII of the *Edizione nazionale delle opere di Ugo Foscolo.* Monnier, Firenze, 1933.

Fiorani, G,
  "L'eccidio del Ministro Prina" *Rendiconti* del Reale Istituto lombardo di scienze e lettere, Ser II, XXVIII (1895), 422-36. Contains letters written by Borda, who was an eyewitness of the Milanese revolution, to his friend Gallotta.

Foscolo, Ugo,
  "Epistolario" *Opere complete di Ugo Foscolo* (2 vols, no publisher given, Napoli, 1860), II, 1-365.

Foscolo, Ugo,
  "Lettera Apologetica" *Opere complete di Ugo Foscolo,* I, 671-715.

Foscolo, Ugo,
  "Prose Politiche" *Opere complete di Ugo Foscolo,* I, 545-670

Freksa, Frederick,
  A Peace Congress of Intrigue (A Vivid, Intimate Account of the Congress of Vienna, composed of the Personal Memoirs of its Important Participants). Century, New York, 1919 Translated by Harry Hansen from Freksa's *Der Wiener Kongress. Nach Aufzeichnungen von Teilnehmern*

und Mitarbeitern. Published in 1917, by the Memoiren-Bibliothek of Stuttgart.

Gallavresi, Giuseppe (edit.),
Carteggio del conte Federico Confalonieri ed altri documenti spettanti alla sua biografia; con annotazione storiche. 3 vols, Ripalta, Milano, 1910-13. The best and most complete collection of Confalonieri's correspondence. An invaluable source.

Gallavresi, Giuseppe (edit.),
Il carteggio intimo di Andrea Borda. Estratto dall'*Archivio Storico Lombardo,* Anno XLVII. Tipogr. Pont. ed Arcio S. Giuseppe, Milano, 1921.

Gallavresi, Giuseppe,
" La rivoluzione lombarda del 1814 e la politica inglese secondo nuovi documenti." *Archivio Storico Lombardo,* Ser. IV, XI (1909), 97-166. An invaluable source for the intrigues of the English agents in Milan in late April and early May, 1814. Consists chiefly of documents

Gallavresi, Giuseppe,
" I ricordi ed il carteggio del conte Ludovico Giovio " *Periodico* della Società storica della Provincia e antica Diocesi di Como, XVII-XVIII (1906-8), 221-50.

Gallavresi, Giuseppe,
" Testimonianze tratte dalle carte Giovio per la storia dei fatti del 1814 " *Bollettino ufficiale* del primo congresso storico del Risorgimento Italiano (1906), 131-37.

Gallavresi, Giuseppe, e V. Sallier de la Tour de Cordon,
Le Maréchal Sallier de la Tour. Mémoires et lettres. Artigianelli, Torino, 1912.

Gebhardt, Bruno,
Wilhelm von Humboldt's politische Denkschriften 2 vols, Behr, Berlin, 1903.

Giornale dipartimentale dell'Adriatico, 1814.

Giornale italiano, of Milan, 1814.

Giornale di Venezia, 1814. All three of the above papers, although they were carefully censored, are of some value

Granville, Paulina B (edit),
Autobiography of A. B. Granville, M.D., F.R.S.,—being eighty-eight years of the life of a physician who practised his profession in Italy, Greece, Turkey, Spain, Portugal, the West Indies, Russia, Germany, France, and England. 2 vols., 2nd ed , King, London, 1874.

Guicciardi, Conte, ex-Chancelier du Sénat,
Relation historique de la révolution du royaume d'Italie en 1814. Traduit de l'Italien par M. Saint-Edme. Corréard, Paris, 1822. This is a

French edition of Armaroli's *Sulla rivoluzione di Milano seguita nel giorno 20 aprile 1814, op cit.*

Hansard, T. C.,
The Parliamentary Debates from the Year 1803 to the Present Time. Hansard, London, 1804——.

Hertslet, Edward,
The Map of Europe by Treaty, showing the various political and territorial Changes which have taken place since the general Peace of 1814. 4 vols., Butterworth and Harrison, London, 1875-91.

Journal historique sur la campagne du Prince Eugène, en Italie, pendant les années 1813 et 1814. Par L. D****, Capitaine attaché à l'État-major du Prince, et Chevalier de la Légion d'Honneur. Plancher, Delaunay, et Guibert, Paris, 1817. A good source for the Italian campaign of 1813-14

Klinkowstroem, Alfons Freiherr von (edit.),
Oesterreichs Theilnahme an den Befreiungskriegen. Ein Beitrag zur Geschichte der Jahre 1813 bis 1815 nach Aufzeichnungen von Friedrich von Gentz, nebst einem Anhang: " Briefwechsel zwischen den Fuersten Schwarzenberg und Metternich." Carl Gerold's Sohn, Wien, 1887

Klueber, Johann Ludwig,
Acten des Wiener Congresses in den Jahren 1814 und 1815. 8 vols., Palm und Enke, Erlangen, 1815-19.

Koch, Christophe G de, et Friedrich Schoell,
Histoire abrégée des traités de paix entre les puissances de l'Europe depuis la paix de Westphalie. 15 vols., Gide, Paris, 1817-18. This work has a good account of the military campaign of 1813-14.

Lemmi, Francesco,
La restaurazione in Italia nel 1814 nel diario del barone von Huegel (9 decembre 1813-25 mai 1814). Albrighi, Segati e Cie, Milano, 1910. Copied from the original in the *Haus- Hof- und Staats- Archiv,* Vienna, *Staatskanzlei, Provinzen, Lombardei-Venedig,* Fasc. 45, Sect. 1. Cited as " Huegel Diary, op. cit." Baron Huegel was aide-de-camp to Marshal Bellegarde. His diary is an invaluable source for the study of the fall of the Kingdom of Italy.

The London Times, 1814. Contains a few reports from Italy that are useful.

Martens, Geo Fréd., et Charles Martens,
Nouveau recueil de traités d'alliance, de paix, de trève, de neutralité, de commerce, de limites, d'échange, etc., et de plusieurs autres actes servant à la connaissance des rélations étrangères des puissances et états de l'Europe 16 vols. and supplements, Dietrich, Gottingue, 1817-42.

Melzi d'Eril, Francesco, Duca di Lodi,
Memorie-documenti e lettere inedite di Napoleone I. e Beauharnais. Raccolte e ordinate per cura di Giovanni Melzi. 2 vols., Brigola, Milano, 1865. A valuable and much cited source.

" Memorie inedite di Giuseppe Bossi." *Archivio Storico Lombardo,* Anno V (1878), 275-307. Bossi was in charge of the Milanese civic guard at the time of the revolution of April 20, 1814.

Memoirs of the Secret Societies of the South of Italy, particularly the Carbonari. Translated from the original MS Murray, London, 1821. Indispensable for a study of the Carbonari.

" La morte del Prina narrata da un locarnese." *Bollettino storico della svizzera italiana,* Anno XXXIII (1911), 105-7.

Oesterreichisch- Kaiserliche privilegirte Wiener- Zeitung nebst Amtsblatt. Cited as the " *Wiener Zeitung."*

Oesterreichischer Beobachter, 1813, 1814. Although carefully censored, both this paper and the *Wiener Zeitung* contain useful material

Orloff, Comte Grégoire [Orlov, Grigorii Vladimirovich],
Mémoires historiques, politiques et littéraires sur le royaume de Naples. 5 vols, Chasserieu et Hecart, Paris, 1819-21

Pedrotti, Pietro,
Note autobiografiche del cospiratore trentino Gioacchino Prati, con annotazioni e commenti. Sulla base di documenti inediti d'archivio. Grandi, Rovereto, 1926.

Pellini, Silvio,
" Il 20 aprile 1814." *Napoleone Rivista storica,* Anno I (1914), 49-53. Contains an anonymous letter which gives a good description of Minister Prina's assassination.

Pellini, Silvio,
Il General Pino e la morte del Ministro Prina. Miglio, Novara, 1905. This is the name given on the title page. On the cover the title is given as *il* [*sic*] *General Pino e l'eccidio del Ministro Prina* Miglio, Novara, 1906. The book consists almost entirely of documents which are indispensable for a study of the Milanese revolution

Pellini, S,
" La sommossa di Milano del 20 aprile 1814 e la morte del Prina secondo un testimonio oculare." *Rivista mensile di lettere, di storia e d'arte* (Casalmaggiore), Anno I (1900), 6-8. Contains letters which Gallone, an eyewitness of Minister Prina's assassination, wrote his friend Bianchini

Pilot, A.,
" Venezia nel blocco del 1813-14 Da noterelle inedite del Cicogna." *Nuovo Archivio Veneto,* Anno XIV (1914), 191-227. Gives an excellent description of conditions in the city of Venice immediately before and after its capitulation on April 20, 1814.

Précis historique des opérations militaires de l'armée d'Italie, en 1813 et 1814, Par le Chef de l'État-Major-général de cette Armée. Barrois, Paris, 1817. Good for the Italian campaign of 1813-14.

Raccolta degli atti del governo e delle disposizioni generali emanate dalle diverse autorità in oggetti sì amministrativi che giudiziarj. Imp regia stamperia, Milano, 1816-19. Contains all the official decrees and regulations of the Milanese government from April 21, 1814, to 1818. Although it has remained almost entirely unused, this source is indispensable. Cited as " *Atti del governo lombardo, op. cit.*"

Rinieri, P Ilario,
Corrispondenza inedita dei cardinali Consalvi e Pacca nel tempo del Congresso di Vienna (1814-1815); ricavata dall'archivio secreto vaticano, corredata di sommarii e note. Precedula da uno studio storico sugli stati d'Europa nel tempo dell'impero napoleonico, e sul nuovo assestamento europeo e da un diario inedito del Mse. di San Marzano. Unione Tipografica, Roma, 1903.

Rota, Ettore,
Il problema italiano dal 1700 al 1815 (L'idea unitaria). Istituto per gli studi di politica internazionale, Milano, [1938]. A collection of selected documents.

Ruffini, G,
" Una lettera di Vincenzo Dandolo sulla seduta del 17 aprile 1814 nel Senato italico " *Archivio Storico Lombardo,* Anno XLVIII (1921), 613-16.

Saint-Edme, M. [Edme, Théodore Bourg],
Constitution et organisation des Carbonari, ou documents exacts sur tout ce qui concerne l'existence, l'origine et le but de cette société secrète. 2nd ed , Brissot-Thivars, Paris, 1822 Indispensable for a study of the Carbonari.

Spadoni, Domenico,
" Gli Statuti della Guelfia in possesso della Polizia austriaca nel 1816." *Rassegna storica del Risorgimento,* Anno XI (1924), 704-38. Indispensable for a study of the origins of secret societies in nineteenth century Italy.

Studi intorno alla storia della Lombardia negli ultimi trent'anni e delle cagioni del difetto d'energia dei Lombardi. Manoscritto in francese di un Lombardo, voltato in italiano da un Franceso No publisher given, Parigi, 1847. Published anonymously, but written by Princess Cristina Belgiojoso-Trivulzio. A much cited and valuable source for the Milanese revolution.

Vane, Charles, Marquess of Londonderry (edit),
Memoirs and Correspondence of Viscount Castlereagh, Second Marquess of Londonderry. The last eight volumes are under the following title: *Correspondence, Despatches, and other Papers of Viscount Castlereagh, Second Marquess of Londonderry.* 12 vols. The first 4 vols published by Colburn, London, 1848-49; the last 8, by Shoberl, London, 1851-53. Cited as " Castlereagh Correspondence, *op. cit.*"

Vaudoncourt, Le général de [Frédéric Guillaume],
Histoire politique et militaire du Prince Eugène Napoléon, vice-roi d'Italie. 2 vols , Mongie, Paris, 1828.

Verri, Conte Carlo,
  Sugli avvenimenti di Milano 17-20 aprile 1814. Scritta in Nizza, Inverno
1817. Reprinted in Casini, Tommaso, *La rivoluzione di Milano dell'aprile
1814. Relazioni storiche di Leopoldo Armaroli e Carlo Verri, Senatori del
Regno italico.* Società editrice Dante Alighieri, Roma, 1897. My citations
are from the Casini edition. This account is perhaps the most important
source on the events occurring in Milan between the 17th and 20th of
April, 1814.

Webster, C. K.,
  *British Diplomacy, 1813-1815 (Select Documents Dealing with the Re-
construction of Europe).* Bell and Sons, London, 1921.

Weil, Maurice H.,
  *Les dessous du Congrès de Vienne, d'après les documents originaux des
archives du Ministère impérial et royal de l'intérieur à Vienne* 2 vols,
Payot, Paris, 1917.

Welden, Ludwig Freiherr von,
  *Der Krieg der Oesterreicher in Italien gegen die Franzosen in den Jahren
1813 und 1814.* Damian u. Sorges' Universitaets- Buchhandlung, Graz, 1853
A good account of the Italian campaign, written by a man who took part
in it.

Wilson, Sir Robert,
  *Private Diary of Travels, Personal Services, and Public Events, during
Mission and Employment with the European Armies in the Campaigns of
1812, 1813, 1814.* 2 vols., Murray, London, 1861. This is the diary of one
of the English agents in Milan in May, 1814.

Special Articles

Bersano, Arturo,
  " Adelfi, Federati e Carbonari. Contributo alla Storia delle Società
segrete " *Atti* della R Accademia delle Scienze di Torino, XLV (1909-10),
409-30.

Bonfadini, R.,
  " Federico Confalonieri." *Nuova Antologia di scienze, lettere ed arti,*
Ser. IV, CLVI (1897), 671-87.

Buccella, M. R.,
  " La congiura e l'offerta dell'impero romano a Napoleone all'isola
d'Elba." *Nuova Antologia. Rivista di lettere, scienze ed arti,* Anno LXV
(1930), 352-62.

Capograssi, Antonio,
  " L'unità d'Italia nel pensiero di Lord William Bentinck." *Rassegna
storica del Risorgimento,* Anno XXI (1934), 227-57.

Castro, Giovanni de,
"I ricordi autobiografici inediti del Marchese Benigno Bossi." *Archivio Storico Lombardo,* Anno XVII (1890), 894-937.

Castro, Giovanni de,
"La restaurazione austriaca in Milano (1814-1817) Notizie desunte da diarj e testimonianze contemporanee." *Archivio Storico Lombardo,* XV (1888), 591-658, 905-79.

Cervellini, G. B.,
"Il periodo veneziano di P. A. Paravia (dal carteggio inedito con G. Monico)." *Archivio Veneto,* Anno LXI (1931), 143-90.

Cessi, Roberto,
"Agli albori del Risorgimento" *Nuovo Archivio Veneto,* XXXII, Pt. II (1916), 223-37

Chiattone, Domenico,
"Nuovi documenti su Federico Confalonieri e per le sue relazioni intime e patriottiche prima del processo" *Archivio Storico Lombardo,* Anno XXXIII (1906), 47-114.

Comandini, Alfredo,
"Un Milanese per l'Italia a Londra nel 1814" *Il Secolo,* 10 aprile 1919. The writer saw a copy of this article in the Milanese *Biblioteca del Risorgimento italiano.*

Ferrero, Guglielmo,
"L'effet de la révolution française sur l'Italie" *Revue Bleu,* February 5, 1928, 65-8

Franchetti, Augusto,
"Della rivoluzione francese e della coscienza politica nazionale in Italia." *Nuova Antologia di scienze, lettere ed arti,* CIV (1889), 417-29.

Gallavresi, Giuseppe,
"La franc-maçonnerie et la formation de l'unité italienne." *Revue des questions historiques,* Année L (1922), 415-37.

Gallavresi, Giuseppe,
"Per una futura biografia di F. Confalonieri." *Archivio Storico Lombardo,* XXXIV (1907), 428-70.

Gallavresi, Giuseppe,
"Ricerche intorno alla rivoluzione milanese del 1814." *Rendiconti* del Reale Istituto lombardo di scienze e lettere, Ser. II, XL (1907), 403-15.

Johnston, R. M,
"Lord William Bentinck and Murat." *The English Historical Review,* XIX (1904), 263-80.
"The Kingdom of Italy." *Eclectic Magazine,* LIII (1861), 145-57.

Lackland, Miss H. M.,
"Lord William Bentinck in Sicily, 1811-12." *The English Historical Review*, XLII (1927), 371-96.

Lackland, Miss H. M,
"The Failure of the Constitutional Experiment in Sicily, 1813-14 " *The English Historical Review*, XLI (1926), 210-35.

Lemmi, Francesco,
"Gioacchino Murat et le aspirazioni unitarie nel 1815 " *Archivio storico per le Province Napoletane*, Anno XXVI (1901), 169-211.

Marchesi, G. B,
"Il podestà di Milano conte Antonio Durini " *Archivio Storico Lombardo*, XIX (1903), 138-76.

Marcolongo, Bianca,
"La massoneria nel secolo XVIII." *Studi Storici*, XIX (1910), 407-77.

Marcolongo, Bianca,
"Le origini della Carboneria e le Società segrete nell'Italia Meridionale dal 1810 al 1820 " *Studi Storici*, XX (1912), 233-348.

Mazziotti, M,
"L'offerta del trono d'Italia a Napoleone I esule all'Elba." *Rassegna storica del Risorgimento*, Anno VII (1920), 1-18.

Monti, Antonio,
"G. D Romagnosi Contributo Biografico " *Nuova Antologia. Rivista di lettere, scienze ed arti*, Anno LIII (1918), 41-50.

Nardi, Carlo,
"La vita di Francesco Saverio Salfi (1759-1832) " *Rassegna storica del Risorgimento*, Anno VII (1920), 161-332.

"L'origine e lo scopo della Carboneria secondo i costituti de'primi Carbonari e Guelfi " *La Civiltà Cattolica*, Anno LXVI (1915), 641-61

Ottolini, Angelo,
"U. Foscolo e la risoluzione dell'esilio." *Archivio Storico Lombardo*, Anno LV (1928), 168-80.

Rinieri, Ilario,
"Le sette in Italia dopo la restaurazione del 1814 La congiura di Macerata (1817) " *Il Risorgimento Italiano*, Anno XIX (1926), 1-76

Salvisenti, Bernardo,
"La missione Porro presso le Alte Potenze nel 1814 " *La Lombardia nel Risorgimento*, Anno I-II (1914), 33-45.

Solitro, Giuseppe,
"Maestri e scolari dell'università di Padova nell'ultima dominazione austriaca (1813-1866)." *Archivio Veneto-Tridentino*, Anno I (1922), 109-93.

Solmi, Arrigo,
   "Francesco Melzi e l'idea unitaria nel 1801." In his *L'idea dell'unità italiana nell'età napoleonica* (In the *Collezione storica del Risorgimento italiano*, Società Tipografica Modenese, Modena, 1934), 77-93.

Solmi, Arrigo,
   "L'idea dell'unità italiana nell'età napoleonica" In his book by the same name, 29-76. Also in *Rassegna storica del Risorgimento*, Anno XX (1933), 1-19.

Solmi, Arrigo,
   "Sul vero autore della 'Storia dell'amministrazione del Regno d'Italia durante il dominio francese.'" In his *L'idea dell'unità italiana nell'età napoleonica*, 145-58.

Solmi, Arrigo,
   "Ugo Foscolo e l'unità dell'Italia." In his *L'idea dell'unità napoleonica*, 97-141.

Soriga, Renato,
   "Augusto Bozzi Granville e la Rivista 'L'Italico'" *Bollettino* della Società pavese di storia patria, Anno XIV (1914), 265-301.

Soriga, Renato,
   "Baglion unitari in Lombardia avanti la restaurazione austriaca (1814)." *Bollettino* della Società pavese di storia patria, Anno XV (1915), 3-18.

Soriga, Renato,
   "La passione italica di Vittorio Barzoni da Lonato (1767-1843)." *Rassegna storica del Risorgimento*, Anno XX (1933), 675-77.

Soriga, Renato,
   "La ristampa milanese della 'Lira focense' di Antonio Ierocades" *Rassegna storica del Risorgimento*, Anno V (1918), 727-38.

Soriga, Renato,
   "Ugo Foscolo e il suo amico anglo-italo Augusto Bozzi Granville." *La Lombardia nel Risorgimento italiano*, Anno XIII (1928), 121-40.

Spadoni, Domenico,
   "Aspirazioni unitarie d'un austriacante nel 1814" *La Lombardia nel Risorgimento italiano*, Anno XVIII (1933), 71-80.

Spadoni, Domenico,
   "Carlo Comelli de Stuckenfeld e il trono de'Cesari offerto a Casa Savoja nel 1814." *Rassegna storica del Risorgimento*, Anno XIV (1927), 593-656

Spadoni, Domenico,
   "Federazione e Re d'Italia mancati nel 1814-15." *Nuova Rivista storica*, Anno X (1931), 398-433.

Spadoni, Domenico,
   "I documenti della congiura milanese carpiti da St. Agnan nel 1814." *Il Risorgimento Italiano*, XIX (1926), 299-326.

Spadoni, Domenico,
"Il gen. bar. Giacomo Filippo de Meester." *Rassegna storica del Risorgimento,* Anno XVI (1929), 847-96.

Spadoni, Domenico,
"Il Foscolo cospiratore nel 1813-14." *Studi su Ugo Foscolo,* editi a cura della R. Università di Pavia nel primo centenario della morte del poeta. (Chiantore, Torino, 1927), 555-600

Spadoni, Domenico,
"Il processo per la congiura bresciano-milanese del 1814." *Atti* del XIII Congresso Nazionale della Società Nazionale per la Storia del Risorgimento italiano, tenutosi in Genova nei giorni 26-28 ottobre 1925, 81-99.

Spadoni, Domenico,
"Il sogno unitario e wilsoniano d'un patriota nel 1814-15." *Rassegna storica del Risorgimento,* Anno XIII (1926), 341-55.

Spadoni, Domenico,
"Le società segrete nella rivoluzione milanese dell'aprile 1814" *Nuova Antologia. Rivista di lettere, scienze ed arti,* Ser. VII, CCLXV (1929), 197-211. Throws new light on the Milanese revolution.

Spadoni, Domenico,
"L'ultimo appello antinapoleonico del Barzoni." *La Lombardia nel Risorgimento italiano,* Anno XV (1930), 65-73.

Trecchi, Dario Biandrà,
"Milano e gli Inglesi nel 1814. La missione del barone Trecchi." *Rassegna storica del Risorgimento,* Anno XV (1937), 521-54.

Verga, Ettore,
"La deputazione dei collegi elettorali del regno d'Italia a Parigi nel 1814" *Archivio Storico Lombardo,* Anno XXXI (1904), 303-33. The best study of the Milanese deputation at Paris.

Weil, C.,
"Les négociations secrètes entre Joachim Murat et le prince Eugène (février-mars 1814)." *Revue d'histoire moderne et contemporaine,* VII (1905-6), 509-23.

Zieger, Antonio,
"I primi risultati delle ricerche austriache sui massoni lombardi nel 1814 e 1815." *La Lombardia nel Risorgimento italiano,* Anno XIII (1928), 5-29

SPECIAL WORKS

Avenati, Carlo Antonio,
La rivoluzione italiana da Vittorio Alfieri a Benito Mussolini. In the *Biblioteca della Società storica subalpina.* Ghirardi, Torino, 1934.

Balfour, Lady Frances,
The Life of George Fourth Earl of Aberdeen. Hodder and Stoughton, London, 1922.

Beer, Adolf,
Die Finanzen Oesterreichs im XIX. Jahrhundert. Nach archivalischen Quellen. Tempsky, Prag, 1877.

Beidtel, Ignaz,
Geschichte der oesterreichischen Staatsverwaltung, 1740-1848. 2 vols, Wagner'schen Universitaets- Buchhandlung, Innsbruck, 1896-98 Is still the best study of the Austrian state administration.

Bianchi, Nicomede,
Storia documentata della diplomazia europea in Italia dall'anno 1814 all'anno 1861. 8 vols., Unione Tipografica, Torino, 1865-72 Although it has been proved that some of the documents included in this book are inaccurate and spurious, it is still a valuable source.

Bruun, Geoffrey,
Europe and the French Imperium, 1799-1814. In *The Rise of Modern Europe* series, edited by William L. Langer. Harper's, New York, 1938.

Caemmerer, Rudolf von,
Die Befreiungskriege, 1813-1815. Ein strategischer Ueberblick. Mittler und Sohn, Berlin, 1907.

Cantù, Cesare,
Il Conciliatore e i Carbonari. Treves, Milano, 1878.

Castro, Giovanni de,
Il mondo secreto. 9 vols, Daelli e C, Milano, 1864.

Castro, Giovanni de,
Principio di secolo: Storia della caduta del regno italico. 2nd ed., Treves, Milano, 1897. A much quoted book.

Ceria, Luigi,
L'eccidio del Prina e gli ultimi giorni del regno italico (1814). Mondadori, Milano, 1937. A popularized account which is, however, based on a careful study of source materials.

Colletta, Pietro,
Storia del reame di Napoli dal 1734 sino al 1825. 2nd ed, 2 vols., Monnier, Firenze, 1848. There is also an English edition, published under the following title· *History of the Kingdom of Naples, 1734-1825* Tr. from the Italian by S. Horner, with a supplementary chapter, 1825-1856. 2 vols, Hamilton, Adams, and Co., London, 1858-60.

Cusani, Francesco,
Storia di Milano dall'origine ai nostri giorni e cenni storico-statistici sulle città e province lombarde. 8 vols., Pirotta, Milano, 1861-84. An old source, superseded by more recent studies, but still worthy of being consulted.

D'Ancona, Alessandro,
 Federico Confalonieri. Su documenti inediti di archivj pubblici e privati.
2nd ed., Treves, Milano, 1898. Is still the standard biography of Confalonieri.

Dito, Oreste,
 *Massoneria, carboneria ed altre società segrete nella storia del Risorgi-
mento italiano, con appendice ed illustrazioni.* Roux e Viarengo, Torino,
1905.

Driault, J. Édouard,
 Napoléon en Italie (1800-1812). In *Études Napoléoniennes.* Alcan, Paris,
1906.

Fabi, Massimo,
 *Milano e il ministro Prina. Narrazione storica del Regno d'Italia
(aprile 1814). Tratta da documenti editi ed inediti.* Pedroli, Novara, 1860.
Contains valuable source material. Indispensable for a study of the
Milanese revolution.

Ferrari, Aldo,
 L'esplosione rivoluzionaria del Risorgimento italiano (1789-1815). Cor-
baccio, Milano, 1925

Fornari, P.,
 *Giuseppe Prina, 20 aprile 1814. Fine del Regno italico. Principio della
dominazione austriaca per 45 anni. Narrazione al Popolo.* Vallardi, Milano,
1914. A popularized account which is of little value.

Fournier, August,
 Napoleon the First, a Biography. Holt, New York, 1903. Translated by
Margaret B. Corwin and Arthur D. Bissell from the German edition, which
is entitled: *Napoleon I., eine Biographie.* 3 vols, Freytag, Leipzig, 1886-89.

Frost, Thomas,
 The Secret Societies of the European Revolution, 1776-1876. 2 vols,
Tinsley Bros., London, 1876.

Gaffarel, Paul,
 Bonaparte et les républiques italiennes (1796-1799). Alcan, Paris, 1895.

Greenfield, Kent Roberts,
 *Economics and Liberalism in the Risorgimento. A Study of Nationalism
in Lombardy, 1814-1848.* Johns Hopkins Press, Baltimore, Md., 1934 The
best study of this subject which has yet been written.

Hayes, Carlton J. H.,
 The Historical Evolution of Modern Nationalism Smith, New York,
1931.

Hazard, Paul,
 La révolution française et les lettres italiennes, 1789-1815. Hachette et
Cie., Paris, 1910

Helfert, Barone von,

La caduta della dominazione francese nell'alta Italia e la congiura militare bresciano-milanese nel 1814. Traduzione consentita dall'autore di L. G. Cusani Confalonieri. Zanichelli, Bologna, 1894. An Italian translation of Helfert's *Ausgang der franzoesischen Herrschaft in Ober-Italien und Brescia-Mailaender Militaer-Verschwoerung,* which was first published in the *Archiv fuer oesterreichische Geschichte,* Vol. LXXVII, Pt. 2, 407-555. Although this work has been in part superseded by Lemmi, it is still indispensable for a study of the fall of the Kingdom of Italy.

Helfert, Josef Alexander Freiherr von,

Joachim Murat, seine letzten Kaempfe und sein Ende. Manz'sche k. k. Hof- Verlags, Wien, 1878.

Helfert, Dr. Josef Alex. Freih. v.,

Kaiser Franz und die europaeischen Befreiungskriege gegen Napoleon I. Prandel u. Ewald, Wien, 1867.

Helfert, Fhr. v.,

Kaiser Franz I von Oesterreich und die Stiftung des Lombardo-Venetianischen Koenigreichs. In *Quellen und Forschungen zur Geschichte, Litteratur und Sprache Oesterreichs und seiner Kronlaender,* herausgegeben von Dr. J. Hirn und Dr. J. E. Wackernell. Wagner'schen Universitaets-Buchhandlung, Innsbruck, 1901. The standard account on the restoration of the Austrian government in Lombardy-Venetia. Has never been superseded.

Helfert, Dr. Jos. Alex. Freih,

Zur Geschichte des Lombardo-Venezianischen Koenigreichs. Vol XCVIII of the *Archiv fuer oesterreichische Geschichte,* herausgegeben von der historischen Kommission der kaiserlichen Akademie der Wissenschaften. Hoelder, Wien, 1908.

Hock, Carl Freiherr von, und Herm. Ign. Bidermann,

Der oesterreichische Staatsrath (1760-1848). Braumueller, Wien, 1879.

Holtz, Oberst Georg Freiherr vom,

Die inneroesterreichische Armee, 1813 und 1814. Vol. IV of Veltzé, Major Alois (edit.), *1813-1815. Oesterreich in den Befreiungskriegen.* Edlinger, Wien, 1912.

Huch, Ricarda,

Das Leben des Grafen Federigo Confalonieri. Insel- Verlag, Leipzig, [1934].

Johnston, R. M.,

· *The Napoleonic Empire in Southern Italy and the Rise of the Secret Societies.* 2 vols., Macmillan, London, 1904.

Koch, Gottfried,

Die Entstehung der italienischen Republik (1801/2). A small pamphlet in the Fournier Collection of the University of California Library, with no evidence given as to where it was taken from or by whom it was published.

Lemmi, Francesco,
  Le origini del Risorgimento italiano (1748-1815). 2nd ed., Hoepli, Milano, 1924.

Lemmi, Francesco,
  La restaurazione austriaca a Milano nel 1814. Zanichelli, Bologna, 1902. The best study of the fall of the Kingdom of Italy which has yet been written.

Leti, Giuseppe,
  Carboneria e massoneria nel Risorgimento italiano. Saggio di critica storica. 2nd ed, Libreria editrice moderna, Genova, 1926.

Luzio, Alessandro,
  La Massoneria sotto il Regno italico e la restaurazione austriaca. Estratto dall'*Archivio Storico Lombardo*, Anno XLIV, Fascicolo II [1917-18, pp. 241-352]. Cogliati, Milano, 1918.

Luzio, Alessandro,
  La Massoneria e il Risorgimento italiano. Saggio storico-critico. Con illustrazioni e molti documenti inediti. 2 vols, Zanichelli, Bologna, 1925. Both this and the preceding work are indispensable for a study of Italian secret societies.

Megaro, Gaudence,
  Vittorio Alfieri, Forerunner of Italian Nationalism. Columbia University Press, New York, 1930.

Meynert, Hermann,
  Kaiser Franz I. Zur Geschichte seiner Regierung und seiner Zeit. Nach Originalmittheilungen und ungedruckten Quellen. Hoelder, Wien, 1872. Old but still one of the best studies of Emperor Francis I.

Oncken, Wilhelm,
  Oesterreich und Preussen im Befreiungskriege. Urkundliche Aufschluesse ueber die politische Geschichte des Jahres 1813. 2 vols, Grote'sche Verlagsbuchhandlung, Berlin, 1876-79.

Ottolini, Angelo,
  La carboneria dalle origini ai primi tentativi insurrezionali (1797-1817). In the *Collezione storica del Risorgimento italiano*. Società Tipografica Modenese, Modena, 1936 A good study not only of the Carbonari but of other Italian secret societies.

Pecchio, Giuseppe,
  Saggio storico sull'amministrazione finanziaria dell'ex-regno d'Italia dal 1802 al 1814. 2nd ed., Sincon, London, 1826.

Pedrotti, Pietro,
  Francesco Melzi d'Eril e la Repubblica Italiana. Ist. di Risorgimento Italiano, Roma, 1937.

Pingaud, Albert,
  Bonaparte, président de la République italienne. Perrin, Paris, 1914.

Ratti, Luigi,
  Il Ministro Prina cento anni dopo la sua morte; su documenti e particolari inediti. Vallardi, Milano, 1914. A popularized account.

Redding, Moses W,
  The Illustrated History of Free Masonry. Redding and Co, New York, 1907.

Ruth, Emil,
  Geschichte des italienischen Volks unter der Napoleonischen Herrschaft als Grundlage einer neuesten Geschichte Italiens. Mayer, Leipzig, 1859

Salvatorelli, Luigi,
  Il pensiero politico italiano dal 1700 al 1870. Einaudi, Torino, 1935.

Sandonà, Augusto,
  Il Regno Lombardo Veneto 1814-1859, la costituzione e l'amministrazione. Studi di storia e di diritto, con la scorta degli atti ufficiali dei dicasteri centrali di Vienna. Cogliati, Milano, 1912 Contains several valuable documents.

Simonyi, Ludwig von,
  Das Lombardisch-Venezianische Koenigreich: Charakteristisch- Artistisch- Topographisch- Statistisch- und Historisch. 2 vols, Redaeilli, Mailand, 1844-46.

Smola, Karl Freiherrn von,
  Das Leben des Feldmarschalls Heinrich Grafen von Bellegarde. Heubner, Wien, 1837.

Sorel, Albert,
  L'Europe et la révolution française. 5th ed., 8 vols., Plon, Nourrit et Cie., Paris, 1885-1904. Still the best study of the diplomacy of the Revolutionary and Napoleonic eras

Soriga, Renato,
  Il primo Grande Oriente d'Italia. Estratto dal *Bollettino* della Società Pavese di Storia Patria, Anno XVII. Fusi, Pavia, 1917.

Spadoni, Domenico,
  Milano e la congiura militare nel 1814 per l'indipendenza italiana: Il moto del 20 aprile e l'occupazione austriaca. In the *Collezione storica del Risorgimento italiano.* Società Tipografica Modenese, Modena, 1936. Cited as " *Il moto del 20 aprile, op. cit.*" An excellent study of the period after April 20, 1814. Shows the part which the secret societies took in instigating the Milanese revolution and in supporting the activities of the " pure Italian " party

Spadoni, Domenico,
Milano e la congiura militare nel 1814 per l'indipendenza italiana: La congiura militare e il suo processo. In the *Collezione storica del Risorgimento italiano.* Società Tipografica Modenese, Modena, 1937. Cited as " *La congiura militare, op. cit.*" The best study of the Brescian-Milanese military conspiracy that has yet been made.

Spadoni, Domenico,
Milano e la congiura militare nel 1814 per l'indipendenza italiana: I giudizi di Mantova e la sorte dei congiurati. In the *Collezione storica del Risorgimento italiano.* Società Tipografica Modenese, Modena, 1937.

Spadoni, Domenico,
Sette, cospirazioni e cospiratori nello stato pontificio all'indomani della restaurazione. Casa Editrice Nazionale, Torino, 1904

Srbik, Heinrich Ritter von,
Metternich, der Staatsmann und der Mensch. 2 vols., Bruckmann, Muenchen, 1925. The best and most complete biography of Metternich.

Tarlé, Eugène,
Le Blocus continental et le Royaume d'Italie. La Situation économique de l'Italie sous Napoléon Ier, d'après des documents inédits. Alcan, Paris, 1928. The standard study of economic conditions in the Napoleonic Kingdom of Italy.

Villari, Luigi,
The Development of Political Ideas in Italy in the Nineteenth Century. A reprint from the *Proceedings* of the British Academy, 1926. Oxford University Press, London, [1926].

Webster, Charles K.,
The Congress of Vienna, 1814-1815. Milford, London, 1919.

Webster, Charles K ,
The Foreign Policy of Castlereagh, 1812-1815; Britain and the Reconstruction of Europe. Bell and Sons, London, 1931. One of the best studies of British diplomatic history during the period.

Weil, Maurice Henri,
Joachim Murat, roi de Naples, la dernière année de règne (mai 1814— mai 1815). 5 vols., Fontemoing, Paris, 1909-10. Contains valuable documents.

Weil, Maurice Henri,
Le prince Eugène et Murat 1813-1814; opérations militaires, négociations diplomatiques. 5 vols., Fontemoing, Paris, 1902. Indispensable. Contains many valuable documents.

Wiedemann-Warnhelm, Adolf von,
Die Wiederherstellung der oesterreichischen Vorherrschaft in Italien (1813-1815). Holzhausen, Wien, 1912. A short but useful study.

Wolf, Adam, u. Hans von Zwiedineck-Suedenhorst,
Oesterreich unter Maria Theresia, Josef II. und Leopold II., 1740-1792.
Grote'sche Verlagsbuchhandlung, Berlin, 1884.

Zanoli, Alessandro,
Sulla milizia cisalpino-italiana. Cenni storico-statistici dal 1796 al 1814.
2 vols, Borroni e Scotti, Milano, 1845.

GENERAL HISTORIES

Bermann, Moriz,
Oesterreich-Ungarn im neunzehnten Jahrhundert. Mit besonderer Beruecksichtigung aller wichtigen Vorfaelle in der Geschichte, Wissenschaft, Kunst, Industrie und dem Volksleben. Engel, Wien, 1884.

Bibl, Viktor,
Kaiser Franz und sein Erbe. Vol. I of his *Der Zerfall Oesterreichs.* Rikola, Wien, 1922 Hostile to Emperor Francis I and his government. Contains interesting material.

Bonfadini, R[omualdo],
Mezzo secolo di patriotismo. Saggi storici. 2nd ed , Treves, Milano, 1886 Old but still worthy of study.

Botta, Carlo,
Storia d'Italia dal 1789 al 1814. 10 vols. in 5, Didot, Paris, 1824. This work was translated into English under the following title: *History of Italy during the Consulate and Empire of Napoleon Buonaparte.* 2 vols , Baldwin and Cradock, London, 1828.
The Cambridge Modern History, Vols. VIII and IX. 13 vols., University Press, Cambridge, 1902-12.

Cantù, Cesare,
Della indipendenza italiana cronistoria. 3 vols , Unione Tipografica Editrice, Torino, 1872-77. A much cited work.

Castro, Giovanni de,
Storia d'Italia dal 1799 al 1814. In *Storia politica d'Italia,* scritta da una società d'amici, Pt. VII. Vallardi, Milano, 1881.

Fiorini, V., e F. Lemmi,
Periodo Napoleonico dal 1799 al 1814. In *Storia politica d'Italia,* scritta da una società di professori, Pt. XVI. Vallardi, Milano, [190-?].

Ghisalberti, Alberto,
Gli albori del Risorgimento italiano (1700-1815). Cremonese, Roma, 1931.

Lavisse, Ernest, et Alfred Rambaud,
Histoire générale du IVe siècle à nos jours, Vols. VII-X. 12 vols., Colin, Paris, 1893-1901.

Leo, Heinrich,
Geschichte der italienischen Staaten. 5 vols., Perthes, Hamburg, 1829-37.

Masi, Ernesto,
Il Risorgimento italiano. 2nd ed., 2 vols , Sansoni, Firenze, 1937. One of the standard shorter studies of the Risorgimento.

Peverelli, P[ietro],
Storia di Venezia dal 1798 sino ai nostri tempi. 2 vols., Castellazzo e Degaudenzi, Torino, 1852.

Reuchlin, Hermann,
Geschichte Italiens von der Gruendung der regierenden Dynastien bis zur Gegenwart. 4 vols., Hirzel, Leipzig, 1859-73.

Springer, Anton,
Geschichte Oesterreichs seit dem Wiener Frieden 1809. 2 vols , Hirzel, Leipzig, 1863-65.

Tivaroni, Carlo,
L'Italia prima della rivoluzione francese (1735-1789). Vol. I of his *Storia critica del Risorgimento italiano* (Roux, Torino, 1888-97). One of the standard works on the period.

Tivaroni, Carlo,
L'Italia durante il dominio francese (1789-1815) Vols. II and III of his *Storia critica del Risorgimento italiano* (Roux, Torino, 1888-97). One of the standard works on the period.

INDEX

money in Italy, 72; views of in
regard to the high taxation in
Venetia, 74; advises Prince Eugene
to make peace, 86-7; visits Prince
Eugene, 125; meetings of with
Milanese deputations, 132-33, 135-
36, 146-48; instructions of to Sommariva and Strassoldo, 142-43, 166-
67, 186; arrival of in Milan, 146;
relations of with the Milanese
provisional government, 148, 149,
151, 155, 156; views of on Lombard public opinion, 173; expressions in favor of Lombard independence by, 135-36, 187, 187-88;
receives word that Lombardy is to
become a Habsburg possession,
187-88; instructions to from Emperor Francis, 201-3; instructions
to from Metternich, 203-4, 205-6;
establishment of Austrian control
in Lombardy by, 204-6; enactments in regard to the Italian
army by, 208-9, 210
Bentinck, Lord William: life of, 32
ftn.; Italian policy of, 32, 164;
propaganda activities of, 33, 36-7,
203; connections of with the
Guelfs, 39-40 ftn.; connections of
with the Carbonari, 41; quarrel of
with Murat, 51-2, 56-9; in the
Italian campaign, 56, 59; Leghorn proclamation of, 56-7; deputations sent by the Milanese to,
132-35, 136, 159-61; activities in
Milan of, 170, 194; instructions of
the British government to, 57 ftn.,
58, 59 ftn., 169-70, 184 ftn, 186;
views of on Lombard public
opinion, 172
Bergamo, 122, 163, 196, 206
Bertoletti, General Antonio, 88, 125,
191, 192
Bologna, Legation of, 15
Bonaparte, See Napoleon
Bormio, Valley of, 15, 197-98
Borromeo, Giberto, 99, 100, 102, 128,
146, 161
Bosisio, Captain, 109
Bossi, Benigno, 85, 99, 102, 112, 145
Bovara, Minister, 20
Breganze, Giacomo, 106
Brescia, 122-23, 144, 196, 206
Brescian-Milanese military conspir-
acy, 105, 214
British agents: liberal and national
propaganda of during the Na-

poleonic period, 31-7; effects on
Milanese public opinion of the
propaganda of, 81-2, 168-69; deputations sent by the Milanese to,
132-35, 159-64; interference in
Milanese affairs by, 165-68; opinion
of Austrian officials of, 57 ftn,
168-69; Milanese opinion of, 168;
departure from Milan of, 169-70;
views of on Lombard public
opinion, 164-65, 171-72; activities
in Venetia of, 178-79
British government: Italian policy
of, 31-7, 59 ftn, 164, 169-70, 171;
orders to Bentinck by, 57 ftn.,
58, 59 ftn., 169-70, 184 ftn, 186;
decision of to give Lombardy-
Venetia to Austria, 180-83, 190-91
Bubna, Count Ferdinand, 194, 197
Business failures, 25
Business tax, See Arts and business
tax

Cadolino, Gaetano Pietro, 163
Campaign: Napoleon's Italian of
1796, 13; of the Second Coalition,
14; Italian, of 1813-14, 45-61
Carascosa, General, 53, 58
Carbonari, 37, 40-2, 104, 105-6, 107,
109
Cariati, Prince, 51
Castiglioni, Senator Alfonso, 94, 95
Castiglioni, Marquis Carlo, 85, 99,
100
Castlereagh, Lord, Marquis of Lon-
donderry, 35-6, 57 ftn, 58, 59 ftn.,
159 ftn, 165, 167, 169, 170, 171,
172, 180, 183, 186, 190, 194, 195
Cavazza, Colonel Antonio, 124
Censorship, 22, 142, 153
Châtillon, Conferences at, 185
Chiavenna, Valley of, 15, 197-98
Ciani, Giacomo, 99, 104, 131, 188, 200
Cicogna brothers, 99, 100, 101 ftn,
102
Cima, Luigi, 109
Cisalpine Republic, 13-14
Cispadane Republic, 13
Civic guard, of Milan, 112, 113, 118
ftn., 121, 122, 144, 145, 162
Clarence, Duke of, 85, 109
Cockade, 128, 151, 206
Communal council, of Milan, 120,
127-28, 131 ftn, 132-33, 135, 143,
159, 160
Como, 123

Lightning Source UK Ltd.
Milton Keynes UK
UKOW07f1642170515

251723UK00004B/102/P